A PASSION FOR HOLINESS

A Passion
for Holiness

J. I. Packer

CROSSWAY BOOKS
CAMBRIDGE

To

Jim and Rita Houston

*who also care
about holiness*

CONTENTS

PREFACE

THIS BOOK HAS GROWN OUT of four talks that I gave at a conference in 1991. This conference was sponsored by the Alliance for Faith and Renewal, an interdenominational organization that seeks to empower pastors and other Christian leaders in building the kingdom of God and in strengthening those they serve in the Christian life. The shape this book has taken reflects my belief that there is need to blow the whistle on the sidelining of personal holiness which has been a general trend among Bible-centered Western Christians during my years of ministry. It is not a trend that one would have expected, since Scripture insists so strongly that Christians are called to holiness, that God is pleased with holiness but outraged by unholiness, and that without holiness none will see the Lord. But the shift of Christian interest away from the pursuit of holiness to focus on fun and fulfillment, ego-massage and techniques for present success, and public issues that carry no challenge to one's personal morals, is a fact. To my mind it is a sad and scandalous fact, and one that needs to be reversed.

With the fading of interest in supernatural holiness, interest has grown in supernatural healing and in the supernatural powers of evil with which Christians must battle. My hope is that this heightened awareness of the reality of the supernatural will soon reconnect with what Walter Marshall, the Puritan, long ago called the "gospel mystery of sanctification." If this book helps in that reconnection, I shall think myself fully rewarded.

I am enormously grateful to my daughter Naomi, who labored at some inconvenience to herself to put the book on computer, and to my wife Kit, who was willing to be neglected for a time so that it might be born.

J.I. Packer
March 1992

1 || What Holiness Is, and Why It Matters

Just as he who called you is holy, so be holy in all you do; for it is written: "Be holy, because I am holy."
1 Pt 1:15-16

Make every effort... to be holy; without holiness no one will see the Lord. **Heb 12:14**

LOSS OF A PRECIOUS PAST

Our grandfather clock, which tells us not only the hours, minutes, and seconds, but also the days of the week, the months of the year, and the phases of the moon, is something of a veteran. Scratched on one of its lead weights is the date 1789—the year of the French Revolution and George Washington's first term as President. I am writing these words in 1991, the 200th anniversary of John Wesley's death: our clock was going before he stopped going, if I may put it so. It is a musical clock, too, of a rather unusual sort. Not only does it strike the hour, but it also has a built-in carillon (knobs on a brass cylinder tripping hammers that hit bells which play a tune for three minutes every three hours). Two of its four tunes we recognize, for we hear them still today. However, the other two, which sound like country dances, are unknown—not just to us but to everyone who has heard them played.

Over the years they were forgotten, which was a pity, for they are good tunes; and we would like to know something about them.

In the same way, the historic Christian teaching on holiness has been largely forgotten, and that also is a pity, for it is central to the glory of God and the good of souls.

It is nearly sixty years since I learned at school the opening verse of a poem by Rudyard Kipling, titled "The Way through the Woods." It goes like this:

> They shut the road through the woods
> Seventy years ago.
> Weather and rain have undone it again
> And now you would never know
> There was once a road through the woods.

I suppose it is because I love walking through woods that these lines move me so deeply. Again and again, when I find myself mourning the loss of a good thing that has perished through stupidity, carelessness, or neglect (and I confess that, both as a conservationist and a Christian, I have that experience often), Kipling's verse jumps into my mind. It haunts me now, as I contemplate the church's current loss of biblical truth about holiness.

Our Christian Heritage of Holiness. There was a time when all Christians laid great emphasis on the reality of God's call to holiness and spoke with deep insight about his enabling of us for it. Evangelical Protestants, in particular, offered endless variations on the themes of what God's holiness requires of us, what our holiness involves for us, by what means and through what disciplines the Holy Spirit sanctifies us, and the ways in which holiness increases our assurance and joy and usefulness to God.

The Puritans insisted that all life and relationships must become "holiness to the Lord." John Wesley told the world that God had raised up Methodism "to spread scriptural holiness throughout the land." Phoebe Palmer, Handley Moule, Andrew Murray, Jessie Penn-Lewis, F.B. Meyer, Oswald Chambers, Horatius Bonar, Amy Carmichael, and L.B. Maxwell are only a few of the leading figures in the "holiness revival" that touched all evangelical Christendom between the mid-nineteenth and mid-twentieth centuries.

On the other side of the Reformation divide, Seraphim of Sarov (Russian Orthodox) and Teresa of Avila, Ignatius Loyola, Madame Guyon, and Père Grou (all Roman Catholics) ministered as apostles of holiness in a similar way. We must realize that, as John Wesley, for one, clearly saw, the Reformation cleavage was much less deep on sanctification and the Spirit than it was on justification and the Mass.

Formerly, then, holiness was highlighted throughout the Christian church. But how different it is today! To listen to our sermons and to read the books we write for each other, and then to watch the zany, worldly, quarrelsome way we behave as Christian people, you would never imagine that once the highway of holiness was clearly marked out for Bible-believers, so that ministers and people knew what it was and could speak of it with authority and confidence. "Weather and rain have undone it again." Now we have to rebuild and reopen the road, starting really from scratch.

In the Old Testament we read how Isaac, forced to relocate his large household, "reopened the wells that had been dug in the time of his father Abraham, which the Philistines had stopped up after Abraham died" (Gn 26:18). Isaac thus secured the water supply without which neither his family, nor his servants, nor his cattle, nor he himself, could have survived. He did not prospect for new wells in a water-divining quest that might or might not have succeeded, but he went straight to the old wells. He knew he would find water in them, once he had cleared them of the earth and debris that malevolent Philistines had piled on top of them.

Isaac's action reflects two simple spiritual principles that apply here in a very direct way:

1. the recovering of old truth, truth which has been a means of blessing in the past, can under God become the means of blessing again in the present, while the quest for newer alternatives may well prove barren;

2. no one should be daunted from attempting such recovery by any prejudice, ill will, or unsympathetic attitudes that may have built up against the old truth during the time of its eclipse.

These are the principles whose guidance I follow in this book. No novelties will be found here. I shall draw, gratefully, from an older Christian wisdom.

The Lost World. Sir Arthur Conan Doyle, the creator of Sherlock Holmes, also wrote an adventure story called *The Lost World*. In it Professor Challenger and his friends climb to a supposedly inaccessible plateau in South America and find there both dinosaurs and a previously unknown pattern of human life. The story was clearly meant for boys from nine to ninety, and I vividly recall being thrilled by it, I think at the age of ten, when I heard it serialized on British radio's Children's Hour. It ends with Challenger battling frozen disbelief among his scientific peers as he tells them what he had found.

In this book I try to testify to the reality of the lost world of authentic Christian holiness. Will what I say about the supernaturalizing of our disordered lives be believed, I wonder? Will my account of what will appear to many as an unknown pattern of human life have any credibility at all? And what sort of spiritual dinosaur shall I be seen as for producing such ancient ideas? Never mind. In the memorable words of Cary Grant, "A man's got to do what a man's got to do." For me that means moving without fuss into my expository task, whether or not I am going to be taken seriously. To this task I now turn.

SCHOOL OF HOLINESS, SCHOOL OF PRAYER

One of the titles I proposed for this book was *With Christ in the School of Holiness*. That was a deliberate echo, almost a steal, of *With Christ in the School of Prayer* by Andrew Murray, a much appreciated South African devotional author of two generations ago. I adapted Murray's title in this manner in order to highlight three truths that to me seem basic to all I propose to say. (Murray would—indeed, did—fully agree with all three, as his own many books make plain.)

First Truth. Holiness, like prayer (which is indeed part of it), is something which, though Christians have an instinct for it through their new birth, as we shall see, they have to learn in and through experience. As Jesus "learned obedience from what he suffered" (Heb 5:8)—learned what obedience requires, costs, and involves through the experience of actually doing his Father's will up to and in his passion—so Christians must, and do, learn prayer from their struggles to pray, and holiness from their battles for purity of heart and righteousness of life.

Talented youngsters who go to tennis school in order to learn the game soon discover that the heart of the process is not talking about tactics but actually practicing serves and strokes, thus forming new habits and reflexes, so as to iron out weaknesses of style. The routine, which is grueling, is one of doing prescribed things over and over again on the court, against a real opponent, in order to get them really right.

Prayer and holiness are learned in a similar way as commitments are made, habits are formed, and battles are fought against a real opponent (Satan, in this case), who with great cunning plays constantly on our weak spots. (That these are often what the world sees as our strong points is an index of Satan's resourcefulness: presumptuous self-reliance and proud overreaching on our part serve his turn just as well as do paralyzing timidity, habits of harshness and anger, lack of discipline, whether inward or outward, evasion of responsibility, lack of reverence for God, and willful indulgence in what one knows to be wrong.) Satan is as good at judo throws as he is at frontal assaults, and we have to be on guard against him all the time.

Second Truth. The process of learning to be holy, like the process of learning to pray, may properly be thought of as a school—God's own school, in which the curriculum, the teaching staff, the rules, the discipline, the occasional prizes, and the fellow pupils with whom one studies, plays, debates, and fraternizes, are all there under God's sovereign providence.

As pushing ahead on the path of prayer and holiness is a prime form of spiritual warfare against sin and Satan, so it is an educational process that God has planned and programmed in order to refine, purge, enlarge, animate, toughen, and mature us. By means of it he brings us progressively into the moral and spiritual shape in which he wants to see us.

Physical education in grade school and adult workouts in fitness centers offer perhaps the closest parallels to what is going on here. They, too, require us to endure things we find it hard to enjoy. As a schoolboy I was gangling and clumsy. I loathed "P.T." (physical training, as it was called in those days). I was in fact very bad at it, but I do not doubt that it was very good for me. Having to heave and bump my dogged way over a period of years through physical jerks that others found easy (and treated as fun and did much better than I could) may well have helped me grasp the virtue of keeping on keeping on in other disciplines that are not immediately gratifying: and God's program of holiness training always includes quite a number of these.

We must be clear in our minds that whatever further reasons there may be why God exposes us to the joys and sorrows, fulfillments and frustrations, delights and disappointment, happinesses and hurts, that make up the emotional reality of our lives, all these experiences are part of his curriculum for us in the school of holiness, which is his spiritual gymnasium for our reshaping and rebuilding in the moral likeness of Jesus Christ.

It is reported that on one occasion when Teresa of Avila was traveling, her conveyance dumped her in the mud. The spunky saint's first words as she struggled to her feet were: "Lord, if this is how you treat your friends, it is no wonder that you have so few!" One of the most attractive things about Teresa is that she could be playful like this with her God. But none knew better than she that the ups and downs of her life were divinely planned in order to mold her character, enlarge her heart, and deepen her devotion. And what was true for her is true for us all.

Third Truth. In God's school of holiness our Lord Jesus Christ (the Father's Son and the Christian's Savior) is with us, and we with him, in a controlling relationship of master and servant, leader and follower, teacher and student. It is crucially important to appreciate this. Why is it that in the school of holiness, as in the schools to which we send our own children, some move ahead faster than others? How are the different rates of progress to be explained? Fundamentally, the factor that makes the difference is neither one's intelligence quotient, nor the number of books one has read nor the conferences, camps, and seminars one has attended, but the quality of the fellowship with Christ that one maintains through life's vicissitudes.

Jesus is risen. He is alive and well. Through his word and Spirit he calls us to himself today, to receive him as our Savior and Lord and become his disciples and followers. Speaking objectively—with reference to how things really are, as distinct from how they might feel at any particular moment—the "there-ness" of Jesus, and the personal nature of his relationship with us as his disciples, are as truly matters of fact as were his bodily presence and his words of comfort and command when he walked this earth long ago. Some, however, do not reckon with this fact as robustly and practically as others do. That is what makes the difference.

I mean this. Some who trust Jesus as their Savior have formed the habit of going to him about everything that comes up, in order to become clear on how they should react to it as his disciples. ("Going to him" is an umbrella phrase that covers three things: praying; meditating, which includes thinking, reflecting, drawing conclusions from Scripture, and applying them directly to oneself in Jesus' presence; and holding oneself open throughout the process to specific illumination from the Holy Spirit.) These Christians come to see how events are requiring them to:

- consecrate themselves totally to the Father, as Jesus did;
- say and do only what pleases the Father, as Jesus did;
- accept pain, grief, disloyalty, and betrayal, as Jesus did;
- care for people and serve their needs without either compromise of principle or ulterior motives in practice, as Jesus did;
- accept opposition and isolation, hoping patiently for better things and meantime staying steady under pressure, as Jesus did;
- rejoice in the specifics of the Father's ways and thank him for his wisdom and goodness, as Jesus did;

and so on.

Kept by this means from bitterness and self-pity, these Christians cope with events in a spirit of peace, joy, and eagerness to see what God will do next. Others, however, who are no less committed to Jesus as their Savior, never master this art of habitually going to him about life's challenges. Too often they start by assuming that their life as children of God will be a bed of roses all the way. Then when the storms come, the best they can do is stagger through in a spirit of real if unacknowledged disappointment with God, feeling all the time that he has let them down. It is easy to understand why those in the first category advance farther and faster in the love, humility, and hope that form the essence of Christ-like holiness than those in the second category.

DEFINING HOLINESS

But what exactly is holiness? We need a full-scale definition, and my next task is to attempt one.[1]

Consider first the word itself. *Holiness* is a noun that belongs with the adjective *holy* and the verb *sanctify*, which means to make holy. (It is a pity in one way that we have to draw on two word-groups in English to cover what is a single word-group in both Hebrew and Greek, but the verb *holify* would be so ugly that maybe we should be glad it does not exist.) *Holy* in both biblical languages means separated and set apart for God, consecrated and made over to him. In its application to people, God's "holy ones" or "saints," the word implies both devotion and assimilation: devotion, in the sense of living a life of service to God; assimilation, in the sense of imitating, conforming to, and becoming like the God one serves. For Christians, this means taking God's moral law as our rule and God's incarnate Son as our model; this is where our analysis of holiness must start.

In his great book *Holiness* (published in 1879, still in print, and going strong), the Anglican Bishop John Charles Ryle set out in simple biblical terms a classic twelve-point profile of a holy person. (Being a Victorian, he said "man," but he meant woman too.) His description runs as follows:

1. Holiness is the habit of being of one mind with God, according as we find his mind described in Scripture. It is the habit of agreeing in God's judgement, hating what he hates, loving what he loves, and measuring everything in this world by the standard of his Word....
2. A holy man will endeavour to shun every known sin, and to keep every known commandment. He will have a decided bent of mind towards God, a hearty desire to do his

will, a greater fear of displeasing him than of displeasing the world, and... will feel what Paul felt when he said, "I delight in the law of God after the inward man" (Rom 7:22)....

3. A holy man will strive to be like our Lord Jesus Christ. He will not only live the life of faith in him, and draw from him all his daily peace and strength, but he will also labor to have the mind that was in him, and to be conformed to his image (Rom 8:29). It will be his aim to bear with and forgive others... to be unselfish... to walk in love...to be lowly-minded and humble.... He will lay to heart the saying of John: "He that saith he abideth in [Christ] ought himself also so to walk, even as he walked" (1 Jn 2:6)....

4. A holy man will follow after meekness, longsuffering, gentleness, patience, kind tempers, government of his tongue. He will bear much, forbear much, overlook much, and be slow to talk of standing on his rights....

5. A holy man will follow after temperance and self-denial. He will labour to mortify the desires of his body, to crucify his flesh with his affections and lusts, to curb his passions, to restrain his carnal inclinations, lest at any time they break loose... (Ryle then quotes Lk 21:34, 1 Cor 9:27).

6. A holy man will follow after charity and brotherly kindness. He will endeavour to observe the golden rule of doing as he would have men do to him, and speaking as he would have men speak to him..... He will abhor all lying, slandering, backbiting, cheating, dishonesty, and unfair dealing, even in the least things....

7. A holy man will follow after a spirit of mercy and benevolence towards others.... Such was Dorcas: "full of good works and almsdeeds, which she did"—not merely purposed and talked about, but *did*... (Acts 9:36).

8. A holy man will follow after purity of heart. He will dread all filthiness and uncleanness of spirit, and seek to avoid all things that might draw him into it. He knows his own

heart is like tinder, and will diligently keep clear of the sparks of temptation....

9. A holy man will follow after the fear of God. I do not mean the fear of a slave, who only works because he is afraid of punishment and would be idle if he did not dread discovery. I mean rather the fear of a child, who wishes to live and move as if he was always before his father's face, because he loves him....

10. A holy man will follow after humility. He will desire, in lowliness of mind, to esteem all others better than himself. He will see more evil in his own heart than in any other in the world....

11. A holy man will follow after faithfulness in all the duties and relations in life. He will try, not merely to fill his place as well as others who take no thought for their souls, but even better, because he has higher motives and more help than they.... Holy persons should aim at doing everything well, and should be ashamed of allowing themselves to do anything ill if they can help it.... They should strive to be good husbands and good wives, good parents and good children, good masters and good servants, good neighbours, good friends, good subjects, good in private and good in public, good in the place of business and good by their firesides. The Lord Jesus puts a searching question to his people, when he says, "What do ye more than others?" (Mt 5:47).

12. Last, but not least, a holy man will follow after spiritual-mindedness. He will endeavour to set his affections entirely on things above, and to hold things on earth with a very loose hand.... He will aim to live like one whose treasure is in heaven, and to pass through this world like a stranger and pilgrim travelling to his home. To commune with God in prayer, in the Bible, and in the assembly of his people—these things will be the holy man's chief enjoyments. He will value every thing and place and company, just in proportion as it draws him nearer to God....[2]

ASPECTS OF HOLINESS

All Ryle's declarations, surely, are abiding and challenging truths with which no sane Christian can quarrel. Building on what he says, and thinking things through from the vantage point to which he has brought us, I now proceed to make on my own account the assertions that follow. I cast them in first-person form, partly to help my readers apply what is said to themselves, and partly because I accept Calvin's dictum that it would be best for a preacher to fall and break his neck as he mounts the pulpit if he is not himself going to be the first to follow God in living his own message. This applies when one preaches on paper no less than when one does so in church, so I need to be preaching to myself as much as to anyone.

Here, then, are my points. There are four of them.

Holiness Has to Do with My Heart. I speak of the heart here in the biblical sense, according to which it means, not the body's blood pump, but the center and focus of one's inner personal life: the source of motivation, the seat of passion, the spring of all thought processes and particularly of conscience. The assertion that I make, and must myself face, is that holiness begins with the heart. Holiness starts inside a person, with a right purpose that seeks to express itself in a right performance. It is a matter, not just of the motions that I go through, but of the motives that prompt me to go through them.

A holy person's motivating aim, passion, desire, longing, aspiration, goal, and drive is to please God, both by what one does and by what one avoids doing. In other words, one practices good works and cuts out evil ones. Good works begin with praise, worship, and honoring and exalting of God as the temper of one's whole waking life. Evil works start with neglect of these things, and coolness with regard to them. So I must labor to keep my heart actively responsive to God.

Of George Herbert, his favorite poet, the Puritan Richard Baxter said: "*heart-work* and *heaven work* make up his books."[3] By "heart-work" Baxter meant cultivating the spirit of grateful, humble, adoring love to one's divine Lover and Savior, as Herbert does in this poem (nowadays a familiar hymn):

> King of glory, King of peace,
> I will love thee;
> And that love may never cease
> I will move [ask] thee.
> Thou hast granted my request,
> Thou hast heard me;
> Thou didst note my working breast,
> Thou hast spared me.
>
> Wherefore with my utmost art
> I will sing thee,
> And the cream of all my heart
> I will bring thee....

This kind of heart-love to God is the taproot of all true holiness.

So asceticism, as such—voluntary abstinences, routines of self-deprivation and grueling austerity—is not the same thing as holiness, though some forms of asceticism may well find a place in a holy person's life. Nor is formalism, in the sense of outward conformity in word and deed to the standards God has set, anything like holiness, though assuredly there is no holiness without such conformity. Nor is legalism, in the sense of doing things to earn God's favor or to earn more of it than one has already, to be regarded as holiness. Holiness is always the saved sinner's response of gratitude for grace received.

The Pharisees of Jesus' day made all three mistakes, yet were thought to be very holy people until Jesus told them the truth about themselves and the inadequacies of their supposed piety. After that, however, we dare not forget that holiness begins in the heart. Who wants to line up with those Pharisees?

Charles Wesley wrote:

> O for a heart to praise my God,
>   A heart from sin set free;

A heart that always feels thy blood
   So freely shed for me;

A heart resigned, submissive, meek,
   My great redeemer's throne,
Where only Christ is heard to speak,
   Where Jesus reigns alone;

A heart in every thought renewed
   And full of love divine,
Perfect and right and pure and good:
   A copy, Lord, of thine.

It is with this focus, and this prayer, that real holiness begins.

Holiness Has to Do with My Temperament. By temperament I mean the factors that make specific ways of reacting and behaving natural to me. To use psychologists' jargon, it is my temperament that inclines me to *transact* with my environment (situations, things, and people) in the way I usually do.

Drawing on the full resources of this jargon, psychologist Gordon Allport defines temperament as "the characteristic phenomena of an individual's nature, including his susceptibility to emotional stimulation, his customary strength and speed of response, the quality of his prevailing mood, and all the peculiarities of fluctuation and intensity of mood, these being regarded as dependent on constitutional make-up, and therefore largely hereditary in origin."[4] Allport's statement is cumbersome but clear. Temperament, we might say, is the raw material out of which character is formed. Character is what we do with our temperament. Personality is the final product, the distinct individuality that results.

Temperaments are classified in various ways: positive and negative, easy and difficult, introverted and extroverted, outgoing and withdrawn, active and passive, giving and taking, sociable and forthcoming as distinct from manipulative and self-absorbed, shy and uninhibited, quick and slow to warm up, stiffly defiant as contrasted with flexibly acquiescent, and so on.

While these classifications are useful in their place, perhaps the most useful of all, certainly to the pastoral leader, is the oldest one which Greek physicians had already worked out before the time of Christ. It distinguishes four basic human temperaments:

- the sanguine (warm, jolly, outgoing, relaxed, optimistic);
- the phlegmatic (cool, low-key, detached, unemotional, apathetic);
- the choleric (quick, active, bustling, impatient, with a relatively short fuse); and
- the melancholic (somber, pessimistic, inward-looking, inclined to cynicism and depression).

It then acknowledges the reality of mixed types, such as the phlegmatic-melancholic and the sanguine-choleric, when features of two of the temperaments are found in the same person. In this way it covers everybody. The ancient beliefs about body fluids that supported this classification are nowadays dispelled, but the classification itself remains pastorally helpful. People do observably fall into these categories and recognizing them helps one to understand the temper and reactions of the person with whom one is dealing.

The assertion that I now make, and must myself face, is that I am not to become (or remain) a victim of my temperament. Each temperament has its own strengths and also its weaknesses. Sanguine people tend to live thoughtlessly and at random. Phlegmatic people tend to be remote and unfeeling, sluggish and unsympathetic. Choleric people tend to be quarrelsome, bad-tempered, and poor team players. Melancholic people tend to see everything as bad and wrong and to deny that anything is ever really good and right. Yielding to my temperamental weaknesses is, of course, the most natural thing for me to do, and is therefore the hardest sort of sin for me to deal with and detect. But holy humanity, as I see it in Jesus Christ, combines in itself the strengths of all four temperaments without any of the weaknesses. Therefore, I must try to be like him in this, and not indulge the particular behavioral flaws to which my temperament tempts me.

Holiness for a person of sanguine temperament, then, will involve learning to look before one leaps, to think things through responsibly, and to speak wisely rather than wildly. (These were among the lessons Peter learned with the Spirit's help after Pentecost.) Holiness for a person of phlegmatic temperament will involve a willingness to be open with people, to feel with them and for them, to be forthcoming in relationships, and to become vulnerable, in the sense of risking being hurt. Holiness for a choleric person will involve practicing patience and self-control. It will mean redirecting one's anger and hostility toward Satan and sin, rather than toward fellow human beings who are obstructing what one regards as the way forward. (These were among the lessons Paul learned from the Lord after his conversion.) Finally, holiness for a melancholic person will involve learning to rejoice in God, to give up self-pity and proud pessimism, and to believe, with the medieval mystic Julian of Norwich, that through sovereign divine grace, "All shall be well and all shall be well, and all manner of things shall be well." What are my temperamental weaknesses? If I am to be holy, as I am called to be, I must identify them (that is the hard part) and ask my Lord to enable me to form habits of rising above them.

Holiness Has to Do with My Humanness. Our Lord Jesus Christ is both God for man and man for God; he is God's incarnate Son, fully divine and fully human. We know him as both the mediator of divine grace and the model of human godliness. And what is human godliness, the godliness that is true holiness, as seen in Jesus? It is simply human life lived as the Creator intended—in other words, it is perfect and ideal humanness, an existence in which the elements of the human person are completely united in a totally God-honoring and nature-fulfilling way. (Since God made humanity for himself, godliness naturally fulfills human nature at the deepest level.

As experience proves, no contentment can match the contentment of obeying God, however costly this may prove.)

Human lives that are lived differently from this, however, though human in a biological and functional sense, are less than fully human in terms of their quality. Holiness and humanness are correlative terms and mutual implicates (as the logicians would put it). To the extent that I fall short of the first, I fall short of the second as well.

All members of our fallen race who, because they do not know Jesus Christ, still live under the power of that self-deifying, anti-God syndrome in our spiritual system which the Bible calls sin, are living lives that are qualitatively subhuman. Sin in our minds says otherwise, but in this, as always, sin is lying.

The twentieth century will doubtless go down in history as the century of secular humanism. It began with the euphoric, sin-spawned confidence that human endeavor in science, education, the harnessing of nature, and the increase of wealth would generate human happiness to the point of achieving something like heaven on earth. It ends, however, with none of these hopes realized, but with sickening memories of many great evils committed, and with hearts everywhere full of restless and gloomy unease regarding humanity's future prospects and life's present worth.

Our proud humanism, so-called, has made the world more like hell than heaven. "What the world hungers for today," say British writers Brain and Warren, rightly, is:

> the discovery of what it means to be truly human. The world sees the destructive effect of devotion to the pursuit of money, sex and power in the lives of many of its heroes. What people long for is a way of integrating the various parts of themselves, and the insights of modern psychology and sociology, in a way that leads to wholeness. Humanism cannot provide the answer. It is through the person of Jesus Christ alone that true humanity can be found.... Holiness is not primarily about submission to authoritarian rules or nar-

row or conformist notions of acceptable behavior. It is about the celebration of our humanity.

To hammer this home, they subjoin a telling quotation from the Scottish preacher James Philip:

> Above all the life of the early church was characterised—and surely this is a paramount need in evangelical life today—by humanity. The deepest word that can be spoken about sanctification is that it is a progress towards true humanity. Salvation is, essentially considered, the restoration of humanity to men. This is why the slightly inhuman, not to say unnatural, streak in some forms and expressions of sanctification is so far removed from the true work of grace in the soul. The greatest saints of God have been characterised, not by haloes and an atmosphere of distant unapproachability, but by their humanity. They have been intensely human and lovable people with a twinkle in their eyes.[5]

The assertion I make, and must now myself face, is that Brain, Warren, and Philip are right. Genuine holiness is genuine Christ-likeness, and genuine Christ-likeness is genuine humanness—the only genuine humanness there is. Love in the service of God and others, humility and meekness under the divine hand, integrity of behavior expressing integration of character, wisdom with faithfulness, boldness with prayerfulness, sorrow at people's sins, joy at the Father's goodness, and single-mindedness in seeking to please the Father morning, noon, and night, were all qualities seen in Christ, the perfect man.

Christians are meant to become human as Jesus was human. We are called to imitate these character qualities, with the help of the Holy Spirit, so that the childish instability, inconsiderate self-seeking, pious play acting, and undiscerning pigheadedness that so frequently mar our professedly Christian lives are left behind. "Holiness, rightly understood, is a beautiful thing, and its beauty is the beauty and tenderness of divine love"[6]—

which is precisely the beauty of truly mature humanity. I need to remember all this, and take it to heart, and set my sights accordingly.

Holiness Has to Do with My Relationships. Sometimes it has been thought that a state of isolation and solitude, permanently detached from ordinary human involvements, is a help, or perhaps even a necessity, for the practice of holiness. It is true that holy living calls for regular times of aloneness with God. But the notion here is that one gains freedom to move ahead with God by cutting oneself off from the communal life of family and church and society, and that does not seem to be true at all. This idea, it seems, broke surface in the fourth century when pioneer Christian monks habitually went off on their own to practice the bodily austerities and spiritual athletics by which holiness was defined at that time. Thus, Antony withdrew into the Egyptian desert for twenty years. Simeon Stylites mounted his pillar and lived on top of it for thirty years. There was much of this kind of thing.

In turn, people in the Middle Ages cherished the thought of holiness as an optional "higher life" of prayerful austerity for the super-serious. They took for granted the propriety of seeking the detachment that was supposedly necessary for such a life by renouncing marriage and wealth and becoming a monk, a nun, or a hermit. It was thus revolutionary for social life and thought when the Reformers reconceived holiness as the fulfilling of one's relationships, the stewarding of one's talents and time, and the maintaining of love, humility, purity, and zeal for God in one's heart. The ideal of isolationism was then jettisoned completely and replaced by an insistence that holiness—viewed now as the consecrated life of the grateful, forgiven sinner—must be worked out in the way in which, as worshiper, worker, and witness, one relates to one's family, church, and wider community. It is not open to dispute, however, that the Reformers had the Bible on their side.

No doubt the Reformers went too far when, in the heat of

their reaction against the prevailing pattern, they sought to close all monasteries and denied there ever was such a thing as a call to serve God in the solitude of withdrawal from the world's affairs. But they were certainly right to negate the idea that such withdrawal is a necessary condition of thoroughgoing holiness, and that involvement in the world rules out all possibility of a full-scale holy life. Biblical holiness is in this sense an unambiguously worldly holiness. Without conforming to the world by becoming materialistic, extravagant, or a grabber and empire-builder of any kind, the Christian must operate as a servant of God in the world, serving others for the Lord's sake. So the assertion I make, and must now myself face, is that the way I relate to others is the essence of my holiness in the sight of God, just as it is one index of it in the sight of men and women.

Here I recall something I once read about a lady who was a popular speaker on holiness platforms and a fluent writer on holiness themes over a hundred years ago. (To avoid scandal, I will not give her name, or reference the quotation that follows.) Her son-in-law wrote that many thought her "a sage and a saint," but he himself "came gradually to think of her as one of the wickedest people I had ever known." Why? His list of reasons began thus: "Her treatment of her husband, whom she despised, was humiliating to the highest degree. She never spoke to him or of him except in a tone that made her contempt obvious. It cannot be denied that he was a silly old man, but he did not deserve what she gave him, and no one capable of mercy could have given it."

The son-in-law was not a Christian, but there is nothing un-Christian about this bit of reasoning. For love to be replaced by resentful contempt between husband and wife, or for that matter between parent and child, or colleague and colleague, is a negation of holiness, whatever stuff one may display in books or relay from pulpits and platforms. I need to remember that, and I do not think I am the only one.

In the book that Brain and Warren cited, James Philip points to the way in which some Christians are unwilling to show any kind of empathetic feelings (the macho-syndrome of those who fancy themselves as God's tough guys), and to give up their love of the limelight and the desire to control others (the Diotrephes disease of 3 John 9); all these things, he tells us, induce a hardness of heart that from God's standpoint ruins their relationships.

> There are many Christians who have never learned to say "Thank you" graciously, and who cause their best friends much distress by their apparent thoughtlessness and lack of gratitude, when they take so much costly love and friend-ship... for granted.... There is nothing so calculated to cause trouble... as persisting in holding unrealistic estimates of oneself... Very often, of course, it is the relentless drive of an inferiority complex that expresses itself in high and exalted ideas of one's own importance, out of all proportion to reality. The problem of inferiority complex is more closely allied to self-centeredness than most of us would like to believe.... We must recognize the root of the problem for what it is. This is why, ultimately, the gospel is the only true psychology, for no less a power can break the tyranny of self in the human heart.

The essential problem is "a self that has not learned to die." But "a true surrender to Christ shrinks our inflated ego to its proper size in relation to him and our fellows, and imparts reality to our lives."[7] Wise words! Let none suppose that they advance in holiness while such lapses in Christian relation-ships still mark their path.

To summarize, then, it appears that Christian holiness is a number of things together. It has both outward and inward aspects. Holiness is a matter of both action and motivation, conduct and character, divine grace and human effort, obedi-ence and creativity, submission and initiative, consecration to God and commitment to people, self-discipline and self-giving, righteousness and love. It is a matter of Spirit-led law-keeping, a walk, or course of life, in the Spirit that displays the fruit of the Spirit (Christ-likeness of attitude and disposition). It is a matter of seeking to imitate Jesus' way of behaving, through depending on Jesus for deliverance from carnal self-absorption and for discernment of spiritual needs and possibilities.

It is a matter of patient, persistent uprightness; of taking God's side against sin in our own lives and in the lives of others; of worshiping God in the Spirit as one serves him in the world; and of single-minded, wholehearted, free and glad concentration on the business of pleasing God. It is the distinctive form and, so to speak, flavor of a life set apart for God that is now being inwardly renewed by his power.

Holiness is thus the demonstration of faith working by love. It is wholly supernatural in the sense of being God's gracious achievement within us, and wholly natural in the sense of being our own true humanness, lost through sin, misconceived through ignorance, and through listening too hard to current culture—but now in process of restoration through the redirecting and reintegrating energy of new creation in Christ through the Holy Spirit. Oswald Chambers called God's gift of holiness "our brilliant heritage." The phrase was well chosen. *Brilliant*—bright, shining, precious, glorious—is the word that fits.

IS HOLINESS IMPORTANT TODAY?

But is holiness really important? Does it matter, in the final analysis, whether Christ's professed followers live holy lives or not?

From watching today's Christian world (and in particular the great evangelical constituency of North America), you might easily conclude that it does not matter. I once had to respond in print to the question, "Is personal holiness passé?" I found it hard not to conclude that most present-day believers deep down think it is passé. Here is some of the evidence for that conclusion.

Preaching and Teaching. What do we Christians mainly preach and teach and produce TV programs and videocassettes about these days? The answer seems to be not holiness, but success and positive feelings—getting health, wealth, freedom from care, good sex, and happy families. I remember seeing in a Christian journal a group of eight new "how-to" books reviewed on a single page. How long, I wonder, is it since you heard about eight new books on holiness? Shall I guess?

Leadership. What do we Christians chiefly value in our leaders—our preachers, teachers, pastors, writers, televangelists, top people in parachurch ministries, money-men who bankroll churches and other Christian enterprises, and other folk with key roles in our set-up? The answer seems to be not their holiness, but their gifts and skills and resources. The number of North American leaders (and other Christians too) who in recent years have been found guilty of sexual and financial shenanigans, and who when challenged have declined to see themselves as accountable to any part of the body of Christ, is startling. Much more startling is the way in which, after public exposure and some few slaps on the wrist, they are soon able to resume their ministry and carry on as if nothing had happened, commanding apparently as much support as before. To protest that Christians believe in the forgiveness of sins and the restoration of sinners is beside the point. What I am saying is that the speed of their reinstatement shows that we value them more for their proven gifts than for their proven sanctity, since the thought that only holy people are likely to be spiritually useful does not loom large in our minds.

More than a century and a half ago, the Scottish parish minister and revival preacher Robert Murray McCheyne declared: "My people's greatest need is my personal holiness." It seems clear that neither modern clergy nor their modern flocks would agree with McCheyne's assessment. In the past when your church has appointed a calling committee to hunt for the next pastor, I am sure that a very adequate profile of required gifts has been drawn up, but how much emphasis has been laid on the crucial need to find a holy man? Shall I guess?

Evangelism. How do we Christians formulate the gospel to others in our evangelism, and to ourselves as born-again believers who are called to live by it? I do not think it can be disputed that while we lay heavy stress on faith (coming to Christ, trusting his promises, believing that God knows what he is doing with our lives, and hoping for heaven), we touch very lightly on repentance (binding one's conscience to God's moral law, confessing and forsaking one's sins, making restitution for past wrongs, grieving before God at the dishonor one's sins have done him, and forming a game plan for holy living). The post-Christian culture of the West doubts whether there are any moral absolutes. It is sure that in any case private morality or immorality really matter to nobody except the persons directly involved. Western Christians act as if they agreed, especially where sex and shekels (H. Hensley Henson's apt phrase) are concerned.

Some even argue that to speak of repentance as a necessity rather than a mere beneficial option, and to affirm that the gospel call to faith is also a call to repentance, is to lapse into anti-Christian legalism.[8] You have heard, I am sure, many, many sermons on faith. How often, I wonder, have you heard a series, or even one, preached on repentance? You have books in your home on living the Christian life successfully. Do they even mention repentance, let alone make much of it as a vital lifelong discipline?

When you explain the gospel to others, do you emphasize repentance, and the holiness by which repentance is expressed, as a spiritual necessity? Shall I guess?

But if we play down or ignore the importance of holiness, we are utterly and absolutely wrong.

Holiness is in fact commanded: God wills it, Christ requires it, and all the Scriptures—the law, the gospel, the prophets, the wisdom writings, the epistles, the history books that tell of judgments past, and the Book of Revelation that tells of judgment to come—call for it.

It is God's will that you should be sanctified. **1 Thes 4:3**

Go now and leave your life of sin. **Jn 8:11**

All Scripture is God-breathed and is useful for teaching, rebuking, correcting and training in righteousness, so that the man of God may be thoroughly equipped for every good work. **2 Tm 3:16**

Do not let this Book of the Law depart from your mouth; meditate on it day and night, so that you may be careful to do everything written in it. **Jos 1:8**

Anyone who breaks one of the least of these commandments and teaches others to do the same will be called least in the kingdom of heaven, but whoever practices and teaches these commands will be called great in the kingdom of heaven. **Mt 5:19**

It is written, "Be holy, because I am holy." **1 Pt 1:16**

In reality holiness is the goal of our redemption. As Christ died in order that we may be justified, so we are justified in order that we may be sanctified and made holy.

The grace of God that brings salvation... teaches us to say "No" to ungodliness and worldly passions, and to live self-controlled, upright and godly lives in this present age, while we wait for the blessed hope—the glorious appearing of our great God and Savior, Jesus Christ, who gave himself for us to redeem us from all wickedness and to purify for himself a people that are his very own, eager to do what is good.

Ti 2:11-14

Christ loved the church and gave himself up for her to make her holy, cleansing her by the washing with water through the word, and to present her to himself as a radiant church... holy and blameless. **Eph 5:25-27**

Holiness is the object of our new creation. We are born again so that we may grow up into Christ-likeness.

We are God's workmanship, created in Christ Jesus to do good works, which God prepared in advance for us to do.

Eph 2:10

You were taught... in accordance with the truth that is in Jesus... to put off your old self, which is being corrupted by its deceitful desires; to be made new in the attitude of your minds; and to put on the new self, created to be like God in true righteousness and holiness. **Eph 4:21-24**

Holiness, as a sign and expression of the reality of one's faith and repentance, and of one's acceptance of God's ultimate purpose, is genuinely necessary for one's final salvation.

Nothing impure will ever enter it [new Jerusalem], nor will anyone who does what is shameful or deceitful. **Rv 21:27**

Without holiness no one will see the Lord. **Heb 12:14**

Holiness is actually the true health of the person. Anything else is ugliness and deformity at character level, a malfunctioning of the individual, a crippled state of soul. The various forms of bodily sickness and impairment that Jesus healed are so many illustrations of this deeper, inward deformity.

Holiness effectively thwarts Satan in his designs on our lives. By contrast, unconcern about holiness and failure to practice the purity and righteousness to which we are called play into his hands every time.

Be self-controlled and alert. Your enemy the devil prowls around like a roaring lion looking for someone to devour. Resist him.... **1 Pt 5:8-9**

Do not give the devil a foothold. **Eph 4:27**

Righteousness, meaning holy integrity and uprightness, is the breastplate in the armor of God that Christians are called to wear in order to counter the devil's attacks (Eph 6:14).

Holiness also gives credibility to witness. But those who proclaim a life-changing Savior will not impress others if their own lives seem to be no different from anyone else's. Holy ways will enhance our testimony, while worldly ways will undermine it. "You are the light of the world.... Let your light shine before men, that they may see your good deeds [good works, backing up good words] and praise your Father in heaven [about whom you told them, and whose power they now see in your living]" (Mt 5:14, 16).

If we want to be fruitful in evangelism, we must cultivate holiness of life.

Finally, holiness is the substance of which happiness is the spin-off. Those who chase happiness miss it, while to those who pursue holiness through the grace of Christ, happiness of spirit comes unasked. "I delight in your commands because I love them.... They are the joy of my heart" (Ps 119:47, 111).

Can anyone still doubt, after all this, that for every Christian without exception holiness is important?

SYSTEMATIC AND TIME-TESTED

The account of holiness in the following chapters is, for better or for worse, that of a systematic theologian. Systematic theology is, in Anselm's famous phrase, faith seeking understanding—faith trying to think everything through, and think it all together, in relation to God the Creator as the central reality. The study of holiness is a mapping of the life of God in the human soul, a study that is nowadays usually called Christian spirituality. (The adjective "Christian" is important there, for every religion has its own spirituality. Christian spirituality, however, stands as far apart from other spiritualities as Christian doctrine does from other forms of belief.) This book should be seen as a venture in systematic spirituality. What is that? It is a subsection of systematic theology in which one tries to think everything through, and think it all together, in terms of communion with God as the central relationship.

As I said at the outset, I regard Christian holiness as a topic on which better teaching was given in the past than in the present, and the lines of thought I shall offer have all been tested by time. I make no apology for drawing on Protestant, Roman Catholic, and Orthodox wisdom from yesterday in order to help us see how the relevant biblical instruction applies to us today. Rather, I urge that this is good sense. By standing on the shoulders of the giants, little people like ourselves may hope to see more than we would if we stayed on the ground.

Exploring Salvation: Why Holiness Is Necessary

But we ought always to thank God for you, brothers loved by the Lord, because from the beginning God chose you to be saved through the sanctifying work of the Spirit and through belief in the truth. He called you to this through our gospel, that you might share in the glory of our Lord Jesus Christ. **2 Thes 2:13-14**

Peter, an apostle of Jesus Christ, to God's elect, strangers in the world... who have been chosen according to the foreknowledge of God the Father, through the sanctifying work of the Spirit, for obedience to Jesus Christ and sprinkling by his blood: Grace and peace be yours in abundance. **1 Pt 1:1-2**

DISEASES AND DELUSIONS

I opened my eyes to find myself lying on my back in a strange bed. Because my head was raised, I could see into the semidarkness beyond the bed. My first thought was that I was in New York's Grand Central railroad station at night. (I had recently seen a photo of the huge Grand Central hall at night, and thought I was recognizing that location.) Then I saw, sitting on the left-hand side of the bed, my mother. She was wearing the big flowered overall and dusting-cap in which she used to clean the house. She did not speak, but smiled and gave me a cold drink through the spout of what looked like a small white teapot. Afterward they told me that I went straight back to sleep.

In fact, as I learned when I woke next, I was nowhere near Grand Central station. I was in the hospital in my English hometown, having had surgery for a depressed fracture of the skull, which was thought to have damaged my brain. What I saw was partly a delusion, for the ward did not really look like the Grand Central station of the photo either by day or by night. The person keeping vigil by my bed had been a nurse in uniform, wearing a frilly headdress, blue frock, and white apron. I saw what I saw (if I shut my eyes I can see it now), but I was not seeing what was there. My shocked and battered brain was playing tricks on me. Reality was different from what I thought it was.

All of that happened in 1933, when I was seven years old. Why do I now hark back to it? Because it illustrates two truths that I find I have to stress over and over again when talking to Christians today.

First Truth. We are all invalids in God's hospital. In moral and spiritual terms we are all sick and damaged, diseased and deformed, scarred and sore, lame and lopsided, to a far, far greater extent than we realize. Under God's care we are getting better, but we are not yet well. The modern Christian likes to dwell on present blessings rather than future prospects. Modern Christians egg each other on to testify that where once we were blind, deaf, and indeed dead so far as God was concerned, now through Christ we have been brought to life, radically transformed, and blessed with spiritual health. Thank God, there is real truth in that. But spiritual health means being holy and whole. To the extent that we fall short of being holy and whole, we are not fully healthy either.

We need to realize that the spiritual health we testify to is only partial and relative, a matter of being less sick and less incapacitated now than we were before. Measured by the absolute standard of spiritual health that we see in Jesus Christ, we are all of us no more, just as we are no less, than invalids in the process of being cured. The old saying that the church is God's hospital remains true. Our spiritual life is at best a fragile convalescence, easily disrupted. When there are tensions, strains, perversities, and disappointments in the Christian fellowship, it helps to remember that no Christian, and no church, ever has the clean bill of spiritual health that would match the total physical well-being for which today's fitness seekers labor. To long for total spiritual well-being is right and natural, but to believe that one is anywhere near it is to be utterly self-deceived.

It is not always easy to grasp that one is ill. I remember how in the hospital in 1933 I was, so to speak, kept in cotton wool for several days by doctor's orders, since nobody knew how much harm might have come to my brain. I also remember how hard it was to think of myself as a sick boy, since at no stage did I feel any ill effects at all. For slipping out of bed to wander round, and for standing on the bed to see how springy it was, I was tongue-lashed, I recall, by the nurse who upbraided me with Welsh eloquence for, in effect, putting my life at risk. After this I remained dutifully bedbound, according to instructions—but still without any conviction inside me that it needed to be that way. (Seven-year-olds can be as opinionated as any adult, and I certainly was.)

In the same way, Christians today can imagine themselves to be strong, healthy, and holy when, in fact, they are actually weak, sick, and sinful in ways that are noticeable not just to their heavenly Father, but also to their fellow believers. Pride and complacency, however, blind us to this reality. We decline to be told when we are slipping; thinking we stand, we set ourselves up to fall, and predictably, alas, we do fall.

In good hospitals, patients receive regular curative treatment as well as constant care, and the treatment determines in a direct way the form that the care will take. In God's hospital the course of treatment that the Father, Son, and Holy Spirit, the permanent medical staff (if I dare so speak), are giving to each of us with a view to our final restoration to the fullness of the divine image, is called *sanctification*. It is a process that includes on the one hand medication and diet (in the form of biblical instruction and admonition coming in various ways to the heart), and on the other hand tests and exercises (in the form of internal and external pressures, providentially ordered, to which we have to make active response). The process goes on as long as we are in this world, which is something that God decides in each case.

Like patients in any ordinary hospital, we are impatient for recovery. The question that forms the title of Lane Adams' wonderful little book on God's sanctifying therapy, *How Come It's Taking Me So Long to Get Better?*,[1] is often our heart-cry to God. The truth is that God knows what he is doing, but sometimes, for reasons connected with the maturity and ministry that he has in view for us, he makes haste slowly. That is something we have to learn humbly to accept. We are in a hurry; he is not.

Second Truth. We are all prone to damaging delusions. On my first night in the hospital, the place was not where I thought it was, and the person by my bed was not whom I thought it was: I was in a state of delusion. The next day I felt well and could not think of myself as ill, but that was delusion too. In the same way believers are often deluded about Christian faith and living.

There are the delusions of direct theological error about God's nature and character and ways and purposes. In liberal and modernist and process theology, to look no further, these abound.

There are the delusions of doubt and unbelief. Something horrible happens, and at once we conclude that God must have forgotten us or turned against us, or perhaps gone out of existence.

There are the delusions of self-confidence. We think we

have finally licked some particular sin or weakness by which we were previously dragged down. We relax, and a sense of well-being, security, and triumph creeps over us. Then comes the double whammy of fresh external pressure and a renewed inner urge, and down we go again.

There are also the delusions that disrupt relationships. We misunderstand each other's motives and purposes. We blame others for causing the tensions and generating the hostility, and are blind to our own part in provoking the difficulties.

There are delusions too, resulting from failure to distinguish things that differ—for example, equating the biblical gospel with Jesus-centered legalism, Jesus-centered lawlessness, Jesus-centered socialism, or Jesus-centered racism; equating secular psychological counseling with biblical pastoral direction; or equating inner passivity as a formula for holiness with the biblical call to disciplined moral effort in the power of the Holy Spirit.[2] All such delusions spell disaster.

And then there are delusions about the Christian life—that it will ordinarily be easy, successful, healthy and wealthy, excitingly punctuated by miracles; that such acts as fornication and tax evasion will not matter as long as nobody finds out; that God always wants you to do what you feel like doing; and so on, and so on. Satan, the father of lies and a past master at deluding, labors constantly to mislead and muddle God's people, so that humble self-suspicion, and the commonsensical hardheadedness that used to be called prudence, and the habit of testing by Scripture things hitherto taken for granted, become virtues of very great importance.

Throughout this book, I shall be appealing to Scripture constantly. It is the only safe way, for we are all as vulnerable to delusions about holiness as we are about anything else.

GOD'S PRESCRIPTION FOR US

The sort of physician I appreciate (and you, too, I expect) takes the patient into his or her confidence and explains his or her diagnosis, prognosis, and treatment. Then he or she tells you what the prescribed medication is meant to do. You are put fully in the picture, and so you know where you are. Not all physicians behave this way, but the best do—and so does the Great Physician of our souls, our Lord Jesus Christ. His therapeutic style, if I may express it this way, is communicative from first to last. The Bible, heard and read, preached and taught, interpreted and applied, is both the channel and the content of his communication. It is as if Jesus hands us the canonical Scriptures directly, telling us that they are the authoritative and all-suffcient source from which we must learn both what we are to do in order to be his followers and also what he has done, is doing, and will do to save us from the fatal sickness of sin. Think of your Bible, then, as Jesus Christ's gift to you; think of it as a letter to you from your Lord. Think of your name, written in the front of it, as if Jesus himself had written it there. Think of Jesus each time you read your Bible. Think of him asking you, page by page and chapter by chapter, what you have just learned about the need, nature, method, and effect of the grace that he brings, and about the path of loyal discipleship that he calls you to tread. That is the way to profit from the Bible. Only when your reading of the written Word feeds into your relationship with the living Word (Jesus) does the Bible operate as the channel of light and life that God means it to be.

Scriptural Framework. The aim of this present chapter is to profile from the Scriptures the whole work of divine grace in the individual, first to last, so that we grasp the frame of reference within which God's summons to holiness is issued. When we see what God through Christ and the Spirit is doing for us and in us, we shall be better placed to understand what it is that he calls us to do for him and with him. Here the distinction between justification and sanctification becomes important. As far as concerns the making of atonement for our sins, and the consequent pardoning and justifying of our person, the work is entirely and exclusively God's. When we confess ourselves lost sinners and cast ourselves on Christ to save us, we are acknowledging by our action that we contribute nothing to our new relationship with God save our need of it, and this is the exact truth. We get into God's favor, not by paying our way, but by accepting his gift of a blood-bought amnesty. However, in sanctification, which is the work of God within us from which our holiness flows, we are called to cooperate actively with God. In order to do this as we should, we need to have some overall awareness of his purpose and strategy for our lives as a whole.

So I offer now a Bible-based account of God's way with us as our Creator and Redeemer, an account built around the questions concerning God and ourselves that all of us ought to be asking (whether or not we actually are). I want this account to function as a hiker's map is meant to function, that is, as a help to determining where we are at the moment and seeing which way we should go. The map is admittedly small-scale (what I pass over in review here fills hundreds of pages in theology textbooks). But small-scale maps are sometimes best for getting clear on the overall lay of the land, and I hope it may be so in this case.

If my attempt to clarify everything at once makes the chapter tough going for you, I apologize, but I beg you to stay with it all the same. It is basic to everything else I shall say.

DEFINING SALVATION

First question then: *what is salvation?*

This is not a hard question to answer. Anywhere that we open the New Testament, we find that from one angle or another salvation is being explained, displayed, and discussed. Salvation is the New Testament's master theme in all of its twenty-seven books. If we compare and correlate their contents, we find that the understanding of salvation that is presented is uniformly clear and virtually unanimous. The idea conveyed by the salvation language is nowhere in doubt. Salvation always means being rescued from jeopardy and misery, so that one is now safe. Thus, in the Old Testament, God is said to have saved Israel from Egypt, Jonah from the fish's belly, and the psalmist from death (Ex 15:2; Jon 2:9; Ps 116:6).

New Testament salvation, however, is salvation from sin and its consequences. It is the work of the God who reveals himself as triune, the God who is Father, Son, and Spirit, in clear personal distinction, though in equally clear unity of being and purpose. The New Testament is explicit that the Savior-God whom it proclaims is Yahweh (Jehovah), the covenant Lord of the Old Testament. But it is no less explicit in displaying him as tripersonal—revealing him to be them, if we may so express it. The God who saves from sin is, so to speak, a team. Part of the glory of each divine person is that of being a team player. The New Testament writers speak out of their own experience of being saved by the Father, the Son, and the Spirit, working together. They expend their strength going over the various aspects of this salvation in the hope of helping their readers to get a better grasp of it, and so to enter into it more fully. Those who do not see this, do not understand the New Testament at all.

New Testament salvation has three tenses: past, present, and future. It is salvation:

- from sin's guilt (the past aspect: exposure to penalty is gone);
- from its power (the present aspect: sin no longer rules us); and
- ultimately from its presence (the future aspect: sin will one day be no more than a bad memory).

Salvation, in other words, is an ongoing process that is currently incomplete. Already Christians have been saved:

- from the wrath of God (from judicial retribution: Rom 5:9; 1 Thes 1:10);

- from eternal death (Rom 6:21, 23);
- from the dominion of sin (Rom 6:14, 18);
- from the life of fear (Rom 8:15); and
- from controlling habits of ungodliness and immorality (Ti 2:11-3:6).

And one day, beyond this world, Christians will be fully conformed to Jesus in both body and moral character (Phil 3:20; 1 Jn 3:2). Then sin will not be in them anymore.

At this moment, however, we who are Christians are very conscious of not yet having reached that happy state. We live joyfully in God's favor, serve and worship him out of gratitude for his grace, and battle with the downdrag of indwelling sin through the energy granted us by the indwelling Holy Spirit (Rom 5:1, 12:1, 8:5-14; Gal 5:16). We often have cause to thank God for fresh victories won, but like Paul we long for the day when the war within will be a thing of the past (Rom 7:24ff., 8:23).

We desire perfect holiness and reach out after it, but for the present our reach exceeds our grasp. God's salvation is from sin: we are into salvation, but salvation is not yet fully into us. The foretaste is ours now; the fullness remains future. That is where I am as I write these words, and where I shall assume that you are too as you read them. I am right, am I not?

In New Testament salvation, Jesus Christ the Savior, who is both God and man (Jn 1:14; Col 1:13-20, 2:9), is the key figure. Salvation is *through* him, in the sense that our forgiveness, justification, reconciliation, pardon, acceptance, access, standing, and fellowship with God (all these terms are used[3]) rest on his death as a sacrifice for our sins—a sacrifice guaranteeing that believers will never come into condemnation, nor be deprived of the communion with the Father and the Son that is now theirs (Jn 5:24; Rom 8:32-39).

Salvation is also *in* him, in the double sense that we are both in solidarity with him as our representative head, who once suffered as our sin-bearer, and now intercedes on our behalf, and are also in vital and vitalizing union with him by faith through the Holy Spirit. Thus he becomes truly our life-giver, who animates us for holiness in a way to which we were strangers before (see Rom 5:12-19; Eph 2:1-10, 4:20-24; Col 1:27, 3:4). Natural life is supernaturalized as the Holy Spirit makes Christ present to us, and reproduces in us the God-oriented desires, aims, attitudes, and behavior patterns that were seen in Christ's own perfect humanity when he was on earth. All Christians who can recall their life before they were converted can point to specific ways in which their mindset in Christ has now become different from what it was before.

Salvation as the Joint Effort of the Trinity. New Testament salvation, as was hinted above, is the joint work of a divine trio, a team consisting of the Father, Son, and Holy Spirit. It is, indeed, in the process of expounding the cooperative saving action of the holy Three that the New Testament brings out their personal distinctness within the unity of God. The truth of the Trinity thus emerges as part of the doctrine of salvation. Their roles are set forth as follows. The Father, who planned everything (Rom 8:28-30; Eph 3:9-11), sent first the Son and then the Spirit into the world to carry out his saving intentions (Jn 3:17, 6:38-40, 14:26, 16:7-15; Rom 8:26). The Son, whose nature and joy it is to always do the Father's will (Jn 4:34, 5:19, 6:38, 8:29), became man in order to die for us, rise for us, reign for us, and one day return for us to take us to the place of happy rest that he has prepared for us (Jn 10:14-18, 14:2, 18-23). In the meantime, he mediates mercy and help to us from his throne (Heb 4:14-16, 7:25). The Holy Spirit, the self-effacing divine executive who engineered creation (Gn 1:2) and now engineers the new creation (Jn 3:3-8), has been at work since Pentecost imparting to believers their first install-ment of heaven's life in and with their Savior (Rom 8:23; Eph 1:13). In addition, the Holy Spirit is changing believers pro-gressively into Christ's image (2 Cor 3:18).

Salvation is thus the threefold activity of the triune God.

Just as mutual love and honor is revealed as the occupation of the Three-in-One (Jn 3:35, 5:20, 14:31, 16:14, 17:1, 4), so loving and honoring the Trinity becomes the eternal vocation of those whom the Three-in-One have saved—starting now! One mark of the saved, therefore, is that they currently give themselves to worship, and they want to go on doing so literally forever. This appears in the joyful anticipation of heaven's eternity described in the hymn "Amazing Grace":

> When we've been there ten thousand years
> Bright shining as the sun,
> We've no less days *to sing God's praise*
> Than when we first begun. (emphasis mine)

SALVATION'S PURPOSE

Second question: *why did we need salvation?*

Why, because we were sinners! and, as such, lost! This has been said already, but the assertion needs now to be amplified.

We were sinners: sinners in practice, because we were sinners by nature. Sin is a universal, transcultural reality, an infection from which no human being anywhere, at any time, is exempt. What is it? Formally, it is what answer fourteen of the *Westminster Shorter Catechism* says it is: "Any want of conformity unto, or transgression of, the law of God."

But it is also an energy, an obsession, an allergic reaction to God's law, an irrational anti-God syndrome in our spiritual system that drives us to exalt ourselves and steels our hearts against devotion and obedience to our Maker. Pride, ingratitude, and self-gratification are its basic expressions, leading sometimes to antisocial behavior and always, even in the nicest and most honorable people, to a lack of love for God at the motivational level. The religious practice of unregenerate mankind, whatever its form, may be and often is conscientious and laborious. It always proves, however, on analysis to be self-seeking and God-exploiting, rather than self-denying and God-glorifying, in its purpose.

Both Old Testament Hebrew and New Testament Greek have a wide range of words for sin, picturing its nonconformity to God in a variety of different ways:

- as rebellion against our rightful owner and ruler;
- as transgression of the bounds he set;
- as missing the mark he told us to aim at;
- as breaking the law he enacted;
- as defiling (dirtying, polluting) ourselves in his sight, so making ourselves unfit for his company;
- as embracing folly by shutting our ears to his wisdom; and
- as incurring guilt before his judgment seat.

The Bible, functioning as a mirror for self-knowledge, shows us ourselves as playing God, by making ourselves, our wishes and advancement, the center of everything; as fighting God, by refusing to submit to him and defying his revealed will; and as hating God in our hearts for the claims he makes on our lives. "The mind of sinful man is death... the sinful mind is hostile to God. It does not submit to God's law, nor can it do so. Those controlled by the sinful nature cannot please God" (Rom 8:6-8).

Lost Sinners. As sinners, *we were lost* in the way that stray sheep are lost: cut off from our true home and out of touch with our true master. We had nothing to look forward to save misery without end. We merited nothing but exclusion and banishment from the presence of the living God whom we had already excluded from our lives. Perhaps we did this through preoccupation with the quest for pleasure and profit, position and possessions, and perhaps even by sheltering behind a smokescreen of religiosity. One way or another, however, we did it, and it is nothing more than justice for God now to shut us out of his life in the way that we shut him out of ours. Made by God for God, and so made that at the deepest level we cannot find contentment save in a love-relationship with God, we were thus "without hope and without God in the world" (Eph 2:12). This is the universal human condition. All Christians know in their heart that everyone in whom fallen nature runs its course is naturally in that lost and hopeless state, and each believer glories accordingly in the "Amazing grace... that saved a wretch like me."

Do all sinners know that they are sinners? Yes—and no. The distinction, important throughout theology, between the order of being and the order of knowing applies here (the distinction, that is, for those who like technical terms, between the ontological and the epistemological dimensions). The death-dealing dominion of sin over us is a reality from birth. It is only known as God's light shines into our hearts, exposing our lack of love for God, and lack of believing obedience to his word. This light shows us how self-focused our real motives are, and how we regularly omit to do what we should do, and instead do what we should not. But such exposure is painful, and we shrink from it. Our first reaction to what the light shows us of our own inner badness is like the common first reaction to a diagnosis of terminal cancer, namely denial.

All have, however, some rudimentary knowledge of God from which these things may be learned. In Romans 1:18-32 Paul tells us that all mankind "knew God"—they were (and are) aware to some extent of his reality and requirements through his universal self-disclosure via creation to everyone's mind and conscience. The entire human race, therefore, is "without excuse" for its embrace of idolatry and immorality. All the non-godliness of the non-Christian and post-Christian world is actually ungodliness and anti-godliness in the Creator's world. It is sin against light, and deep down people know this, though many are so out of touch with themselves that if asked, they would affirm that they do not.

Those, however, who have been instructed in God's law and gospel, as found in the Bible, will ordinarily have a more vivid awareness of their sinfulness, and of their particular sins, because the divine light that shines on them from Scripture to show them to themselves is brighter. This is one reason (there are others) why converted Christians regularly experience deeper conviction of sin after their conversion than they knew before, and why one dimension of spiritual growth, as we shall shortly see, is growth downward into a more thorough humility and more radical repentance. Though not much is said about this nowadays, a deepening sense of one's sinfulness remains a touchstone of the genuine Christian life.

GOD'S PLAN FOR SALVATION

Third question: *what is God's strategy in salvation?* What sequence of steps and stages has he followed, and will he follow, in order to carry through his saving purpose in each Christian's life, and so complete the "good work in you" that he has started (Phil 1:6)? From Scripture we may formulate an answer to both parts of our question. As with the previous question, the biblical answer has been hinted at already, but needs now to be expanded.

History of Salvation. First, then, how did God bring me into the salvation that I now enjoy? The Bible tells me that at the start of the first century of our era, in Galilee, the northern part of Palestine, "when the (appointed) time had fully come" (Gal 4:4), the divine incarnation took place. The Son of God, without ceasing to be God the Son, became Jesus of Nazareth through the virgin birth (see Lk 1:29-35; Jn 1:14; Gal 4:4). As the God-man, Jesus' vocation was to be the mediator between his Father and ourselves (1 Tm 2:5), revealing his Father to us, teaching and modeling the way of godliness, communicating mercy and help from God to people in need, and finally making himself a sacrificial ransom for our sins (Mk 10:45; Mt 26:28; 1 Tm 2:6).

At the close of his three-year ministry, after announcing the kingdom of God and giving the announcement credibility through miraculous works of grace, mostly healings, Jesus was crucified as a political subversive (which he was not). On the cross the penal retribution due to us for our sins was laid on him and became his experience, by his Father's own action. By thus suffering as our substitutionary sacrifice, he redeemed us from evil, reconciled us to the Father, and quenched forever the Father's judicial hostility (wrath) towards us (see Rom 3:21-26; 5:6-11).

The historic *Anglican Prayer Book* celebrates Jesus' atoning death on the cross as "a full, perfect, and sufficient sacrifice, oblation, and satisfaction for the sins of the whole world." This magnificent phrase expresses a magnificent truth: because Christ suffered in our stead, our sins may be forgiven and we be saved—"saved by his precious blood" (his precious sacrificial death, which is what the New Testament means whenever it speaks of the blood of Christ). As Calvin expressed it, in a manner beyond our understanding God loved us even when he hated us. The measure of his love was, and is, the gift of his Son to die for our sins (Jn 3:16; Rom 5:8; 1 Jn 4:8-10).

Jesus' death was not the end of the story. On the third day after his crucifixion, he was raised from the dead by his Father's power. He left the tomb in a body with mysteriously enhanced capacities. In that body, mysteriously once more, he came and went in moments of ministry to his disciples for the next forty days. Then he ascended to the Father (Jn 20:17; Acts 1:1-11; Eph 4:10), being taken from human sight by an upward movement into a cloud. C.S. Lewis somewhere speaks of his being withdrawn through "a fold in space."

From that day forward he has been exercising dominion over the created order in his Father's name and on his Father's behalf. (That is why he is called "Christ": the title designates him as God's anointed Savior-King.) As an initial act of his dominion, both demonstrating and furthering it, he poured out the Holy Spirit on his disciples at nine o'clock on Pentecost morning, some ten days after he had ascended to his throne (Acts 2:1-21,33). Ever since then the Holy Spirit has been active in the world, witnessing to Jesus by prompting and blessing human testimony to Jesus' saving ministry, and drawing people to Jesus by his work of new creation and new birth (Jn 3:3-8; 2 Cor 5:17; Ti 3:4-7). This means that he renews them at the core of their personhood, so that they come actively to trust Jesus, obey him, and love him as their living Savior, divine King, and heavenly Friend. It is through this activity of the Holy Spirit that you, I, and all the Christians that have ever been, became believers as we did.

What happens here is that through the Spirit's work in people's hearts, once the message that invites them to faith in Christ has gotten into their heads, they become certain that Jesus Christ is fact, not fancy; that he lives to save those who turn from sin to be his; and that there is no salvation save through personal trust in him. So they do in fact actively and deliberately commit themselves to him, not only because they know they need to, but because they find themselves so changed that they want to.

For some, like the present writer, this commitment occurs as a clear and conscious break with an unconverted past. For others, it emerges as a focusing of what has been implicit in their life for some time, perhaps from infancy. But that difference makes no difference to the reality of what takes place. One way or another, out of changed hearts there issues a commitment to live changed lives, while the Spirit within us witnesses both to Jesus' reality, as the mighty Savior who is there for us, and to our own renewal, as penitent sinners who have now made him the object of our wholehearted loyalty.

New Life. The New Testament goes on to explain to us the newness of our life in Christ as a real and radical alteration of our personal being. It tells us that believers have been united to Christ, and are now "in" him, having died (finished with their old life) and been raised (started off in a new life) with their Lord (Rom 6:3-11; Eph 2:4-10; Col 2:11-14). In Christ they enjoy a new status. They are:

- *justified* (pardoned and accepted);
- *adopted* (made God's children and heirs); and
- *cleansed* (fitted for fellowship with their holy Creator).

All aspects of their new status become real by virtue of Christ's suffering for them on the cross (see Rom 3:21-26, 5:1, 8:15-19; Gal 4:4-7; Jn 15:3; 1 Jn 1:3-7). This is momentous. To be justified means that, by God's own judicial decision, I stand before him now and forever "just as if I had never sinned." To be adopted means that now I may call my Creator-Judge "Father," in the intimacy of his beloved family, and know myself to be an heir of his glory—"heirs of God and co-heirs with Christ" (Rom 8:17). To be cleansed means that nothing in my past imposes any restraint on my fellowship with God in the present.

Nor is that all. In Christ believers are also involved in a process of character change. The Holy Spirit (through whose agency faith was engendered in them) and Christ (through whom the new life was won for them, and became consciously real to them) now indwell them to transform them "into his (Christ's) likeness with ever-increasing glory." Christ and his Spirit empower them to put sinful habits to death and bring forth in them the new behavior patterns that constitute the Spirit's "fruit" (see Rom 8:9-13; 2 Cor 3:18; Gal 5:22-26). This, too, is momentous.

We who believe have to wake up to the fact that the ministry to us of the Father and the Son through the Spirit has turned us into different people from what we were by nature. Our present task is, as it is sometimes put, to be what we are—to live out what God has wrought in, expressing in action the new life (new vision, motivation, devotion, and sense of direction) that has now become ours. Or, as Paul puts it, "Live a life worthy of the calling you have received" (Eph 4:1). The thought is the same.

The hearts of saved persons will always affirm that their conversion, or new birth, or renewal (different people use different words at this point) was the work of God from first to last. All the searching and struggling that went into it will be felt to have been no less divinely orchestrated than were its final stages of conviction, commitment, and assurance. Ever since the fifth century, Western Christians have used Augustine's term for God's initiative of life-giving love within the soul, giving thanks for his *prevenient grace:* grace that moves in as a renovating force to make the spiritually blind see, the spiritually deaf hear, and the spiritually dumb speak. (Prevenient means "coming before"—coming to one, before one is spiritually alive, in order to impart life.)

God's Purpose. The sense that God has thus invaded one's own darkness and lostness in order to bring salvation naturally prompts the question that was poignantly posed in a modern gospel song—"But, Jesus, why me?" The New Testament faces and answers this question by pointing backward and upward to an eternal purpose of sovereign divine love to sinful individuals, a purpose that has its source in God's own free decision. It is manifested by the prevenient grace that brings each one to faith and salvation, and guarantees their final glory. New Testament writers do not tell me why God chose to save me. They only tell me to be thankful that he did.

Here is Paul celebrating God's loving purpose as he summons the Gentile believers at Ephesus to join him in doxology:

> Praise be to the God and Father of our Lord Jesus Christ, who has blessed us in the heavenly realms with every spiritual blessing in Christ. For he chose us in him before the creation of the world to be holy and blameless in his sight. In love he predestined us to be adopted as his sons through Jesus Christ, in accordance with his pleasure and will—to the praise of his glorious grace, which he has freely given us in the One he loves. In him we have redemption through his blood, the forgiveness of sins, in accordance with the riches of God's grace that he lavished on us.... And you also

were included in Christ when you heard the word of truth, the gospel of your salvation. Having believed, you were marked in him with a seal, the promised Holy Spirit, who is a deposit guaranteeing our inheritance until the redemption of those who are God's possession—to the praise of his glory. **Eph 1:3-7, 13-14**

This is how he formulates the same eternal purpose for the encouragement of Christians who face suffering and feel themselves weak:

We know that in all things God works for the good of those who love him, who have been called according to his purpose. For those God foreknew he also predestined to be conformed to the likeness of his Son, that he might be the firstborn among many brothers. And those he predestined, he also called; those he called, he also justified; those he justified, he also glorified. **Rom 8:28-30**

Jesus himself has precisely this purpose in view when he says:

All that the Father gives me will come to me, and whoever comes to me I will never drive away. For I have come down from heaven not to do my will but to do the will of him who sent me. And this is the will of him who sent me, that I shall lose none of all that he has given me, but raise them up at the last day. For my Father's will is that everyone who looks to the Son and believes in him shall have eternal life, and I will raise him up at the last day.... No one can come to me unless the Father who sent me draws him, and I will raise him up at the last day.... Everyone who listens to the Father and learns from him comes to me. **Jn 6:37-40, 44-45**

God's plan to save individual sinners through his work of sovereign grace is sometimes seen as a theme for anxious debate. The truth that God has such a plan is thought to threaten those who do not yet believe, by implying that should they turn to God they might find that he has no mercy for them, because they are not among his elect. But this fear is unreal, for no one ever turns to God—"no one can come to me," says Jesus—apart from the sovereign grace that implements God's merciful plan.

In actual fact, all are invited to enter God's kingdom, with the assurance that if they seek enabling from the Holy Spirit to repent and believe they will find it. Prevenient grace—the Holy Spirit, already in action—stirs whatever positive response the invitation brings. Believers, as we saw, know for sure that without prevenient grace they would not be believers, and that prevenient grace touched their lives because of God's plan to save them. So it is no wonder that in the New Testament God's plan appears not as a matter for debate and doubt, but for doxology—directing those who now believe to humility, homage, and hope, and imparting to them both determination and delight as their minds dwell on it. Article 17 of the Anglican 39 expresses this in a clear (if lumpy) way:

> ... the godly consideration of Predestination, and our Election in Christ, is full of sweet, pleasant, and unspeakable comfort to godly persons, and such as feel in themselves the working of the Spirit of Christ, mortifying the works of the flesh, and their earthly members, and drawing up their mind to high and heavenly things, as well because it doth greatly establish and confirm their faith of eternal Salvation to be enjoyed through Christ, as because it doth fervently kindle their love towards God....

GOD'S SAVING PLAN

The question as to how God brought me into the salvation that I now enjoy is thus fully answered, so we move to our next question about God's saving strategy: *what will God go on to do, here and hereafter, in order to finish what he has begun and complete the salvation he has in store for me?* To establish the proper perspective for answering that question, I quote Thomas Binney's well-known hymn.

Eternal light! Eternal light!
How pure the soul must be
When, placed within thy searching sight,
It shrinks not, but with calm delight
Can live and look on thee!

The spirits that surround thy throne
May bear the burning bliss;
But that is surely theirs alone,
Since they have never, never known
A fallen world like this.

O how shall I, whose native sphere
Is dark, whose mind is dim,
Before the ineffable appear,
And on my naked spirit bear
The uncreated beam?

There is a way for man to rise
To that sublime abode—
An offering and a sacrifice,
The Holy Spirit's energies,
An advocate with God.

These, these prepare us for the sight
Of holiness above;
The sons of ignorance and night
May dwell in the eternal light
Through the eternal love.

God's Future Plan of Salvation. The lesson to be learned here is that our thinking about the future part of God's saving plan must start where Binney starts: namely, with recognition that the triune God is *light.* This means that he is holy—pure and perfect, loving all good and hating all evil. Also, it means that he constantly searches out all that is in us, so that "everything is uncovered and laid bare before the eyes of him to whom we must give account" (Heb 4:13). (The exposing of what would otherwise lie hidden in darkness is one of the thoughts that the biblical image of *light* regularly conveys: see John 3:19-21; Ephesians 5:11-14.) So no unholiness in us will go unnoticed.

The triune God who is *light* is also *love*—holy love. (See 1 John 1:5, 4:8, 16.) What does this mean? It means that only what is actually holy and worthy can give God actual satisfaction. As the love that binds spouses in a good marriage is an evaluative love that appreciates the excellence of the loved one, so the love that binds Father, Son, and Spirit is an evaluative love whereby each delights in the holiness of the other two, and in the holiness of the holy angels. That love will not have full joy of us who are Christ's until we are holy too. Nor can we fully love God, and fully enjoy him as we love him, while we know ourselves to be still in the grip of moral weaknesses and perversities. To know oneself, here and now, to be, in Luther's phrase, *simul justus et peccator*—a justified sinner, right with God though sinning still—is a wonderful privilege. But the hope set before us is yet more wonderful, namely to be in the presence of God, seeing him and fellowshiping with him, as one who is a sinner no longer. What God plans for us in the present is to lead us toward this goal.

So the divine agenda for the rest of my life on earth is my sanctification. As has already been hinted, I have been raised from spiritual death and born again in Christ so that I might be changed into his moral likeness. "You were taught," Paul tells me (for I, like all other Bible-readers, stand with the Ephesian Christians at this point), "with regard to your former way of life, to put off your old self... to be made new... and to put on the new self, created to be like God in true righteousness and holiness" (Eph 4:22-24; see also Col 3:9-10). The detailed moral directives in each of Paul's letters show me that he means this in the most literal and down-to-earth sense.

Increasing conformity to the image of Christ—to his righteousness and holiness, his love and humility, his self-denial and single-mindedness, his wisdom and prudence, his boldness and self-control, his faithfulness and strength under pressure—is the sum and substance of the "good works" for which Christians have been created (that is, re-created) in Christ (Eph 2:10). It is also the "good" for which in all things God works in the lives of those who love him (Rom 8:28). The God in whose hands I am, willy-nilly, and whom I have in fact gladly and penitently put in charge of my life, is in the holiness business. Part of the answer to the question that life's roller coaster ride repeatedly raises, *why has this happened to me?* is always: it is moral training and discipline, planned by my heavenly Father to help me forward along the path of Christ-like virtue (see Heb 12:5-11).

Many years ago a wise man explained to me that the Christian life—meaning, as we have just seen, the life of growth into Christ-likeness—is like a three-legged stool, which can only stand if all three legs are in place. He spoke of the three legs as D, E, and P—doctrine, experience, and practice.

Doctrine. This refers to the truth and wisdom that we may constantly receive from God through Bible study, Bible-based meditation (not the same thing, be it said), and the ministry of the biblical Word.

Experience. This means the many-sided fellowship with God to which divine truth and wisdom lead when brought to bear on our lives: the faith, the penitence, the renewed sense of sin, the restored joy of salvation, the distress at our repeated failure to be for Christ all we wanted to be, the sorrow we feel at others' need and misery as we pray for them, the delight we feel when others are blessed. It also includes the moments of strong assurance and longing for heaven, the learning of new lessons about God's way through the pain and distress of suffering, the fear of proving oneself to be an unconverted hypocrite after all, the deeper awareness of God's reality that a heart-to-heart exchange with another believer will impart, the vivid sense of Christ's closeness that comes through corporate praise, particularly through serious sharing in the Lord's Supper, and so forth.

Practice. This involves setting oneself to obey the truth and follow the path of wisdom in one's relationships, one's day-to-day self-management, one's family involvement, one's church commitment, one's role in the community, one's wage-earning employment, and so on.

The teaching is true. A Christian who comes short in D, E, or P is inescapably in trouble, one way or another. Where people are ignorant of God's truth and wisdom, or have no conscience about giving it practical expression, or omit to seek God constantly in terms of it and deal with him on the basis of it, there the Christian life has come to grief. The stool has fallen down. Distorted development is thwarting God's plan for healthy spiritual growth.

Renewal of the Church. It seems clear that at least part of God's purpose in movements of church renewal is always the recovering of D and/or E and/or P in individual lives. Such movements are not truly perceived and realistically assessed until this is seen. The Reformation movement, for instance, is often viewed as a technical theological conflict, rarefied and remote, expressing nothing nobler than nationalistic passion. But its leaders saw it, and vast numbers experienced it, as a grass roots revival of pure religion. More obvious examples are: the devotional revival embracing both Counter-Reformation Catholicism and Protestant Puritanism in the early seventeenth century; the British Methodist revival and New England's Great Awakening in the mid-eighteenth century; and the so-called "holiness revival," with its many mutations of Methodist motifs, that touched the entire Protestant world between 1850 and 1950. A current illustration is the ongoing Holy Spirit renewal of our own time.

What should one say of the worldwide charismatic movement of the past thirty years? Laying aside matters of detail,[4] I believe that God has generated it in order to counter and correct the death-dealing fashions of thought which, starting with theologians and spreading everywhere, for the past century have done damage by demurring at the truth of the Trinity, diminishing the deity of Jesus Christ, and for practical purposes discounting the Holy Spirit altogether.

To deal with these theoretical errors, and the spiritual deadness to which they have given rise, God has raised up this movement of uninhibited and flamboyant Holy Spirit life, whereby the truth of the Trinity is vindicated (D), fellowship-union with the divine Christ through the Spirit as the focus of spiritual life is freshly explored (E), and the thought of Christianity as a supernatural life in the Spirit, singing, sharing, and serving, has again become respectable (P). Those who maintain the errors mentioned are thus comprehensively outflanked, not to say upstaged. How wise is the strategy of God!

Signs of Spiritual Growth. With regard to the future of Christians much is mysterious. Spiritual growth, like its physical counterpart, is ordinarily a gentle and imperceptible process. One neither sees nor feels it happening. The most that can be said about the subjective side of it is that every now and then, believers realize they are different in this or that way from what they once were. The long-term effects of particular insights, experiences, chastenings, moments of shock, sustained routines, and ongoing relationships, cannot be calculated in advance.

Some Christians change at surface level far faster and more dramatically than others, but how much corresponding change takes place at a deep level cannot be monitored either by the agent or by any human observer. Only God knows, for he alone can search hearts down to the bottom. The spotlight of consciousness enables us to know only a small part of ourselves. The Holy Spirit's transforming work reaches deep into that large part of ourselves to which we have no access. No wonder, then, that we constantly misconceive and misjudge what God is and is not doing in us, with us and for us, just as we constantly err when we try to assess what God is doing through us in ministry to others.

Further factors hide from us the work of God within us. In all of us, the body and the soul (the principle of conscious personal life) are closely linked, more closely than we can ever understand, and the influence of each on the other further obscures the Spirit's sanctifying action. I think here of a wide range of afflictions in which a physical condition adversely affects the mind, from depression and schizophrenia to Down's syndrome, senile dementia and Alzheimer's disease.

Then death, the departure of the person from his or her physical embodiment, comes at different times and in different ways to different people. The complaint that no rhyme or reason appears in the way that one Christian is taken while another is left is all too familiar. God has already fixed the time and manner of our death. Beyond death he will finish eliminating sin from our system and conforming us dispositionally to Christ. Our transformed and reconstructed selves will in due course be given resurrection bodies to match, and through them we shall be able to express all that we then shall be as fully renewed persons. This is a certainty, but a certainty of faith, not of sight. What it will mean for us we cannot at present imagine. We must be content to wait and see.

Two things, therefore, must be said together with regard to the future work of God that will complete our salvation. The first is that *we know the formula*. We have reviewed it earlier. It is crisply summarized for us in the following extract from John Stott's comment on 1 John 3:2: "Now we are children of God, and what we will be has not yet been made known. But we know that when he appears, we shall be like him, for we shall see him as he is." Stott writes as follows:

Already the image of God, marred by the fall, has been stamped on us again. The new man, which we assumed at our conversion, was "created after the likeness of God in true righteousness and holiness" (Eph 4:24, RSV; cf. Col 3:10). And since that day, in fulfilment of God's predestinating purpose that we should be "conformed to the image of his Son" (Rom 8:29), the Holy Spirit has been transfiguring us "into his likeness from one degree of glory to another" (2 Cor 3:8, RSV; cf. 1 Jn 2:6).

In this latter passage the transformation is said to be due to the fact that we are "with unveiled face beholding the glory of the Lord;" so it is understandable that when we shall see Him as He is, and not our face only but His too is unveiled, we shall be finally and completely like Him, including our bodies (Phil 3:29; cf. 1 Cor 9:49). "Vision becomes assimilation" (Law). This is all John knows about our final, heavenly state. Paul concentrates in his Epistles on the truth that in heaven we shall be "with Christ" (2 Cor 5:8; Phil 1:23; Col 3:4; 1 Thes 4:17; cf. Lk 23:43; Jn 14:3, 17:24). It is enough for us to know that on the last day and through eternity we shall be both with Christ and like Christ; for the fuller revelation of what we shall be we are content to wait.[5]

The second truth, however, is that although we know the formula *we do not know the scenario*. We can state in theological terms what awaits us, according to God's revealed will of purpose. But we cannot say in circumstantial terms what awaits us, according to his secret will of events. A song of my youth had this line in it: "Anything can happen, and it probably will"— and that is the truth about the Christian life. We do not know what a day may bring, hence we have to be ready for anything. That nothing whatever can separate us from the love of Christ, and that God makes absolutely everything work for our spiritual good (see Rom 8:35-39, 28), is certain. That we face the possibility of encountering "trouble... hardship... persecution... famine... nakedness... danger... sword" is also certain (see again Rom 8:35). So, for every Christian everywhere facing the unknown future, the word of wisdom is the Boy Scouts' motto, which is also the good mountaineer's maxim: *be prepared!*

What does being prepared involve? In a word, God-centered realism about living—and actual holiness of life. Following the statement, "We know that when he appears, we shall be like him, for we shall see him as he is," John writes: "Everyone who has this hope in him purifies himself, just as he is pure" (1 Jn 3:3). And again: "No one who lives in him keeps on sinning.... He who does what is sinful is of the devil.... The reason the Son of God appeared was to destroy the devil's work..." (1 Jn 3:6, 8). Those who cope best with pressures and difficulties will ordinarily be those whose life-quest is to be holy, imitating the Son to the glory of the Father both from gratitude for the tripersonal love that has brought them from spiritual death to spiritual life, and from a desire to be ready every moment to meet the Lord Jesus and give account to him, should he choose that moment to return, or to summon us into his nearer presence. If we want to live and die in peace, holiness is in truth a necessity.

Appreciating Salvation: Where Holiness Begins

O LORD, truly I am your servant...
you have freed me from my chains.
I will sacrifice a thank offering to you
and call on the name of the LORD.
I will fulfill my vows to the LORD
in the presence of all his people. **Ps 116:16-18**

O UR PLAIN MAN'S SKETCH of God's plan of salvation for the individual, as the Bible presents it in its past, present, and future aspects, is now complete. But who is this "plain man" to whom I direct it? The phrase goes back to *The Plaine Man's Pathway to Heaven* (1601), a famous book on Christian basics by Arthur Dent, an Elizabethan Puritan. The "plaine man" for whom Dent wrote then, and for whom I write now, is a straightforward, unsubtle, honest person whose heart says with John Wesley, "I am a creature of a day, soon to drop into eternity; I want to know one thing, the way to heaven." And surely this is the best and wisest desire that anyone can ever feel! But if that is so, there is no better course for the present writer than to try to be his own plain man. So I propose once more to speak for myself. In this chapter I reflect on the reactions that knowing God's plan of salvation should call forth from me.

I said reactions, in the plural, for four at least are in order.

Christian holiness embraces all four, which means that our own endeavors after holiness will be radically flawed by the absence of any one of them.

AWE AT GOD'S GREATNESS

First, I must learn from this plan of salvation to be *awestruck at the greatness of my Maker.*

Often during the past thirty years, I have found myself publicly lamenting the way in which this twentieth century has indulged unwarrantably great thoughts of humanity and scandalously small thoughts of God. Our time will surely go down in history, at least as far as the West is concerned, as the age of the God-shrinkers. Mainstream thinkers, inside as well as outside the church, have affirmed either the bloodless deism of a God who is cool, faraway, and uninvolved, and who lets his world run free; or the static monism of a God whose achievement is limited to unifying reality by linking all entities and processes with himself in an interdependent whole; or the pathetic impotence of a God who is revealed in Jesus as an unsuccessful lover; or the faceless force of a God who animates all religions equally, so that none should dream of displacing any other.

There have been lay theologians like G.K. Chesterton, Charles Williams, Dorothy L. Sayers, C.S. Lewis, and Peter Kreeft, and academic theologians like Leonard Hodgson, Oliver Quick, Karl Barth, Cornelius van Til, G.C. Berkouwer, and Donald Bloesch, who have proclaimed the twin truths of the Trinity and Incarnation, and the twin hopes of personal resurrection and cosmic renovation under God's sovereignty, in recognizable form. However, they have been a minority. They have often looked like the Danish king of England a millennium ago, King Canute, vainly forbidding the tide to come in while the waves of scaled-down theologies continue to break and swirl on all sides with ever-increasing impact. Please God, the tide will turn—perhaps it is beginning to turn already—but the God-shrinking trend has long prevailed. Its result is that belief in God's sovereignty and omniscience, the majesty of his moral law and the terror of his judgments, the retributive consequences of the life we live here and the endlessness of the eternity in which we will experience them, along with belief in the intrinsic triunity of God and the divinity and personal return of Jesus Christ, is nowadays so eroded as to be hardly discernible. For many in our day, God is no more than a smudge.

But the plan of salvation, which tells me how my Creator has become my Redeemer, sets before me in fullest glory the transcendent majesty that the churches have so largely forgotten. It shows me a God who is infinitely great in wisdom and power—who knew from all eternity what fallen humanity's plight would be—and who before creating the cosmos had already schemed out in detail how he would save not only me, but each single one of the many billions whom he was resolved to bring to glory. The plan tells me of a vast program for world history, a program involving millennia of providential preparation for the first coming of a Savior, and millennia more of worldwide evangelism, pastoral care, Christianizing of culture, demonstration of God's kingdom, spiritual warfare against its enemies, and building up of the church, before the Savior returns.

The plan sets before me the Father sending the Son to redeem, and the Spirit to quicken, the lost and guilty living dead—dead souls like mine, dead in transgressions and sins, led by the devices and desires of a corrupt heart, and often putting up a smoke screen of religious formalism to keep the light of God from reaching my conscience. The plan covers not only (1) the three-hour agony of Jesus on the cross, vicariously enduring Godforsakenness so that sinners like me would never have to endure it; but also (2) the permanently transforming bodily resurrection of Jesus and the permanently transforming heart-regeneration of everyone who is saved—two demonstrations of the power that made the world that are, be it said, wholly inexplicable in terms of the created forces that operate in the world. (Here then, is where apologetics should start.) Finally, the plan reaches into the future, promising everyone a new, undying body. In addition, it promises saved sinners like me a new heaven and earth, a vast perfected society, and the visible presence of Jesus, to enjoy through that new body forever.

Such are the wonders of the plan of salvation. God's call to holiness begins by telling me to dwell on these great and awesome realities until I find myself truly awestruck at the greatness of my God, who is making it all happen. In this way I will learn to give him glory (in the sense of praise) for the greatness of his glory (in the sense of self-display) as the One whose revealed wisdom and power, in redemption as in creation, dazzle, surpass, and overwhelm my understanding. The triune God of the plan is great—transcendent and immutable in his omnipotence, omniscience, and omnipresence. He is eternal in his truthfulness and faithfulness, wisdom and justice, severity and goodness—and he must be praised and adored as such. Praise of this kind is the doxological foundation of human holiness, which always starts here. Just as there could be for Jesus no crown without the cross, so there can be for us no holiness without the praise.

The Bible Emphasizes Praise. Scripture is full of passages requiring and rehearsing the praises that redeemed people owe to God. Here are a few from the Old Testament:

> I will sing to the LORD, for he is highly exalted.... I will exalt him.... Who is like you—majestic in holiness, awesome in glory, working wonders?... The LORD will reign forever and ever. **Ex 15:1-2, 11, 18**

> How awesome is the LORD Most High, the great King over all the earth! **Ps 47:2**

> Great is the LORD, and most worthy of praise. **Ps 48:1**

The LORD reigns... he sits enthroned.... Great is the LORD in Zion; he is exalted over all the nations. Let them praise your great and awesome name—he is holy. The King is mighty.... Exalt the LORD our God and worship at his footstool; he is holy.   **Ps 99:1-5**

Praise the name of the LORD.... Praise the LORD, for the LORD is good....I know that the LORD is great.... The LORD does whatever pleases him.... Your name, O LORD, endures for ever, your renown, O LORD, through all generations.... Praise the LORD.   **Ps 135:1, 3, 5-6, 13, 19**

I will praise you, O LORD, with all my heart.... I will bow down toward your holy temple and will praise your name for your love and your faithfulness, for you have exalted above all things your name and your word.... May all the kings of the earth praise you, O LORD, when they hear the words of your mouth.   **Ps 138:1-2, 4**

Praise the LORD. How good it is to sing praises to our God, how pleasant and fitting to praise him!... Great is our Lord and mighty in power; his understanding has no limit.... Extol the LORD.... Praise the LORD.   **Ps 147:1, 5, 12, 20**

Sing to the LORD, for he has done glorious things.... Shout aloud and sing for joy, people of Zion, for great is the Holy One of Israel among you.   **Is 12:5-6**

No one is like you, O LORD; you are great, and your name is mighty in power. Who should not revere you, O King of the nations? This is your due.   **Jer 10:6-7**

And there is, as sales catalogs say, much, much more: all of Psalms 145-150, for instance, could well be cited here. But we have to move on.

The New Testament also periodically breaks forth into praise. Here are some samples:

My soul glorifies the Lord [declares him great, extols him] and my spirit rejoices in God my Savior... for the Mighty

One has done great things for me—holy is his name.

Lk 1:46-47, 49

Oh, the depth of the riches of the wisdom and knowledge of God! How unsearchable his judgments, and his paths beyond tracing out!... from him and through him and to him are all things. To him be the glory for ever! Amen.

Rom 11:33, 36

Now to the King eternal, immortal, invisible, the only God, be honor and glory for ever and ever. Amen.   1 Tm 1:17

To the only God our Savior be glory, majesty, power and authority, through Jesus Christ our Lord, before all ages, now and forevermore! Amen.   Jude 25

Worthy is the Lamb, who was slain, to receive power and wealth and wisdom and strength and honor and glory and praise!... To him who sits on the throne and to the Lamb be praise and honor and glory and power for ever and ever.

Rv 5:12-13

Great and marvelous are your deeds, Lord God Almighty. Just and true are your ways, King of the ages. Who will not fear you, O Lord, and bring glory to your name? For you alone are holy. All nations will come and worship before you, for your righteous acts have been revealed.   Rv 15:3-4

It was a sound Christian instinct that led Horatius Bonar, author of the little classic *God's Way of Holiness*, to pray for praise:

Fill thou my life, O Lord my God,
In every part with praise,
That my whole being may proclaim
Thy being and thy ways.

Not for the lip of praise alone,
Nor e'en the praising heart,
I ask, but for a life made up
Of praise in every part;

Praise in the common things of life,
Its goings out and in;
Praise in each duty and each deed,
However small and mean.

Fill every part of me with praise:
Let all my being speak
Of thee and of thy love, O Lord,
Poor though I be and weak.

So shalt thou, Lord, from me, e'en me,
Receive the glory due;
And so shall I begin on earth
The song for ever new.

Exactly so: real consecration to a realistic life-purpose of pleasing and glorifying God starts here. The life of true holiness is rooted in the soil of awed adoration. It does not grow elsewhere. That which grows elsewhere is not true holiness, whatever else it is. No blend of zeal, passion, self-denial, discipline, orthodoxy, and effort adds up to holiness where praise is lacking.

GRATITUDE FOR GOD'S MERCY

Second, I must learn from this plan of salvation to be *grateful for the mercy of my God.*

It is safe to say that no religion anywhere has ever laid such stress on the need for thanksgiving, nor called on its adherents so incessantly and insistently to give God thanks, as does the religion of the Bible in both its Old and New Testament forms. The psalmists are constantly giving thanks (Ps 35:18; 75:1; 119:62) and summoning others to do the same (Ps 95:2; 100:4; 105:1; 106:1; cf. 47; 107:1, 21ff.; 118:1, 29; 136:1-3, 26; 147:7). Paul similarly gives thanks over and over again (Rom 1:8, 6:17, 7:25; 1 Cor 1:4, 14, 14:18, 15:57; 2 Cor 2:14, 8:16, 9:15; Eph 1:16; Phil 1:3; Col 1:3; 1 Thes 1:2, 2:13, 3:9; 2 Thes 2:13; 1 Tm

1:12; 2 Tm 1:3; Phlm 4) and directs Christians to do the same (Eph 5:20; Phil 4:6; Col 2:7, 4:2; 1 Thes 5:18).

The reason why glorifying God through thanksgiving (see Ps 69:30; 2 Cor 4:15) is so emphasized is not hard to see. The divine gifts and blessings that Scripture sees as given in the good experiences of natural life and the amazing mercy of supernatural salvation, are far richer and more abundant, and involve far more of divine generosity, than are dreamed of by any other faith.

Our acts of thanksgiving, therefore, are not to be hollow formalities. On the contrary, to be acceptable, they must be genuine expressions of gratitude in the heart for all God's giving—gratitude for what the General Thanksgiving of the *Anglican Prayer Book* verbalizes as "our creation, preservation, and all the blessings of this life; but above all for thine inestimable love in the redemption of the world by our Lord Jesus Christ, for the means of grace and for the hope of glory." Of this "inestimable love," the plan of salvation is the chart.

Love (*agapē*), in the Christian sense of that word, has been defined as a purpose of making the loved one great. We learn this definition from the revelation of God's love in Christ, the love that saves. As love to sinners deserving hell, it was mercy. As a purpose of raising them from spiritual destitution to the dignity of forgiveness and restoration, acceptance and adoption into God's family, it was costly—not to us, but to God himself, as Scripture makes very clear.

> God so loved the world [humans in their godless and corrupt state] that he gave his one and only Son, that whoever believes in him shall not perish but have eternal life. **Jn 3:16**

> God demonstrates his own love for us in this: While we were still sinners, Christ died for us. **Rom 5:8**

> God is love. This is how God showed his love among us. He sent his one and only Son into the world that we might live through him. This is love, not that we loved God, but that he loved us and sent his Son as an atoning sacrifice [the

Greek says "propitiation," meaning quencher of divine wrath] for our sins.   1 Jn 4:8-10

He... did not spare his own Son, but gave him up for us all.
Rom 8:32

The measure of all love is its giving. The measure of the love of God is the cross of Christ, where the Father gave the Son to die so that the spiritually dead might have life.

Our Motivation. The secular world never understands Christian motivation. Faced with the question of what makes Christians tick, unbelievers maintain that Christianity is practiced only out of self-serving purposes. They see Christians as fearing the consequences of not being Christians (religion as fire insurance), or feeling the need of help and support to achieve their goals (religion as a crutch), or wishing to sustain a social identity (religion as a badge of respectability). No doubt all these motivations can be found among the membership of churches: it would be futile to dispute that. But just as a horse brought into a house is not thereby made human, so a self-seeking motivation brought into the church is not thereby made Christian, nor will holiness ever be the right name for religious routines thus motivated. From the plan of salvation I learn that the true driving force in authentic Christian living is, and ever must be, not the hope of gain, but the heart of gratitude.

The plan of salvation teaches me, not merely that I can never do anything to earn, increase, or extend God's favor, or to avoid the justified fury of his wrath, or to wheedle benefits out of him, but also that I never need to try to do any of these things. God himself has loved me from eternity. He himself has redeemed me from hell through the cross. He himself has renewed my heart and brought me to faith. He himself has now sovereignly committed himself to complete the transformation of me into Christ's likeness and to set me, faultless and glorified, in his own presence for all eternity. When almighty love has thus totally taken over the task of getting me home to glory, responsive love, fed by gratitude and expressed in thanksgiving, should surface spontaneously as the ruling passion of my life. It will be my wisdom to brood on and mull over the marvelous mercies of God's plan until it does.

A little verse once taught to teenagers tells me where I ought to be in my response:

> I will not work my soul to save,
>   For that my Lord has done;
> But I will work like any slave
>   For love of God's dear Son.

In Romans 12, Paul makes clear that this is how it should be. He has proclaimed the righteousness of God (God's work of setting sinners forever right with himself: Rom 1:17, 3:21, 10:3) in its relation to historical atonement (Rom 3:21-26), eternal election (Rom 8:29-39), personal vocation (that is, the "calling" that engenders faith: Rom 1:6, 8:28-30, 9:24), and the place of Jew and Gentile in the covenant community (Rom 9:1-11:36). Now he asks for reader-response as follows: "I urge you, brothers, in view of God's mercy [the Greek says "mercies," meaning acts expressing mercy], to offer your bodies [meaning, total selves] as living sacrifices, holy and pleasing to God—this is your spiritual act of worship" (Rom 12:1).

Christians, says Paul, are to be moved and stirred to consecrated living by their knowledge of God's love, grace, and mercy—the mercy of sovereign salvation, whereby God pardons, accepts, and exalts the undeserving and wretched, at fearsome cost to himself. Insofar as there is a difference of nuance between the terms love, grace, and mercy of God, love means his outgoing to bless those whom he sees as having no claim on him; grace means his outgoing to bless those whom he sees as meriting his rejection; and mercy means his outgoing to bless those whose state he sees to be miserable. *Love* expresses God's self-determining freedom, *grace* his self-generated favor, and *mercy* his compassionate kindness. Paul has dwelt on God's sovereign mercy to sinners in Romans 9:15-18, 11:30-32. Now he says, in effect: "You who know this mercy in your own lives must show yourselves truly grateful for it by the thoroughness of your commitment to God henceforth. This thoroughness is your holiness, for holiness means giving your all to God as God has given, is giving, and will give his all to you. And this thoroughness will please God, for it will show your appreciation and affection for him, and so will be the real essence, Spirit-taught and Spirit-wrought, of your worship of him."

It is important to be clear that, as praise to God for his transcendent greatness is the doxological basis of holiness, so commitment to spend one's life expressing gratitude for God's grace, every way one can, is its devotional basis. No reordering of life that does not spring out of such a commitment adds up to holiness, admirable though it may be by other standards and from other points of view.

It thus appears that, as the Puritans used to say, the heart of holiness is holiness in the heart. The holy sacrifice that gives God pleasure is the Christian whose heart never ceases to be grateful to him for his grace. God is pleased with the Christian whose aim every day is to express that gratitude by living to him, through him, and for him, and who is constantly asking, with the psalmist, "How can I repay the LORD for all his goodness to me?" (Ps 116:12). Such a Christian was the Scottish saint Robert Murray McCheyne, who wrote:

Chosen, not for good in me;
Wakened up from wrath to flee;
Hidden in the Saviour's side,
By the Spirit sanctified;
Teach me, Lord, on earth to show,
By my love, how much I owe.

That is the kind of Christian that I must seek to be.

ZEALOUS FOR HIS GLORY

Third, I must learn from this plan of salvation to be *zealous for the glory of my Savior.*

It is often said that God's goal in the plan of salvation is to exalt himself by exalting us whom he saves, and that is true. But the New Testament goes further, insisting that the Father's prime purpose throughout is to exalt the Son, whom we know in his incarnate being as Jesus Christ our Lord. The Son of God, who is God the Son (second person of the Godhead), was and is the agent of all the Father's works in creation, providence, and grace. He is the mediator of all the goodness and mercy that has ever flowed from God to men and women. The New Testament identifies his life, death, resurrection, and enthronement as the hinge of world history, just as it depicts his throne itself as heaven's centerpiece (Rv 4, 5). As the Father loves the Son and expresses that love by honoring him in the eternal fellowship of the Trinity, so he intends that through the outworking of the plan of salvation, in which Jesus is the focal figure, "all may honor the Son just as they honor the Father" (Jn 5:23).

To that end, and in direct acknowledgment of the perfection of the Son's costly obedience in making atonement for human sin, "God exalted him to the highest place and gave him the name that is above every name, that at the name of Jesus every knee should bow, in heaven and on earth and under the earth, and every tongue confess that Jesus Christ is Lord, to the glory of God the Father" (Phil 2:9-11).

Writing to the Colossian Christians, who were being told to worship angels alongside Jesus, Paul spells out the Father's plan for "the Son he loves" (Col 1:13) to have supreme honor at every level as follows:

> All things were created by him and for him. He is before all things, and in him all things hold together. And he is the head of the body, the church; he is the beginning and the

firstborn from among the dead, so that in everything he might have the supremacy. For God was pleased to have all his fullness dwell in him, and through him to reconcile to himself all things, whether things on earth or things in heaven, by making peace through his blood, shed on the cross. **Col 1:16-20**

We proclaim him, admonishing and teaching everyone with all wisdom, so that we may present everyone perfect in Christ... in whom are hidden all the treasures of wisdom and knowledge. **Col 1:28, 2:3**

In Christ all the fullness of the Deity lives in bodily form, and you have been given fullness in Christ, who is the head over every power and authority. **Col 2:9-10**

You died, and your life is now hidden with Christ in God. When Christ, who is your life, appears, then you also will appear with him in glory. **Col 3:3**

You have taken off your old self with its practices and have put on the new self, which is being renewed in knowledge in the image of its Creator. Here there is no Greek or Jew, circumcised or uncircumcised, barbarian, Scythian, slave or free, but Christ is all, and is in all. **Col 3:9-11**

Let the peace of Christ rule in your hearts.... Let the word of Christ dwell in you richly.... And whatever you do, whether in word or deed, do it all in the name of the Lord Jesus, giving thanks to God the Father through him.

Col 3:15-17

From these texts, which together constitute the "plotline" of Colossians, the centrality and supremacy of Jesus Christ in the plan of salvation are plain to see.

The Book of Revelation shows us the same thing (as indeed do all the New Testament books of any length: but I limit myself to this one further example). Starting with the vision of Christ in glory, dictating personal letters to each of seven churches (chapters 1-3), it moves on to depict him as the Lion of Judah in the form of the slain Lamb, enthroned as Redeemer and Lord of history (chapter 5), to whom songs of praise are repeatedly addressed. In due course the Lamb appears as the conquering Word of God, "King of Kings and Lord of Lords" (Rv 19:11-16). The book closes with Jesus speaking in his own person as the Lord of all, just as he does in the three opening chapters, and declaring: "Behold, I am coming soon! My reward is with me, and I will give to everyone according to what he has done. I am the Alpha and the Omega, the First and the Last, the Beginning and the End.... I, Jesus, have sent my angel to give you [recipients of the book] this testimony for the churches. I am the Root and Offspring of David, and the bright Morning Star" (Rv 22:12, 16).

What I have to learn, then, is this: my salvation, from start to finish, is through Jesus Christ and in Jesus Christ ("in" signifying there a personal communion that is also an enlivening union, willed and wrought by divine action). God the Father planned it this way, for the glory and praise of Christ, his eternal Son. The mercies of election, redemption, regeneration, and justification are mine in Christ (Eph 1:4, 7, 2:4-10; Gal 2:17).

I have died with Christ, God thereby terminating within me the old way of living that I renounced. I have been made to share Christ's resurrection life through the Holy Spirit, so that though I am still who I was, I am no longer what I was, but am now inwardly a different person altogether (Rom 6:2-11, 7:4-6; Gal 2:20; Eph 4:20-24; Col 2:11-13, 20, 3:1-4, 9-11). My business henceforth, in all of my living, is to trust Christ, obey Christ, love Christ, exalt Christ, worship Christ, draw strength from Christ (2 Cor 12:9; Phil 4:13; Col 1:11; 1 Tm 1:12; 2 Tm 4:17), rejoice in Christ (Phil 3:1, 4:4), give him thanks, abide ("stay put") in Christ (Jn 15:4-7), and look forward in hope to the day when Christ will come to take me to be at home with him (Jn 14:1-3; Phil 1:23; 2 Cor 5:6-8). I know that Christ views his disciples as his friends (Jn 15:15). I must show my appreciation of this fantastic privilege of friendship with the world's reigning Lord. I must seek to honor and glorify him every way I can.

I should not, indeed, so focus on the Son that I forget, or ignore, the Father and the Spirit, for then I would be what is sometimes called a Jesusolater (one who worships Jesus in a way that is false to the Bible view of God). Equally, however, I should not so focus on the Father and/or the Spirit that I fail to keep central in my gaze the unique glory of Christ, as the Father and the Spirit want me to do (see Jn 5:23, 16:14). Both mistakes have been made in the past, and are still being made in some quarters. I have to try to avoid them, or I shall grieve my God, and starve my soul.

Salvation and Holiness. Exalting Christ, then, by worship, witness, and service, as the main focus of our uplifting of the triune God, should be our constant aim. Failure here means missing the path of holiness, for a life commitment, deliberate, zealous, and daily renewed, to glorify the Lord Jesus is the dedicatory basis of holiness. There is no holiness without a Christ-centered, Christ-seeking, Christ-serving, Christ-adoring heart. And the plan of salvation requires us to get our hearts into this frame and keep them there.

How can we do that? It is far, far more easily said than done! One help is to think often about the cross. Charles Wesley says this as it should be said:

Behold him, ye that pass him by,
  The bleeding Prince of life and peace!
Come, sinners, see your Maker die,
  And say, was ever grief like his?
Come, feel with me his blood applied:
My Lord, my Love, is crucified.

Then let us sit beneath his cross,
  And gladly catch the healing stream,

All things for him account but loss,
   And give up all our hearts to him.
Of nothing think or speak beside:
   My Lord, my Love, is crucified.

Another help is to soak one's soul constantly in the four Gospels, where the majesty and beauty of Jesus are projected with electrifying power. (Why don't we make more use of the Gospels than we do?) A third help is use of a good hymnbook in one's personal prayers, alongside (of course!) God's own hymnbook, the Psalms. In the hymnbooks I know, up to half the songs express praise and love for Jesus in an explicit way. Weaving them into my prayers (a habit learned from Wesley's Methodists) moves my heart in the desired direction. Love of great hymns, especially those of men like the two Wesleys, Isaac Watts, and John Newton (of "Amazing Grace"), has many good effects, and the zeal for the glory of Christ that you catch from them is one of the best helps to holiness that I know.

LIVING NATURALLY AS A CHILD OF GOD

Fourth, I must learn from God's plan of salvation to be *natural in the living of my life.*

What does it mean to behave naturally? The question is more tricky than it might appear at first. Once the members of my college fellowship group agreed to take turns sharing a major personal interest with the rest of us, and one sought to initiate us into religious dance. We sat down on the floor, and were told that when the music started, we were to move our limbs in any way that seemed a natural response to it. Soon all were wriggling and writhing like snakes emerging from the basket at the snake charmer's piping—all, that is, except me.

What was going on? Well, music has never suggested to me that I do anything except stop and listen to it, like Coleridge's wedding guest who was stopped by the Ancient Mariner and mesmerized into listening quietly to his albatross story. As a child I found it irritating to have to march to music at school and run around chairs to music at parties, instead of being able to stand still and listen without distraction. As an adult I have always felt that dancing to music is disrespectful to it. I suppose that helps to explain why I have never been able to do it (I still cannot dance). So there I sat, a glum dummy, watching my fellow students shimmy from the waist up and flap their hands, and in due course get up and hop around. Nothing occurred to me to do, so I did nothing. Was I showing contempt for the instructor, or for the activity? Not at all. In a way that my wife (who likes dancing) would, perhaps rightly, describe as most unnatural, I was being "natural" in the way that is natural to freaky me. For being natural is not a matter of doing what is expected, or what others are doing. It is a matter of doing, or not doing, what one's own inner nature prompts.

What sort of behavior, now, is natural to the child of God?

The Christian's Nature. A widespread but misleading line of teaching tells us that Christians have two natures: an old one and a new one. They must obey the latter while denying the former. Sometimes this is illustrated in terms of feeding one of your two dogs while starving the other. The misleading thing here is not the reminder that we are called to holiness and not to sin, but that the idea of "nature" is not being used as it is used both in life and in Scripture (see, for example, Rom 2:14; Eph 2:3). The point is that "nature" means the whole of what we are, and the whole of what we are is expressed in the various actions and reactions that make up our life. To envisage two "natures," two distinct sets of desires, neither of which masters me till I choose to let it, is unreal and bewildering, because it leaves out so much of what actually goes on inside me.

The clearer and more correct thing to say, as we have seen already, is this: we were born sinners by nature, dominated and driven from the start—and most of the time unconsciously—by self-seeking, self-serving, self-deifying motives and cravings. Being united to Christ in new birth through the regenerating work of the Spirit has so changed our nature that our heart's deepest desire (the dominant passion that rules and drives us now) is a copy, faint but real, of the desire that drove our Lord Jesus. That was the desire to know, trust, love, obey, serve, delight, honor, glorify, and enjoy his heavenly Father—a multi-faceted, many-layered desire for God, and for more of him than has been enjoyed so far.

The focus of this desire in Jesus was upon the Father, whereas in Christians it is upon the Father and the Son together (and the latter especially). But the nature of the desire is the same. The natural way for Christians to live is to let this desire determine and control what they do, so that the fulfilling of the longing to seek, know, and love the Lord becomes the mainspring of their life.

Augustus Toplady, one of the pioneers of England's evangelical revival in the eighteenth century, showed that he understood this when he wrote:

Object of my first desire,
  Jesus, crucified for me;
All to happiness aspire,
  Only to be found in thee.
Thee to praise, and thee to know,
Constitute my bliss below;
  Thee to see, and thee to love,
  Constitute my bliss above.

Whilst I feel thy love to me,
  Every object teems with joy;
May I ever walk with thee,
  For 'tis bliss without alloy.
Let me but thyself possess,
Total sum of happiness:
  Perfect peace I then shall prove,
  Heaven below and heaven above.

The momentous truth that thus emerges is that to "walk with Christ," as Toplady puts it, in the path of holy discipleship, is the life for which the hearts of Christians truly long. From this follows the equally momentous truth that obeying the promptings of indwelling sin (the sin that still marauds in the systems of Christians though it no longer masters their hearts) is not what they really want to do at all, for sinning is totally unnatural to them.

Why then do we ever do it?—let alone make a habit of doing it, as notoriously we sometimes do? Partly, no doubt, because we fail to recognize sin for what it is, through ignorance of God's standards. Partly too because we yield to the nagging pull of temptation, giving way though we know that we should not and need not. But partly too because we let ourselves be deceived into supposing that to give way to this or that inordinate desire—for food, drink, pleasure, ease, gain, advancement, or whatever—is what we really want to do.

Again and again it appears that Christians are not sufficiently in touch with themselves. They do not know themselves well enough to realize that, because of the way in which their nature has been changed, their hearts are now set against all known sin. So they hang on to unspiritual and morally murky behavior patterns, and kid themselves that this adds to the joy of their lives. Encouraged by Satan, the grand master of delusion, they feel (feelings as such, of course, are mindless and blind) that to give up these things would be impossibly painful and impoverishing, so though they know they should, they do not. Instead, they settle for being substandard Christians, imagining they will be happier that way. Then they wonder why their whole life seems to them to have become flat and empty.

The truth is that they are behaving in a radically unnatural way, one that offers deep-level violence to their own changed nature. In doing what they think they like, they are actually doing what their renewed heart—if they would only let it speak—would tell them that it dislikes intensely, not only because it brings guilt and shame before God but, more fundamentally, because it is in itself repulsive to the regenerate mentality. The regenerate heart cannot love what it knows God hates. So these Christians are behaving unnaturally, occupying themselves in activities against which their own inner nature revolts. Such behavior is always bad medicine, producing sadness, tension, and discontent, if not worse.

Backsliding. There is a venerable Christian term for this condition: *backsliding,* a recurring word-picture in Jeremiah (see Jer 2:19, 3:22, 5:6, 14:7, 15:6). Particularly pertinent to our present discussion is the first of these passages, where God says through the prophet: "'Your wickedness will punish you; your backsliding will rebuke you. Consider then and realize how evil and bitter it is for you when you forsake the LORD your God and have no awe of me,' declares the LORD, the LORD Almighty."

Three centuries ago the Puritan commentator Matthew Henry spelled out the implication of these words as follows:

Observe here, (1) The nature of sin; it is forsaking the Lord as our God; it is the soul's alienation from him, and aversion to him. Cleaving to sin is leaving God. (2) The cause of sin; it is because his fear [awe] is not in us.... Men forsake their duty to God, because they stand in no awe of him, nor have any dread of his displeasure. (3) The malignity of sin; it is an evil thing and a bitter... an evil that is the root and cause of all other evil.... It is not only the greatest contrariety to the divine nature, but the greatest corruption of the human nature.... (4) The fatal consequences of sin; as it is in itself evil and bitter, so it has a direct tendency to make us miserable.... [It] will certainly bring trouble upon thee; the punishment will so inevitably follow the sin, that the sin shall itself be said to punish thee... and the justice of the punishment shall be so plain, that thou shalt not have a word to say for thyself.... (5) The use and application of all this; "Know, therefore [consider, then], and see it, and repent of thy sin, that so the iniquity... may not be your ruin."

The unnatural act of backsliding, then, is always to be avoided, both because it provokes our holy heavenly Father to discipline and correct us in a punitive way (as is further explained in Heb 12:5-10), and also because, at some stage and in some measure, bitterness and misery are its ultimate and inescapable fruit. We must realize that all sin has the nature of suicidal, self-impoverishing madness, in the Christian life no less than elsewhere. To see this, and accordingly to commit oneself to follow one's heart by running in the path of God's calling and commands as hard and as fast as one can, is the directional basis of holiness. Since that is the most truly natural course for any Christian to follow, it holds out a hope of deep happiness, heart-happiness, here and now, that can never be attained otherwise.

Cheerful Holiness. A paradox of Christian holiness that mystifies outsiders is that, despite the privations that Jesus described as self-denial, cross-bearing, cutting off one's hand and foot, gouging out one's eye, leaving wealth and security for poverty and some measure of persecution, holiness is essentially a happy business. Now we see why this is so. Gloomy self-immolation is not holy living, any more than is Pharisaic posturing. Real holiness is a cheerful matter of following one's heart in thinking and planning, and prayerfully doing, what comes most naturally at heart level—namely, praising God, and loving and serving him and others, as we have already seen. Whereas the world's naturalness takes the form of godless self-indulgence, the Christian's naturalness takes the form of Christian holiness. That is the fourth truth that the plan of salvation requires me to learn in my head, and then live out from my heart.

So we reach the end of this long overview, in which we have taken our bearings in God's plan of salvation. We can see that (1) adoration of God for his greatness, (2) gratitude for the grace that saves, (3) zeal to exalt Jesus, "my Savior and my Friend" as the hymn calls him, and (4) wholehearted pursuit of God and godliness according to the natural desire of the regenerate heart, are the four foundations of holy living. These are the first lessons that we have to learn in Christ's school of holiness. They are lessons to which we need to keep coming back, since they slip out of our memories and mind-sets so easily. But they are basic lessons. It is from them that we have to move forward, and where they have not yet been learned to some degree, holiness has not yet begun to be formed in us as God intends. So we start here! Are you still with me? I hope so. Let us proceed.

4 Holiness: The Panoramic View

You are my portion, O LORD;
I have promised to obey your words.
I have sought your face with all my heart;
be gracious to me according to your promise.
I have considered my ways
and have turned my steps to your statutes.
I will hasten and not delay
to obey your commands. **Ps 119:57-60**

Take my yoke upon you and learn from me, for I am gentle and humble in heart, and you will find rest for your souls. For my yoke is easy and my burden light. **Mt 11:29-30**

May God himself, the God of peace, sanctify you through and through. May your whole spirit, soul and body be kept blameless at the coming of our Lord Jesus Christ. The one who calls you is faithful and he will do it. **1 Thes 5:23-24**

THE PANORAMA UNFOLDS

One of life's best experiences is climbing to the head of a

sides closing in on you, as if defying you to squeeze through. At last, however, you reach the top, and suddenly (it is usually sudden, happening as you take a mere two or three steps), a great new landscape unfolds in front of you. You stop. You gaze. Maybe you gasp. Certainly you are thrilled.

I think of two places in North Wales where the head-of-the-pass experience never fails to delight me. Since there are passes all over the world, I expect nearly all my readers have known a similar delight at some time. Panting from your climb, you stand drinking in the view, swiveling your eyes from one feature to another to make sure that you really see all that you are looking at. The joy of the great sight puts energy into you for the next stage of your hike.

To readers who have struggled with me through what has been said so far, I want to announce the good news that we have reached the head of the pass. The landscape of holiness now lies open to our view.

My job for the rest of this book is simply to sharpen the focus on particular bits of the panorama that you can, I believe, already see, at least in outline. Some of them, to be sure, lie a fair distance from where we are standing at the moment—that means that we need the equivalent of field glasses to inspect them. But there is no problem in that. My wife, who is a zealous bird-watcher, uses field glasses constantly to bring far-off birds closer to her line of vision. She loves to pass the glasses to me so that I can inspect the birds too. From now on I seek to play a similar role with regard to holiness. I invite you to look through my glasses, as it were, at a number of particular matters that I want to bring close to your mind and heart.

Basic Truths. It will help us, however, if we first glance back at some of the basic, stage-setting truths that have emerged by way of hints and pointers at least (and mostly by explicit statement) in the course of our ascent to the vantage point that we have now reached.

We have seen, to start with, that holiness is every Christian's calling. It is not an option, but a requirement. God wants his children to live up to his standards and to do him credit in the eyes of the watching world, so he says explicitly to us all: "Be holy, because I am holy" (1 Pt 1:16). Personal holiness is thus an issue for every believer without exception. "I am really expected to be so much like Jesus Christ that others will know at once and unmistakably that I am a Christian."[1] Each of us must reckon on going to school with Jesus our Lord to learn how to practice holiness.

We have seen that holiness is basically a relationship to God, which God himself graciously imparts to us. It is a relationship established by our justification (God's once-for-all act of pardoning and accepting us): hereby he claims us, or rather reclaims us, as his own, through the saving mediation of our Lord Jesus Christ, and so sets us apart for himself. Holiness or sanctification in this sense is always, only, and entirely the free gift of God. It is one aspect of the newness of life that union with Christ effects.

Believers are positionally holy (separated by God for himself) from the word "go." Their obligation to practice moral and spiritual holiness on a day-to-day basis is derived from that fact. Our setting ourselves apart for God, in purposed separation from the world, the flesh, and the devil, is our proper response—our only proper response—to the knowledge that God has already claimed us by right of redemption. He gives us his Spirit as a pledge and foretaste of glory. "Do you not know that your body is a temple of the Holy Spirit, who is in you, whom you have received from God? You are not your own; you were bought at a price. Therefore honor God with your body" (1 Cor 6:19-20). "Do not grieve the Holy Spirit of God, with whom you were sealed for the day of redemption" (Eph 4:30).

We have seen also that holiness of life is not precisely a human achievement, however much it demands of human effort. It is a work of the Holy Spirit, who prompts and energizes the human effort as part of it. It is a supernaturalizing of our natural lives, a matter of becoming and so of being what we are as new creatures in Christ—a living out behaviorally of what God is working in us transformationally. We do not sanctify ourselves. On the contrary, conscious recognition that apart from Christ we can do nothing (Jn 15:6), and prayerful dependence on him to enable us to do each thing that we know we should do, is a *sine qua non* of the holy life. Self-reliance is not the way of holiness, but the negation of it. Self-confidence in face of temptation and conflicting pressures is a sure guarantee that some sort of moral failure will follow.

We have seen, in all this, that holiness involves the two related but distinct aspects of Christian existence that are nowadays labeled spirituality and ethics. Spirituality includes everything that has to do with implementing a Christian's fellowship with God—meditation; prayer; worship; self-discipline; use of the means of grace; exercising faith, hope, and love; maintaining purity, peace, and patience of heart; seeking and serving God in all one's relationships; and giving God glory and thanks. Ethics covers the delineating of God's standards, the determining of his revealed will, and the development and display of those character qualities that constitute God's image in us who were made to be his image-bearers.

Spirituality without ethics corrupts itself by becoming morally insensitive and antinomian, more concerned to realize God's presence than to keep his law. Ethics without spirituality corrupts itself by becoming mechanical, formalistic, proud, and unspiritual. It follows the Pharisees in settling for self-righteous role-play and forgetting that holiness requires a humble heart. Holiness is an arch that rests on spirituality and ethics as its two pillars, and crashes down the moment either pillar crumbles.

Further, we have seen that holiness is the imitation of Christ in his virtues of love to God and humanity, trust in the Father's goodness, acceptance of his will, submission to his providence, and zeal for his honor and glory. "Basically," wrote Stephen Neill,

> we are faced with just the same situation as Jesus—the temptation to choose the easier rather than the harder way; the

demands of daily existence in a very material world; the intrusive claims of family that sometimes set themselves up against the claims of God; the bitterness of misunderstanding and hostility; the simple joys of friendship and companionship. How should a man act in all these situations? There are no rules to cover all situations. But there is a life that was actually lived, and... one of the essential ingredients in Christian holiness is steady patient contemplation of Jesus as he was in the fullness and simplicity of his human life."[2]

Carefully and prayerfully modeling our attitudes and responses to pressure after those of Jesus is part of what holiness means. "I want to be like Jesus in my heart," say the words of a classic spiritual, and true holiness always wants that.

Personal Wholeness. We have seen, finally, that personal holiness is personal wholeness—the ongoing reintegration of our disintegrated and disordered personhood as we pursue our goal of single-minded Jesus-likeness; the increasing mastery of our life that comes as we learn to give it back to God and away to others; the deepening joy of finding worthwhileness in even the most tedious and mundane tasks when tackled for the glory of God and the good of other people; and the peace that pours from the discovery that, galling as failure in itself is, we can handle our failures—we can afford to fail, as some daringly put it—because all along we live precisely by being forgiven, and we are not required at any stage to live any other way.

There is hope too, in the sense of knowing that one is destined, both here and hereafter, to see more of the glory of God in Christ than one has seen as yet. This is part of the holy wholeness of the believer. Robert Louis Stevenson said that to travel hopefully is better than to arrive, as if arrival is always an anticlimax because the destination disappoints. But the Christian travels hopefully in the confidence of arriving at a destination that will be climactically and unceasingly wonderful in every respect, so that however good the hopeful traveling is, arrival will be better still. Cherishing of this hope when the traveling proves rough has an integrating and exhilarating effect that is simply glorious (no other word fits). In all these ways holiness appears as the true health and fulfillment of the individual human being.

In an earlier book, I laid down seven principles about holiness:

1. The nature of holiness is transformation through consecration.
2. The context of holiness is justification through Jesus Christ.
3. The root of holiness is co-crucifixion and co-resurrection with Jesus Christ.
4. The agent of holiness is the Holy Spirit.
5. The experience of holiness is one of conflict.
6. The rule of holiness is God's revealed law.
7. The heart of holiness is the spirit of love.[3]

All these truths have danced before our minds in what has been said so far. It is within this frame of reference that we now proceed.

LIVING A HOLY LIFE

As the landscape of holiness unfolds before us, the practical question becomes sharper and more pressing: just what, then, are we to do? We know ourselves to be justified through faith in Christ, adopted into God's royal family, united to Christ, regenerated, sealed, and indwelt by the Holy Spirit. We know that God is at work in us sanctifying us, changing us into Christ's likeness from one degree of glory (divine self-display in us) to another, and energizing us for works of love and obedience. We know that we are called to cooperate with what our God is doing in our lives. What from one standpoint is our cooperation with the process is from another standpoint a part of the process itself.

What form, then, should our cooperation be taking? How are we to "work out" our salvation (express, exhibit, and advance it) with appropriate "fear and trembling" (awe and reverence in God's presence—*not* panic and alarm in our hearts!)? What is the relevance of the reminder that "it is God who works in you to will and to act according to his good purpose" (Phil 2:13)? "Be holy," says God, and that, as we have seen, is a summons to obedience—consecration to God's service, with conformity to his standards. But what does this mean, in practical terms? Just what are we to do?

Two Extremes. Scripture and experience warn us that here we have to steer our course between two opposite extremes of disaster. On the one hand, there is the legalistic hypocrisy of Pharisaism (God-serving outward actions proceeding from self-serving inward motives), and on the other hand there is the antinomian idiocy that rattles on about love and liberty, forgetting that the God-given law remains the standard of the God-honoring life. Both Pharisaism and antinomianism are ruinous. Scripture and experience warn us that all Christians are at all times more weak, frail, foolish, undiscerning, and more vulnerable to temptations than they realize. None of us escape the attentions of the devil—that malicious marauder who constantly manipulates the seductions of the world and the flesh in order to lay us as low as he can. How, then, in face of all this, should holy living be conceived, described, and practiced? Our high and privileged calling is to do the will of God in the power of God for the glory of God. When life is so full of traps and pitfalls and false trails, how can this ever be achieved?

To get a handle on this question, think for a moment of diet charts—those intimidating products of modern knowledge about proteins, fats, carbohydrates, vitamins, calories, cholesterol, metabolism, and what not. The noteworthy fact about diet charts is that there are so many of them. The Western world is full of diet charts, all designed to regulate one's food intake in such a way as to produce a desired physical effect, such as weight loss or weight gain or increased energy. Not only are there different diet charts for different bodily needs, there are different charts for dealing with the same condition, like so many alternative routes to a single destination. For weight loss in particular, there exist many different diets to try, and I dare say they all have some merit. But I am much more sure of this: human nature being what it is, each diet has a body of supporters who see it as the only word of wisdom for would-be reducers. They take for granted that the diet they follow will work for everybody, and that no other diet will work as well, so they dismiss out of hand all other diet charts in order to promote their own.

For it is human nature to be exclusive, to dislike alternatives, to claim finality for whatever has benefited us personally, and to be suspicious and standoffish toward other recommended ways of producing the same result. I do not ask you to decide whether this mindset is virtuous or vicious, sensible or silly (it might be a bit of both, but never mind that now). I ask you simply to note that it is a fact. The jealous advocates of the various dieting routines are there to prove it. So also are the advocates of various routines for holy living, which is the matter that concerns us now.

Two Journeys. For the better part of two thousand years Christians who know their business (always some, sometimes many) have been seeking to live holy lives in the strength and to the glory of their triune Savior-God. They have seen that the Christian life is two journeys, not just one. They have perceived that alongside the outward journey from the cradle to the grave through what philosophers call the external world, there is an inward journey into God-knowledge and Christ-knowledge that they need to take as well. They have identified this second journey as the first stage of an eternity of love and adoration, service and joy. They have also grasped that the outward life of loving one's neighbor and the inner life of loving one's God belong together, in such a sense that failure in either inescapably weakens the other.

Over the centuries these born-again believers (for such they have been, even when they did not use those words and when the details of their belief were flawed) have taken the inward journey in ways which, though related at root level, were different to a degree. Because human individuals differ from each other, no two marriages are ever identical, and in the same way no two lives of fellowship with God are ever quite the same. Every Christian must ultimately find his or her own way in the relationship, with such help as can be gained from friends, pastors, and those who since the seventeenth century have been called "spiritual directors" (nowadays more often described as "soul-friends").[4] Part of the story, however, is that the different ways exist as traditions that developed in relative isolation from each other—Protestant from Catholic, West from East, Lutheran from Calvinist, Wesleyan from Reformed, mystically oriented from ethically focused, socially alert from individualistic, charismatic from mainstream, and so on. This explains the existence of a number of prescribed paths of holiness that are in themselves complementary and mutually enriching (call them all spiritual diet-and-exercise charts if you wish), but which get presented to us as complete and self-sufficient, with the added innuendo that none of the formulae really work save the one that the speaker is currently peddling. This results in instructors in the spiritual life regularly omitting things that their audiences would be helped by hearing, just because those things are anchored in another tradition. It is an unhappy state of affairs, narrowing those who settle for it and harrowing those who do not.

As one of those who do not, I now proceed to list six differently focused characterizations of the holy life—this Christlike, humble, loving, patient life, in which thought and desire, heart and hand, motive and action, are linked and integrated as they should be. They come from different sources in different eras. Each has been treated from time to time as self-sufficient. It will be evident from the way I present them that I believe they belong together, since the thrust of each is part of the total truth. Let the reader judge.

HOLINESS AS THE REDIRECTING OF DESIRE

Desire is the "I-want" state of consciousness. In this line of teaching (which goes back at least to Origen in the third century, Augustine in the fifth, and Gregory the Great in the sixth), holiness is viewed first and foremost as the detaching of desire from created things in order to attach it through Christ to the Creator, for expression and satisfaction in and through God-centered prayer. Important as the outward life of justice, integrity, and neighbor-love is, the inner life of pure-hearted prayer is held (surely rightly) to be far more important. God calls on his children to give him their hearts. Finding their fullness of life here and now in the relationship of knowing, loving, and enjoying him will be a foretaste of their life in heaven. Prayer is thus the top priority in the life of holiness. Indeed, only insofar as prayer is the breath, heartbeat, and energy source of one's inner being can one be said to be living a life of holiness at all.

Achieving and maintaining steady, God-centered prayerfulness is a struggle. Christians find themselves in constant conflict with the devil and his hosts, who by God's permission tempt us to sin and distract us from obedience in order to obstruct and destroy holiness in our inner life. Honest prayer comes only from honest hearts, hearts that are set against sin and that practice regular self-search lest they be self-deceived. So the essence of Satan's strategy is to prevent us being honest in heart. (He does not mind our behavior being blameless in human eyes as long as our hearts are crooked before God; proud self-absorption and self-indulgence in our fantasies and motivations are all he needs to get his effect.) God allows us to be thus infiltrated and assaulted partly, at least, so that we may be toughened, matured, and anchored in him more deeply, through the experience of fighting back in his strength. This is spiritual warfare, in the true meaning of that phrase (see Eph 6:10-20).

Desiring God. The teaching under review assumes that desiring and contemplating our Savior-God in the reciprocity of love is life's highest and noblest activity. In developing that thought, it makes two further affirmations: first, Christians often forfeit enjoyment of this relationship through their own negligence and preoccupation with other things; second, God sometimes withholds the sense of his presence and love which he gives at other times, in order to teach us lessons about patience and pure-heartedness that we would not otherwise learn. A variety of presentations have been developed to articulate these truths. We glance now at some of these.

The importance of distancing oneself from what has held one's heart has often been expressed in terms of withdrawing into the "desert" of solitude, where desire is purified. The same point has been made in the West by directing Christians to strip off (renounce, leave behind) all the distracting things that overlay the "cone" or "apex" of their souls, and in the East by requiring *apatheia* (not inner impassivity, but the self-mastery that redirects passion into the pursuit of God). Paths of thought and prayer for detaching desire from the magnetic pulls of this world in order to attach it more firmly to God in Christ have been mapped by Augustine, Bernard, and Thomas à Kempis; Roman Catholics like Ignatius Loyola and Francis de Sales; and Puritans such as Richard Sibbes, Richard Baxter, Thomas Goodwin, and John Owen, with many others before and since.

The relationship between, on the one hand, verbal meditation and petition and on the other, post-verbal and non-verbal contemplation and self-offering to the Lord whom one knows, trusts, and loves, has been explored by teachers of the "spiritual marriage." They have developed the analogy of love-language and love-communion between the sexes and applied it to one's relationship with God. In the same connection, Cistercians, Franciscans, and others have highlighted the links between loving contemplation of God and compassionate action among men and women, while Jonathan Edwards' *Treatise on Religious Affections* sets up tests that show whether strong driving feelings in a devotional context are authentically spiritual (stemming from the Holy Spirit's work in the heart) or not. All of this instruction seeks, one way or another, to mark out the path to that enjoyment of God which is life's supreme value and glory.

Unfulfilled Desire. On God's use of the discipline of dryness and temporarily unfulfilled desire for himself as a means of strengthening the inner life of his servants, other classic presentations have been made. Teresa of Avila and John of the Cross described different stages or phases in the life of prayer, including the "dark night of the soul" that may precede the joy of realized union with God. Puritan teaching on "spiritual desertion" was substantially the same as that of the two Spanish mystics just cited. John Wesley formulated a two-level account of the inner life whereby, through seeking and agonizing for the post-conversion blessing of "perfect love," the Christian's heart is totally purged of sin and imbued with an all-consuming passion of love God and fellow human beings.

The variations on this "second blessing" theme (concepts of entire sanctification, the clean heart, Spirit-baptism, Spirit-filling, and eradication of sin) have been vastly influential in popular Protestantism, and more recently in the global charismatic movement. One does not have to give full endorsement to any of these formulations[5] to recognize the recurring pattern: God brings on dryness, with resultant restlessness of heart, in order to induce a new depth of humble, hopeful openness to himself, which he then crowns with a liberating and animating reassurance of his love—one that goes beyond anything that was sensed before. As Christ's humiliation and grief on the cross preceded his exaltation to the joy of his throne, so over and over again humbling experiences of impotence and frustration precede inward renewing, with a sense of triumph and glory, in the believer's heart. Thus, with wisdom adapted to each Christian's temperament, circumstances, and needs, our heavenly Father draws and binds his children closer to himself. Consider the words of Paul and the psalmist on this theme:

> Whatever was to my profit I now consider loss for the sake of Christ.... I consider everything a loss compared to the surpassing greatness of knowing Christ Jesus my Lord, for whose sake I have lost all things. I consider them rubbish, that I may gain Christ and be found in him.... I want to know Christ. **Phil 3:7-10**

> Earth has nothing I desire besides you.... God is the strength of my heart and my portion for ever. **Ps 73:25-26**

These statements are classic transcripts of genuinely holy hearts. The redirecting of desire so that it focuses on fellowship with the Father and the Son, and the strengthening of desire so redirected, is the real essence of holiness. All mature forms of Christian holiness teaching down the centuries have started here, seeing this as the true foundation to everything else in the Christian life, and insisting that the only truly holy people are those with a passion for God. We today have to start here too.

HOLINESS AS THE CULTIVATING OF VIRTUES

Holiness means not only desiring God, but also loving and practicing righteousness, out of a constant exercise of conscience to discern right from wrong and an ardent purpose of doing all that one can to please God. One line of holiness teaching (not usually given under that name) that stems from medieval scholastics and post-Reformation Anglicans in particular, sees holiness in primarily ethical terms. The focus is on the practice of praiseworthy behavior patterns called virtues, which are understood as good habits expressing good character.

Thomas Aquinas delineated holiness as the manifesting of three "theological" virtues (virtues imparted supernaturally by the Holy Spirit to Christians alone) within a frame established by the four "cardinal" virtues (cardinal meaning pivotal, from the Latin for hinge) that Aristotle described, and that the non-Christian world knows at least to some degree. The theological virtues are faith, hope, and love, of which love is the greatest (1 Cor 13:13). The cardinal virtues are prudence (wisdom and common sense), temperance (self-control), justice (fairness, honesty, truthfulness, trustworthiness), and fortitude (courage and resilience, as in the John Wayne film title *True Grit*, or as C.S. Lewis renders it, "guts"). The four cardinal virtues define the manner and spirit of the holy person's exercise of faith, hope, and love. Thus stated, the scheme assumes that nature and grace dovetail, the latter augmenting and perfecting the former. Sin is thought of as a lack of strength rather than a perverted energy. Exponents of a more radical doctrine of sin would feel compelled to make adjustments at this point. But the rightness of insisting that there is no holiness without morally upright and conscientious behavior, grounded in stable character, is surely beyond dispute.

The view of the healthy inner life that accompanies this outlook regularly makes more of ordered steadiness in seeking to please God, than it does either of experiences involving communion and union, or of spiritual warfare against satanic attacks. Teachers in this tradition usually concentrate on sensitizing and educating consciences to judge what is right and wrong, engendering the practical compassion that perceives others' needs and moves in to do something about them, and soft-pedaling any suggestion that emotional intensity is a measure of holiness.

Tension easily arises between those who maximize and who minimize the place of feelings in holiness, and between those who make much or little of particular experiences of God that come the Christian's way. But in terms of the big picture, which is our present concern, all that needs to be said is that the desire for God, with love of Christ, and the doing of good, with love of righteousness, are equally essential ingredients in a holy life.

HOLINESS AS THE FOLLOWING OF THE HOLY SPIRIT'S URGINGS

Here we move into the world of impressions, impulses, inner pressures, and personal promptings—a world where it is not easy to keep one's footing and where many fearful mistakes have been made. But there is truth here too, truth that it is important to bring out: namely, the truth of life supernatural-ized at its motivational level.

During the Reformation and the century that followed, jus-tice was done to this truth in a sober and profound way, be-cause the link, basic to Reformation theology, between the Spirit and the Word (biblical teaching), was conscientiously kept in mind. The danger of following supposed promptings by the Spirit that did not square with the Word was fully appre-ciated. Calvin was not the only one to underline the impossibil-ity of the Spirit in the heart going against his own instruction in the Word, and to draw the conclusion that the impulses driv-ing some ardent individuals and groups outside the main-stream of Christianity came from the spirit of wickedness rather than the Spirit of God.[6]

But the magisterial Reformers, and even more the Puritans of the next century, recognized that when God through the Holy Spirit calls sinners to faith in Christ, their hearts are changed. Henceforth the heart-changing Spirit *indwells* them (sustains a constant energizing, empowering, prayer-generating, Christ-imparting relationship to them at the core of their being). This indwelling has the effect not only of making

Christ's presence a reality to them, but also causing the mind and motivation of Christ to grow within them. This means, as the Reformers and Puritans saw the matter, that only a whole-souled response to the biblical revelation of God's redeeming love and moral will, a response that is grateful, reverent, imaginative, and creative, is adequate. Such a response aims explicitly at pleasing and glorifying God in one's own life-situation, which is something that every Christian deep down wants to do. This supernatural prompting to love, serve, and please is one facet of the reality of a holy life.

Luther's Teaching. The above emphasis first broke surface in the teaching of Martin Luther. Luther's mature thought radiated from a single center like many spokes from the hub of a wheel. He usually referred to this center as the knowledge of Christ, or at one stage, the theology of the cross. On one occasion at least he called it the wonderful exchange. Today we usually call it justification by faith, but it is the same thing, whichever label it bears. It can be stated thus: in virtue of the substitutionary bearing of our sins by Jesus Christ on the cross, and through the divine gift of faith in him and in his achievement, God imparts the further gift of present pardon and acceptance, so that believing sinners now find themselves set right with God the holy judge, even though they actually fall short of perfect righteousness every moment. Luther's famous phrase to describe the Christian's position, one on which he rang many changes, is *simul justus et peccator* (just—accepted and treated as righteous by God—while still a sinner). Luther's teaching here is biblically correct and brilliant. I have already incorporated it into earlier chapters of the present book.

On this basis, Luther went on to affirm that the indwelling Holy Spirit, who first caused our faith to blossom (Luther conceived faith as crystalizing in the convicted sinner's assurance of present acceptance through Christ's cross), now spontaneously moves Christians to a life of self-giving service to God and their fellow human beings, out of grateful love to the

Father and the Son. For Luther the performance of evangelically motivated "good works" in home, church, and society was the essence of a holy life. Faith, he affirmed, engages tirelessly and endlessly in such works. That was his way of saying that the Spirit's witness in the Christian's heart to the reality of gracious acceptance through Christ, and the Spirit-sustained urge to answer God's love by loving others for his sake, was for him (Luther) the Christian's motivating dynamic. It has not always been appreciated how strongly Luther affirmed this ministry, and indeed other ministries, of the Holy Spirit in the Christian's life.[7]

Luther was clear that God's law states God's standards and that lawless living cannot please him, yet he was so anxious to avoid legalism and to present Christian motivation as evangelical that he left his flanks relatively unguarded against the idea that nudges from the Holy Spirit make it needless to look to the law to learn what God wants of us. However, he rejected that idea out of hand when it was actually put forward. Luther was no antinomian, but held always to biblical standards of morality as he understood them. He was as forthright as Calvin in insisting that the motivation by the Spirit which is basic to holiness is motivation only to do according to the Word. For Luther, to follow supposed nudges of the Spirit that do not relate to, or even fly in the face of, biblical standards and requirements is not holiness but unholiness, the devil's distorting and lampooning of God's ideal.

We need to be clear that, in stressing thankfulness to God for salvation as the holy person's controlling motivation, Luther was saying something of enormous importance. To put it in terms of a later controversy, he was affirming that the sense in which Christians work *for* life (to get to heaven) is determined by the sense in which they work *from* life (to show gratitude for the grace that is theirs already). Holy people practice good works, not to earn God's present or future favor, but as a way of laying hold of that for which Christ has laid hold of them. Self-justifying legalism, the false rationale of righteousness that had spread like wildfire through popular Christianity in the centuries before the Reformation, was thus eliminated and banished as a motivating principle forever.

All ventures in holiness go rotten at the core when gain in any form, rather than gratitude, motivates them. The true tap-root of holiness is always the Spirit-prompted urge to show love to God and others by doing what is right out of gratitude to God for Jesus Christ, just as Luther saw. As this was truth for his time, so it is for ours.

HOLINESS AS THE OVERCOMING OF SIN'S DOWNDRAG

This perspective has never been more thoroughly explored than it was by the English Puritans (some of whom, of course, relocated in New England in the course of their ministry). The Puritans as a body constitute a Reformed school of thought, but one marked by their own distinctive interests (theological and pastoral), their own distinctive style (plain and analytical), and their own distinctive flavor.[8]

With Calvin, they analyzed God's work of sanctifying sinners as, on the negative side, *mortification*, the progressive killing of sin as it manifests itself in each rebellious and self-indulging habit, plus, on the positive side, *vivification*, the inculcating and strengthening in us of all Christ-like habits ("graces"), in particular the ninefold pattern of habitual reaction to life's pressures —love, joy, peace, patience, kindness, goodness, faithfulness, gentleness and self-control—that Paul in Galatians 5:22 calls the "fruit" of the Spirit (cf. Mt 12:33).

With Calvin also, the Puritans stressed that God justifies in order to sanctify. Every part of the Christian's life—his relationship to God and God's creation; all his relationships with others, in the family, the church, and the world; and also his relationship to himself, in self-discipline and self-management across the board—must become "holiness to the Lord." With Calvin too, they classed as hypocrites any professing Christians in whom the twofold transformation of mortification and vivification was not taking place. Finally, with Calvin they insisted that God's moral law as set forth by Moses, the prophets, Christ, and the New Testament letters was the family code for all God's children at all times. There was, however, a different nuance. Whereas Calvin regularly referred to Christian holiness as progress in faith and fortitude, the Puritans characteristically depicted it as an increasing measure of deliverance from sin.

The Puritan View of Sin. The Puritans as a body manifested an acute awareness of the holiness, righteousness, hatred of sin, and judicial severity against sin that marks the great, gracious, omniscient, and omnipresent God of the Bible. Their sharp-eyed discernment of the pervasiveness, repulsiveness, and deadliness of sin sprang directly from this deep sense of God as holy. Their sensitivity to sin as an inner force, devious and wily, tyrannizing the unconverted and tormenting the saints, was extraordinary. They remain Christianity's past masters in this particular field of understanding. They saw sin as a perverted energy within people that enslaves them to God-defying, self-gratifying behavior, and by distraction, deceit, and direct opposition weakens and overthrows their purposes of righteousness. They perceived sin as the moral equivalent of a wolf in sheep's clothing, presenting itself to us again and again as good, desirable, and a necessity of life, thereby corrupting our conscience so that we lose the sense of its guiltiness, and cherish it as if it were a friend rather than an enemy.

In *The Great Divorce* C.S. Lewis pictures a man with a lizard on his shoulder, representing lawless lust. The lizard whispers in his ear about how essential it is to his continued well-being. When the angel asks, "Shall I kill it?" the man's first response is to say no. (One thinks of Augustine's prayer: "Give me chastity, but not yet.")

The Puritans would have applauded Lewis's lizard as a perfect projection of the way sin entrenches its various forms of expression in Christians' lives. Puritan theology affirmed that in Christians sin has been dethroned but not yet destroyed. Now sin takes on, as it were, a life of its own, seeking to re-establish the dominion it has lost. Its power appears both in bad habits, which are often deep-rooted and linked with temperamental weaknesses, and in sudden forays and frontal assaults at points where one thought oneself invulnerable. Of itself sin never loses its strength. The most that happens is that with advancing age, ups and downs of health, and shifting personal circumstances, indwelling sin finds different modes of expression. But wherever it appears, in whatever form, Christians are charged, not just to resist it, but to attack it and seek to do it to death—in other words, to mortify it, in the biblical sense of that word (see Rom 8:13; Col 3:5).

Puritan teaching on mortifying the lusts that tempt us is businesslike and thorough. It includes the disciplines of self-humbling, self-examination, setting oneself against all sins in one's spiritual system as a preliminary to muscling in on any one of them, avoiding situations that stoke sin's boiler, watching lest you become sin's victim before you are aware of its approach, and praying to the Lord Jesus Christ specifically to apply the killing power of his cross to the particular vicious craving on which one is making one's counterattack. "Set faith at work on Christ for the *killing* of thy sin," wrote the greatest Puritan teacher, John Owen. "His blood is the great sovereign remedy for sin-sick souls. Live in this, and thou wilt die a conqueror; yea, thou wilt, through the good providence of God, live to see thy lust dead at thy feet."[9]

The Puritans have always had a bad press. Their emphasis on each Christian's lifelong war to the death with "besetting" (habitual) sins has sometimes been dismissed as Manichean (denying the goodness of created human nature), morbid (denying the joy of natural behavior), and morally unreal (obsessed with self-flagellation, in disregard of everything else). But all of this is factually incorrect, and the idea that fighting sin was all the Puritan saints ever thought about is quite wrong.

Love for God, joyful assurance, spiritual-mindedness, honesty and public spirit, quiet acceptance of God's will, the pathway of persistent prayer, and the power of the hope of glory, are among the many themes that are greatly developed in Puritan teaching about holiness. It was not all harping on a single note. Yet it is true that a drumbeat stress on detecting, resisting, and overcoming sin's downdrag appears everywhere. This obtrusive emphasis has kept many in the past from seeing that Puritan holiness is fundamentally a cheerful affair of peace, joy, worship, fellowship, and growth. The solemn business of self-scrutiny and suffering, inward and outward, as one strives and struggles against sin is only one side of it. But in an age in which self-ignorance, secular-mindedness, moral slackness and downright sin are as common among Christians as they are today, it is doubtless from the stern side of Puritanism—the side that forces on us realism about our sinfulness and our sins—that we have most to learn.

HOLINESS AS THE EXERCISING OF FAITH FOR A "SECOND BLESSING"

Holiness always involves the exercising of faith by praying for specific benefits. In a broad sense, all accounts of Christian holiness except the Pelagian (which reduces holiness to unaided self-discipline, and is heretical, and will not be considered here) involve this exercise of faith. They all see sanctification as God's work. They all hold that holy living is only ever achieved by divine grace, power, and help, through the Holy Spirit, and they all agree that only believers who pray enjoy this assistance. Concepts of faith in action, however, are often inadequate, varying as they do from the ill-conceived Catholic formalism of "trust the church implicitly" to the ill-conceived Protestant subjectivism of "face the future fearlessly." Only when the living Christ and the truths of Scripture are the focus of belief, trust, and reliance is it Christian faith at all.

The witness of Reformation theology over almost half a millennium is that only when faith specifically trusts God's promises is it in proper shape.

Looking for, and trusting to, God's fulfillment of his "very great and precious promises" (2 Pt 1:4) is a basic exercise of faith as Scripture portrays it. (See what is said about Abraham, the model man of faith, in Romans 4:18-21; Galatians 3:6-9, 16-18, cf. 22, 29; Hebrews 6:13-15, 11:1, 11, 13, 17-19, cf. 33.) Promise-focused faith both glorifies God by honoring his faithfulness and forms the soul in that Godward attitude of realized dependence and eager expectancy that is seen in many of the psalms. That in itself is one dimension of holiness, whereby trust and hope rest in God alone. In truth there is no real holiness without this constant exertion of heart in God-centered, faithfilled prayer.

Second Blessing. The correlation between faith and promise has been characteristic of all mainstream evangelical Protestantism. But it has been given a particularly striking development in the historic Wesleyan account of "scriptural holiness" and in its many latter-day modifications. The distinctive thesis of this whole school of thought is that through a second "experience" (experiential event, triggered by God), those who became Christians through a first "experience," namely new birth, may enter upon an upgraded quality of Christian living. Through this second experience, the sense of God's love is more vivid, one's own love to God and humanity is stronger, and sin ceases to control any of one's behavior because by the power of the Holy Spirit temptation, discouragement, apathy, and gloom are regularly overcome. Full and genuine holiness of life (so it is claimed) only becomes reality after the second experience has occurred.

The original form of this teaching was Wesley's doctrine of entire sanctification ("Christian perfection," or "perfect love"), mentioned earlier in this chapter, according to which the second experience roots sin out of the born-again person's heart, so that perverse desires and mixed motives become a thing of the past. No passion, purpose, or power operates in one's life henceforth save that of love only. This, said Wesley, is part of the blessing of heaven, which those who seek will find here on earth. During the so-called "holiness revival" between the mid-nineteenth and mid-twentieth centuries, "Keswick" and "higher life" teachers modified Wesley's idea of eradication of sin into mere counteraction of it, thus redefining the second blessing ("Spirit-filling" as they usually called it) as finding one's way into a God-empowered perfection of act in spite of a continuing imperfection of motive.

But both versions of this two-stage view of the Christian life insisted that the way to enter and maintain the sanctified state is through a focused, expectant, importunate, promise-pleading exercise of faith in prayer, whereby one waits on God to do what he has undertaken to do in specific statements of his written Word. Honoring God by "believing for the blessing," and holding on to him in one's petitions until he bestows it, rather than ceasing to pray through unbelief of his willingness to do what he promised, is the action called for. Spokesmen for both views allow that God may keep us waiting once he has stirred us, out of hatred for our own unholiness, to start praying in this way, but they insist that no one ever enters into the true holiness of stage two without such prayer. It is only seekers, they say, who find.

Both versions of this two-stage understanding of "scriptural holiness" seem misconceived. To start with, nowhere does Scripture teach the universal need of a "second blessing," or imply that there is no real holiness without it. Then, eradication ascribes to God too much (no continuance of depravity in the heart), while counteraction ascribes to him too little (no lessening of depravity in the heart). The biblical teaching is rather that the Christian's total self is progressively renewed and restored throughout the sanctifying process—refocused on God, reintegrated with God at the center, reconstructed in character, habits, and reaction patterns, sensitized to God's values, redirected into God-glorifying purposes, and made more alert to others' needs and miseries. At no point is the process complete in any Christian, but it starts and goes forward in them all (see 2 Cor 3:18).

That, in God's mercy, momentous post-conversion experiences come to some Christians, bringing assurance, liberty of heart, new spiritual joy and energy, with new power for life and witness, is beyond doubt. These, however, seem to be the particular discretionary dealings of a gracious heavenly Father with his individual children. They are not universal requirements, not prescribed patterns of experience for all, not hoops through which every Christian must try to jump. Those who have had no momentous "second experience," therefore, should not see themselves as necessarily inferior to those who have been thus blessed. History confirms that some of God's finest servants have been enriched in this way, while others, equally fine, have not.

So when Wesleyan and Keswick spokesmen define holiness as the second blessing, or as a quality of life that will only appear after the second blessing, and when people from the Pentecostal-charismatic world speak of holiness as a life that cannot be lived without a post-conversion Spirit-baptism (not all say this, but some do), I demur.[10] When, however, these same persons maintain that just as one gets into the life of holiness by specific, focused, persistent, reason-giving, promise-oriented verbal prayer, so in the life of holiness each needed benefit and enablement must be sought in the same way, I am right with them. That kind of prayer is indeed modeled and displayed throughout Scripture as an integral element in holy life. I think their account of holiness itself is flawed and incorrect, but I could not agree more with what many of them say about prayer itself. There is, I believe, no genuine holiness that does not have at its heart constant, focused prayer, in which faith is being exercised for the bestowing of particular benefits and the meeting of particular needs.

HOLINESS AS THE PRACTICING
OF SPIRITUAL DISCIPLINES

Verbally, this is a very contemporary perspective, though the point being made goes right back to the earliest years of Christianity. But the recovery of this historic emphasis at the present time is badly needed. The latter years of the twentieth century have seen a tidal wave of hedonism and a random approach to living swamp the West, both outside and inside the church. The bad effect of affluence, about which the Bible constantly warns us, is thoughtless self-indulgence of all sorts in private life. This bad effect is currently visible everywhere. Thoughtlessness has become a mark of our society, and the younger generation of Christians, who culturally speaking have never known anything but affluence, prove again and again to be the morally crippled victims of the materialism, consumerism, and hedonism of the world in which they were brought up.

No wonder then that Richard Foster's *Celebration of Discipline* (1978), the first forthright challenge offered to this modern mindset, struck a nerve for so many. Foster's basic point—that Christians must learn deliberately and regularly to do what makes for their spiritual well-being (use the means of grace and learn self-control, as earlier generations would put it)— was not new, but it hit home as a word in season. Others have since taken it up.

It is interesting to see how the theme is handled by its various exponents. Foster himself explored twelve disciplines in three groups: the *inward* disciplines of meditation, prayer, fasting, and study; the *outward* disciplines of simplicity, solitude, submission, and service; and the *corporate* disciplines of confession (meaning accountability), worship, guidance, and celebration. His *Money, Sex and Power* (1985) then modeled discipline for these three particular headache areas.

More recent exponents of the theme of discipline seem to be standing on Foster's shoulders. Donald Whitney's *Spiritual*

Disciplines for the Christian Life (1991) works over more than half Foster's topics, and adds stewardship and journaling to the list. R. Kent Hughes, once Foster's colleague, in *Disciplines of a Godly Man* (1991) [*Man* meaning *Male!*] reviews sixteen disciplines for men under the headings: purity, marriage, fatherhood, friendship, mind, devotion, prayer, worship, integrity, tongue, work, church, leadership, giving, witness, and ministry. Elisabeth Elliot, in *Discipline: The Glad Surrender* (1982), deals with the discipline of the body, the mind, place (meaning status), time, possessions, work, and feelings. Dallas Willard, in *The Spirit of the Disciplines* (1988), pursues the thought that we will become like Christ if we live as he did, maintaining a rhythm of solitude and silence, prayer, simple and sacrificial living, meditation on Scripture, and service to others.

Kent Hughes, having noted that his survey of disciplines lays on the male conscience "over 100 do's!" speaks wisely about the effect that such a review of the Christian calling should have:

How then are we to respond? Certainly not with "do nothing" *passivity* which has become increasingly characteristic of the American male....

On the other hand, an equally deadly response is self-sufficient *legalism*. Admittedly, it is less a statistical danger than passivity.... [You can say that again, Dr. Hughes!] God save us from the *reductionism* of such legalism which enshrines spirituality as a series of wooden laws and then says, "If you can do these six, sixteen, or sixty-six things, you will be godly." Christianity, godliness, is far more than a checklist. Being "in Christ" is a relationship, and like all relationships it deserves disciplined maintenance, but never legalistic reductionism.

God save us also from self-righteous *judgmentalism*.... There is a universe of difference between the motivations behind legalism and discipline. Legalism says, "I will do this thing to gain merit with God," while discipline says, "I will do this because I love God and want to please him." Legalism is man-centered; discipline is God-centered.[11]

True, Godly Discipline. These discussions of discipline confront us with the truth that the call of God to develop fellowship with him, in face of pressures and restraints imposed on us by our condition, our company, and our circumstances, along with our weaknesses and blind spots and the multitude of traps set for us by the devil, make imperative a planned, orderly, thoughtful approach to the business of daily living. Only then can we ever ensure that there is room in our lives for all the things we ought to be doing. Only then shall we ever learn to think ahead, and prepare ourselves for what may come, and work out before God what our reactions to this and that should be.

The Christians who realize that it is Christ-like wisdom to think ahead in this way are few and far between, but it is so all the same. Experience confirms that those who have already adjusted their minds to the fact that troubles may come, are able to keep their footing and handle their feelings better when troubles do come. As the children of this world, fired by personal ambition, set themselves career goals and then work very hard to achieve them, so God's children, fired by the greatness of divine love, should have before their minds the goal of discipline in daily living, and work equally hard, planning, praying, and trying things out, to make it a reality. The alternative is to live like a pilot flying blind—always being taken by surprise and tyrannized by the immediate, the urgent, and the unexpected—experiencing life as a succession of emergencies that one is never ready to meet.

Thoughtless, undisciplined living is either frantic or happy-go-lucky, according to whether one feels threatened by the flow of events or not. But it is not Christ-like, nor gratifying to ourselves, nor glorifying to God. Sanctified thoughtfulness is a prime element of holy life, for it is here that true discipline begins.

COMPLETING THE PANORAMIC SURVEY

At this point, we close our survey of the view from the head of the pass. We have not yet seen everything, but we have seen the main things. We have trained our spiritual binoculars on the leading features of the landscape of holiness. Thus we begin to get the entire overwhelming panorama into some sort of focus, so that our notion of what we are looking at is now clearer.

What has emerged is a sort of identikit profile of a person:

• who can never love God enough;
• whose adoration of him is unceasing;
• who is always seeking to live nobly, lovingly, and honorably for God;
• who reveres the indwelling Holy Spirit;
• who battles constantly against indwelling sin;
• who pleads God's promises and waits expectantly for their fulfillment; and
• who practices self-discipline maturely and thoughtfully.

Passion and compassion, prayer and prudence, gentleness and generosity, all enter into the portrait. The reflections of Jesus Christ, the apostle Paul, and David and his fellows in the Psalms (to look no further) are surely too plain to miss. Such is the outline of the holiness that is learned in the school of Christ.

Let us give it a further human face. Universal holiness, as they called it, was the chief concern of the Puritans of history. Three and a half centuries ago, when character-drawing on paper was a much-admired literary art, *The Character of an Old English Puritane or Nonconformist* was set down as follows (I retain the quaint old spellings):

The Old English Puritane was such a one that honored God above all, and under God gave everyone his due. His first care was to serve God, and therein he did not what was good in his own, but in God's sight, making the word of God the rule of his worship.... He made conscience of all God's ordinances.... He was much in praier; with it he began and closed the day. In it he was exercised in his closet, family and publike assembly.... He esteemed reading of the word an ordinance of God both in private and publike....

The Lord's day he esteemed a divine ordinance, and rest on it necessary so far as it induced to holinesse. He was very consciencious in the observance of that day as the Mart [market] day of the Soul [i.e., the day when one secures supplies for the coming week].... The Lord's Supper he accounted part of his soul's food: to which he laboured to keep an appetite. He esteemed it an ordinance of nearest communion with Christ, so requiring most exact preparation....

He accounted religion an engagement to duty, that the best Christians should be the best husbands, best wives, best parents, best children, best Masters, best servants, best Magistrates, best subjects, that the doctrine of God might be adorned not blasphemed. His family he endeavoured to make a Church... admitting none into it [i.e., as servants or lodgers] but such as feared God; and labouring that those that were born in it, might be born again to God.... He was a man of a tender heart, not only in regard of his own sin, but others' misery, not counting mercy arbitrary, but a necessary duty; wherein as he prayed for wisdom to direct him, so he studied [resolutely aimed] for cheerfulnesse and a bounty [liberal generosity] to act....

In his habit [dress] he avoided costlinesse and vanity... desiring in all things to express gravity [a serious approach to living, as opposed to irresponsible frivolity]. His whole life he accounted a warfare, wherein Christ was his captain, his arms, praiers and tears. The Crosse his Banner and his word [motto] *Vincit qui patitur* [he who suffers conquers].[12]

This is how holiness was conceived by England's most robust Christians in Puritan times. It is surely plain that only a little adjustment is needed to bring the model right up-to-date.

Now we move on from our vantage point in order to come closer to some of the realities that we have viewed from afar. That is the agenda for the next chapters.

CHAPTER	Growing Downward
5	to Grow Up: The
	Life of Repentance

Now I am happy, not because you were made sorry, but because your sorrow led you to repentance. For you became sorrowful as God intended and so were not harmed in any way by us. Godly sorrow brings repentance that leads to salvation and leaves no regret.... See what this godly sorrow has produced in you: what earnestness, what eagerness to clear your - selves, what indignation, what alarm, what longing, what concern, what readiness to see justice done.

2 Cor 7:9-11

Those whom I love I rebuke and discipline. So be earnest, and repent.   **Rv 3:19**

GROWING UP AND GROWING DOWNWARD

From time to time during our son's teen years he would stand with his back to the dining room doorpost, and we would record his height in pencil on the white wood. He was growing up physically, getting taller as each month went by, and he was excited about it. So were we. Watching your children grow up is, after all, an exciting business. Had we not been interested in the way he was gaining height there would have been something wrong with us. But this chapter is not about growing up:

119

it is about growing *down*, something that every Christian must learn to do.

Growing *down*, or *downward*, is doubtless an odd-sounding phrase in a culture like ours. We celebrate the fact of growing *up* physically and urge those who have slipped into childish petulance to grow *up* emotionally. It is also our habit to speak of growing *up* spiritually, and our English Bible does the same. The New International Version (NIV) follows the King James Version (KJV) and all revisions of it in rendering a Greek verb that has nothing of "up" about it as "grow *up*" in Ephesians 4:15 ("we will in all things grow *up* into him who is the Head, that is, Christ"), and in 1 Peter 2:2 it does the same ("Like newborn babies, crave pure spiritual milk, so that by it you may grow *up* in your salvation").

Yes, to speak of growing downward against this background does sound odd, I grant you. But my phrase is there to strike a spark and make a point. What we have to realize is that we grow *up* into Christ by growing *down* into lowliness (humility, from the Latin word *humilis*, meaning low). Christians, we might say, grow greater by getting smaller.

Of his own ministry, in relation to that of the Lord Jesus, John the Baptist declared: "He must become greater; I must become less" (Jn 3:30). Of our lives as believers, something similar has to be said. Pride blows us up like balloons, but grace punctures our conceit and lets the hot, proud air out of our system. The result (a very salutary result) is that we shrink, and end up seeing ourselves as less—less nice, less able, less wise, less good, less strong, less steady, less committed, less of a piece—than ever we thought we were. We stop kidding ourselves that we are persons of great importance to the world and to God. We settle for being insignificant and dispensable.

Off-loading our fantasies of omnicompetence, we start trying to be trustful, obedient, dependent, patient, and willing in our relationship to God. We give up our dreams of being greatly admired for doing wonderfully well. We begin teaching ourselves unemotionally and matter-of-factly to recognize that we are not likely ever to appear, or actually to be, much of a success by the world's standards. We bow to events that rub our noses in the reality of our own weaknesses, and we look to God for strength quietly to cope. This is part, at least, of what it means to answer our Lord's call to childlikeness.

The Scottish scholar James Denney once said that it is impossible at the same time to leave the impression both that I am a great preacher and that Jesus Christ is a great Savior. In the same way it is impossible at the same time to give the impression both that I am a great Christian and that Jesus Christ is a great Master. So the Christian will practice curling up small, as it were, so that in and through him or her the Savior may show himself great. That is what I mean by growing downward.

Downward Growth. The life of holiness is one of downward growth all the time. When Peter writes, "Grow in the grace and knowledge of our Lord and Savior Jesus Christ" (2 Pt 3:18), and when Paul speaks of growing into Christ (Eph 4:15) and rejoices that the Thessalonians' faith is growing (2 Thes 1:3), what they have in view is a progress into personal smallness that allows the greatness of Christ's grace to appear. The sign of this sort of progress is that they increasingly feel and say that in themselves they are nothing and God in Christ has become everything for their ongoing life. It is into this framework, this continual shrinkage of carnal self, as we may call it, that the thesis of the present chapter fits.

What I intend to argue is that Christians are called to a life of habitual repentance, as a discipline integral to healthy holy living. The first of Luther's ninety-five theses, nailed to the Wittenberg church door in 1517, declared: "When our Lord and Master Jesus Christ said, 'Repent' [Mt 4:17], he willed that the whole life of believers should be one of repentance." Philip Henry, a Puritan who died in 1696, met the suggestion that he made too much of repentance by affirming that he hoped to carry his own repentance up to the gate of heaven itself. These two quotations indicate the wavelength we are now tuning into.

In my part of British Columbia, where rainfall is heavy, roads on which the drains fail soon get flooded and become unserviceable. Repentance, as we shall see, is the drainage routine on the highway of holiness on which God calls us all to travel. It is the way we get beyond what has proved to be dirt, rubbish, and stagnant floodwater in our lives. This routine is a vital need, for where real repentance fails, real spiritual advance ceases, and real spiritual growth stops short.

In speaking of habitual repentance, I do not mean to imply that repentance can ever become automatic and mechanical, as our table manners and our driving habits are. It cannot. Every act of repentance is a separate act and a distinct moral effort, perhaps a major and costly one. Repenting is never a pleasure. Always, in more senses than one, it is a pain, and will continue so as long as life lasts. No, when I speak of habitual repentance, I have in mind the forming and retaining of a conscious habit of repenting as often as we need to—though that, of course, means (let us face it) every day of our lives. It is the wisdom of churches that use liturgies to provide prayers of penitence for use at all services. Such prayers are always words in season. In our private devotions, daily penitential prayer will always be needed too.

Little is said these days about the discipline of regular repentance. The writers on the spiritual disciplines have noticeably not dealt with it, and the standard *Dictionary of Christian Spirituality,* now published in the United States as the *Westminster Dictionary,* has no entry on the subject. Yet it is a basic lesson that has to be learned in Christ's school of holiness. The theme is a vital one for spiritual health, as has already been said. So let us try to understand it well.

WHAT IS REPENTANCE?

What is repentance? What does it mean to repent?

The term is a personal and relational one. It signifies going back on what one was doing before, and renouncing the misbehavior by which one's life or one's relationship was being harmed. In the Bible, repentance is a theological term, pointing to an abandonment of those courses of action in which one defied God by embracing what he dislikes and forbids. The Hebrew word for repenting signifies turning, or returning. The corresponding Greek word carries the sense of changing one's mind so that one changes one's ways too. Repentance means altering one's habits of thought, one's attitudes, outlook, policy, direction, and behavior, just as fully as is needed to get one's life out of the wrong shape and into the right one. Repentance is in truth a spiritual revolution. This, now, and nothing less than this, is the human reality that we are to explore.

Repenting in the full sense of the word—actually changing in the way described—is only possible for Christians, believers who have been set free from sin's dominion and made alive to God. Repenting in this sense is a fruit of faith, and as such a gift of God (cf. Acts 11:18). The process can be alliteratively analyzed under the following headings:

1. Realistic recognition that one has disobeyed and failed God, doing wrong instead of doing right. This sounds easier than it actually is. T.S. Eliot spoke the truth when he observed: "Humankind cannot bear very much reality." There is nothing like a shadowy sense of guilt in the heart to make us passionately play the game of pretending something never happened, or rationalizing to ourselves action that was morally flawed. So, after David had committed adultery with Bathsheba and compounded it with murder, he evidently told himself that it was simply a matter of royal prerogative and, therefore, nothing to do with his spiritual life. So he put it out of his mind, until Nathan's "You are the man!" (2 Sm 12:7) made him realize, at last, that he had offended God. This awareness was, and is, the seed bed where repentance grows. It does not grow elsewhere. True repentance only begins when one passes out of what the Bible sees as *self-deception* (cf. Jas 1:22, 26; 1 Jn 1:8) and modern counselors call *denial*, into what the Bible calls *conviction of sin* (cf. Jn 16:8).

2. Regretful remorse at the dishonor one has done to the God one is learning to love and wanting to serve. This is the mark of the contrite heart (cf. Ps 51:17; Is 57:15). The Middle Ages drew a useful distinction between *attrition* and *contrition* (regret for sin prompted by fear for oneself and by love for God respectively; the latter leading to true repentance while the former fails to do so). The believer feels, not just attrition, but contrition, as did David (see Ps 51:1-4, 15-17). Contrite remorse, springing from the sense of having outraged God's goodness and love, is pictured and modeled in Jesus' story of the prodigal's return to his father (Lk 15:17-20).

3. Reverent requesting of God's pardon, cleansing of conscience, and help to not lapse in the same way again. A classic example of such requesting appears in David's prayer of penitence (see Ps 51:7-12). The repentance of believers always, and necessarily, includes the exercise of faith in God for these restorative blessings. Jesus himself teaches God's children to pray "forgive us our sins... and lead us not into temptation" (Lk 11:4).

4. Resolute renunciation of the sins in question, with deliberate thought as to how to keep clear of them and live right for the future. When John the Baptist told Israel's official religious elite: "Produce fruit in keeping with repentance" (Mt 3:8), he was calling on them to change direction in this way.

5. Requisite restitution to any who have suffered material loss through one's wrongdoing. Restitution in these circumstances was required by the Old Testament law. When Zacchaeus, the renegade Jewish taxman, became Jesus' disciple, he committed himself to make fourfold retribution for each act of extortion, apparently on the model of Moses' requirement of four sheep for every one stolen and disposed of (Ex 22:1; cf. Ex 22:2-14; Lv 6:4; Nm 5:7).

An alternative alliteration (as if one were not enough!) would be:

1. *discerning* the perversity, folly, and guilt of what one has done;
2. *desiring* to find forgiveness, abandon the sin, and live a God-pleasing life from now on;
3. *deciding* to ask for forgiveness and power to change;
4. *dealing* with God accordingly;
5. *demonstrating,* whether by testimony and confession or by changed behavior or by both together, that one has left one's sin behind.

Such is the repentance—not just the initial repentance of the adult convert, but the recurring repentance of the adult disciple—that is our present theme.

REPENTANCE AND THE REFORMATION

The Reformation era was one time in the Christian past when the life of repentance was well understood. Luther's rediscovery of present justification by faith, based on Christ's finished work of substitutionary atonement, led him to challenge the popular idea that there was no more to repentance than the formality of sacramental confession and absolution, with performance of whatever "penance" the priest might impose. Though never officially endorsed, these notions had gained the sanction of custom and consensus; and Luther's challenge was timely and much needed. As we have already seen, he maintained that repentance was meant to be a constant, lifelong activity, and he argued that, like faith, it has to be an exercise of the heart.

One who picked up this insight and ran with it was John Bradford, who in 1555, at the age of forty-five, was burned at the stake in London as part of Queen Mary's campaign to purge England of Protestants. Bradford was a Christian in the full sense for six years only. During that time, however, he gained distinction among the English Reformers both as a preacher and as an outstandingly saintly man, one for whom, quite specifically, repentance was a way of life. Thomas Sampson, the friend who led him to faith, wrote a foreword to the second printing of Bradford's *Sermon of Repentance* (in *Two Sermons...*, 1574). Headed "To the Christian Reader, Tho. Sampson wisheth the felicity of speedy and full conversion to the Lord," this foreword shares something of the reality, and the secret, of Bradford's holiness. "Such a pattern was Master Bradford," writes Sampson "of this... repentance which...he teacheth, that I which did know him familiarly must needs give God this praise for him, that among men I have scarcely known one like unto him."[1]

He goes on to explain this in words that merit extensive quotation.

> ... it pleased God with great speed to make him ready and ripe to martyrdom, in which through Christ he has now gained the crown of life. But... he was much helped forward by a continued meditation and practice of repentance and faith in Christ, in which he was kept by God's grace notably exercised all the days of his life.

> ... our Bradford had his daily exercises and practices of repentance. His manner was, to make himself a catalogue of all the grossest and most enorme (*sic*) sins, which in his life of ignorance he had committed; and to lay the same before his eyes when he went to private prayer, that by the sight and remembrance of them he might be stirred up to offer to God the sacrifice of a contrite heart, seek assurance of salvation in Christ by faith, thank God for his calling from the ways of wickedness, and pray for increase of grace to be conducted (i.e., led on) in holy life acceptable and pleasing to God.

Such a continual exercise of conscience he had in private prayer, that he did not count himself to have prayed to his contentation, unless in it he had felt inwardly some smiting of heart for sin, and some healing of that wound by faith, feeling the saving health of Christ, with some change of mind into the detestation of sin, and love of obeying the good will of God....

... Let us learn by Bradford's example to pray better, that is, with the heart, and not with the lips alone... as Cyprian saith: *"Because God is the hearer of the heart and not of the voice"*: that is to say, not of the voice alone without the heart, for that is but lip-labour....

Another of his exercises was this: he used to make unto himself an ephemeris (i.e., diary) or a journal, in which he used to write all such notable things as either he did see or hear each day that passed. But... he did so pen it that a man might see in that book the signs of a smitten heart. For if he did see or hear any good in any man, by that sight he found and noted the want thereof in himself, and added a short prayer, craving mercy and grace to amend. If he did hear or see any plague, or misery, he noted it as a thing procured by his own sins, and still (i.e., always) added... "Lord, have mercy upon me."

[This seems to be the origin of the later, unconfirmed story that when Bradford saw criminals being led out to execution he would say, "There but for the grace of God goes John Bradford."]

He used in the same book to note such evil thoughts as did rise in him; as of envying the good of other men, thoughts of unthankfulness, of not considering God in his works, or harshness and unsensibleness of heart when he did see others moved and affected. And thus he made to himself and of himself a book of daily practices of repentance....[2]

According to Sampson, repentance was Bradford's focal theme throughout the six years of his Christian life. He preached it (his last words, Sampson tells us, spoken as "the flames of fire did fly about his ears," were "Repent, England"[3]); and he lived it. For his involvement, as a member of Sir John Harrington's staff, in an act of fraud "to the detriment of the king" in the days before he came alive to God, Bradford insisted on restitution: "He could never be quiet till, by the advice of Master Latimer [Hugh Latimer, once Bishop of Worcester, whose sermon on restitution had first stirred his conscience] a restitution was made. Which thing to bring to pass"—though the fraud had been Harrington's, not his, and it was eventually Harrington who repaid—"he did willingly forbear and forego all the private and certain patrimony which he had in earth."[4] Thus "his life was a practice and example, a provocation to repentance."

Then, in his ministry Bradford pressed the need for repentance

> not only in public preaching, but also in private conference and company. For in all companies where he did come, he would freely reprove any sin and misbehaviour which appeared in any person, especially swearers, filthy talkers.... And this he did with such grace and Christian majesty, that ever he stopped the mouths of the gainsayers. For he spake with power, and yet so sweetly, that they might see their evil to be evil and hurtful unto them, and understand that it was good indeed to which he laboured to draw them in God.[5]

Sampson's profile of Bradford, written nineteen years after the Reformer was burned, is fascinating in more ways than one. In the first place, it narrates what seems to be the first historical appearance of the personal spiritual journal. It shows Bradford as the pioneer of a kind of journaling in which the Puritans later came to specialize—namely, one that in effect turns the journal into a private confessional, designed to keep one honest with oneself and with God. (Honesty about one's sins and follies is hard to come by, as we have already noted; a journal kept as Bradford kept his can be of great help here. That was true in his day, and is equally true in ours.) Then, in the second place, there is great fascination in the light that Sampson's words throw on Bradford himself, and his vivid sense of the holiness and graciousness of God.

Bradford's Sensitivity to Sin. It is clear that Bradford's grasp of the holiness of God and the hatefulness of sin was very firm indeed. Some moderns dismiss this sharp-edged sensitivity to holiness and sin (rare in itself, yet typical of the sixteenth century's spiritual leaders), as the spin-off of a neurotic culture. Certainly the fear of God's wrath was a most potent reality throughout Europe at that time, but to treat Bradford's sense of divine purity and human impurity as merely weird is perverse prejudice. Bradford was doing no more than facing up to what God tells us over and over again in the pages of Scripture, namely that he hates sin in all its forms, and impenitence on the part of those who have sinned calls forth his "wrath" (judicial hostility, rejection, and retributive judgment).

Let Bradford set this before us in his own way. Here are some excerpts from his "Prayer on the Wrath of God against Sin."

O Almighty and everlasting Lord God, the dear Father of our Saviour Jesus Christ, "which hast made heaven and earth, the sea and all that therein is"; which art the only Ruler, governor, conserver and keeper of all things.... O holy, righteous, and wise; O strong, terrible, mighty, and fearful Lord God, Judge of all men... whose eyes are upon the ways of all men, and are so clean that they cannot abide impiety; thou "searchest the hearts"... of all men. Thou hatest sin and abhorrest iniquity: for sin's sake thou hast grievously punished mankind... as thou hast declared by the penalty of death laid upon all the children of Adam; by the casting out of Adam and his offspring forth of paradise;

by the cursing of the earth; by the drowning of the world; by the burning up of Sodom and Gomor(rah)....

[Bradford here adds several more examples of God's punitive justice in biblically recorded history.]

But, of all spectacles of thine anger against sin, the greatest and most notable is the death and bloody passion of... Jesus Christ. Great is thine anger against sin, when in heaven and earth nothing could be found which might appease thy wrath, save the blood-shedding of thy only and most dearly beloved Son, in whom was and is all thy delight.... If in Christ, in whom was no sin, thy wrath was so fierce for our sin that he was constrained to cry, "My God, my God, why hast thou forsaken me?" how great and importable (i.e., unbearable) then is thine anger against us, which are nothing but sinful![6]

Bradford's trembling awe in his address to the mighty Creator who displays this energy of punitive hatred toward all manifestations of the morally disruptive energy of sin, is no doubt out of tune with the gentler ideas of God and cooler attitudes towards him that are currently common. It was not, however, in any way unique in the Protestant England of his day.

The same attitude finds classic expression in the prayer confessing sin that Thomas Cranmer wrote two or three years earlier for his Order of Communion (1548)—a prayer that has appeared, more or less intact, in all versions of the Anglican Book of Common Prayer from Cranmer's day to ours. With Bradford-like poignancy, Cranmer's confession speaks thus:

Almighty God, Father of our Lord Jesus Christ, Maker of all things, Judge of all men: We acknowledge and bewail our manifold sins and wickedness, Which we from time to time most grievously have committed, By thought, word, and deed, Against thy Divine Majesty, Provoking most justly thy wrath and indignation against us. We do earnestly repent,

And are heartily sorry for these our misdoings; The remembrance of them is grievous unto us; The burden of them is intolerable. Have mercy upon us, Have mercy upon us, most merciful Father; For thy Son our Lord Jesus Christ's sake, Forgive us all that is past; And grant that we may ever hereafter Serve and please thee in newness of life, To the honour and glory of thy Name; Through Jesus Christ our Lord.[7]

Otto's Perceptions on Holiness. In his groundbreaking book, *The Idea of the Holy* (1923), Rudolf Otto maintained that the religious person's perception of the "numinous" (his word for the sense of divine holiness) has in it something of fear (the feeling of awe and danger that flows from knowing one is in God's hands for weal or woe, and that God is neither subservient nor tame), but fear wedded to fascination (the feeling of being allured, even entranced, by God's beauty, goodness, mercy, and love). Now it must be said at once that most present-day Western religion, particularly of the theosophical, New Age, liberal Protestant and modernistic Catholic stripes, is too culture-bound, immanentistic, sentimental, and bland to yield any form of numinous experience. It casts the Deity in the role of a nice man (or in feminist theology, a nice woman), and has no sense of God uniting in himself the two aspects of transcendence that Otto picked out. But then the verdict has to be, not that Otto's analysis is wrong, but that a good deal of modern Western religion is, in certain basic respects, irreligious.

For Otto's analysis squares with Scripture. Think, for instance, how Moses, Elijah, Isaiah, and Ezekiel met God (see Ex 3; 1 Kgs 19; Is 6; Ez 1), and how Paul met Jesus on the Damascus road (see Acts 9, 22:6-21, 26:12-23). Note how the sense of God's transcendent sovereignty and glory shone through all their subsequent ministry.

Otto's analysis is also validated by the sense of God that becomes vivid in revivals and renewal movements, where God is felt to have drawn near once more and no longer to be keeping himself at a distance. Such movements always depend on, indeed are sparked by, a quickened apprehension of God: one in which awesomeness (God as almighty apportioner of destiny) and attractiveness (God as rich in loving mercy) are always found blended. The Reformation itself was one such renewal movement. The analysis Otto offers is certainly accurate with regard to the magisterial Reformers, Luther and Calvin, and Bradford and Cranmer with them, and the Puritans after them; it is accurate too for great numbers of people who have been caught up in the successive evangelical revivals that have enriched the Protestant world from the eighteenth century to our own present day.

Godly Christians have always been marked by a two-sided perception of the numinous. On the one hand, the transcendent glory of God's purity and love, as focused in the plan of salvation, fascinates them. On the other hand, the transcendent glory of God's sovereignty, as focused in the divine threat of judgment for impiety, alarms them. This characteristically Christian sense of the mercy and the terror (fear) of the Lord is the seed-bed in which awareness grows that lifelong repentance is a "must" of holy living. That awareness will not grow under any other conditions. Where it is lacking, any supposed sanctity will prove on inspection to be flawed by complacency about oneself and short-sightedness about sin. Show me, then, a professed Christian who does not see and insist on the need for ongoing repentance, and I will show you a stunted soul for whom God is not as yet the Holy One in the full biblical sense. For such a person, true Christian holiness is at present out of reach.

Bradford's Other Foundation. But all of this is still only half the story. As Sampson tells us, and as Bradford's literary legacy of letters, sermons, meditations, and prayers confirms, there was another foundation on which Bradford's insight into repentance as a life's work rested. What triggered it not only was his sense of God's holiness according to Otto's formula, but also the motives of gratitude for grace received, and love to the God of grace who had redeemed him through the cross and called him to faith in Christ for salvation. On this aspect of holiness, about which Otto had less to say, Bradford was a shining example.

As is often true with God's saints, there was a marked individuality, even eccentricity by ordinary social standards, in the devotional focus of his life. This should be seen as natural rather than strange. Holy people who love God, like couples in love who have eyes and thoughts only for each other, are apt to act oddly in company. Pursuing the one relationship that really matters to them, they will ignore everything and everyone else for long periods, for they are pre-empted by love. Bradford's heart was altogether for God, and his behavior showed the love that was there. Sampson describes how he would meditate in public:

> ... they which were familiar with him might see how he, being in their company, used to fall often into a sudden and deep meditation, in which he would sit with a fixed countenance and spirit moved, yet speaking nothing a good space. And sometimes in this silent sitting plenty of tears should trickle down his cheeks. Sometimes he would sit in it and come out of it with a smiling countenance. Oftentimes have I sitten (*sic*) at dinner and supper with him... when... he hath fallen into these deep cogitations: and he would tell me in the end such discourses of them that I did perceive that sometimes his tears trickled out of his eyes, as well for joy as for sorrow.[8]

Of his life of prayer, while he was a tutor at Cambridge, Sampson writes:

> he used in the morning to go to the common prayer in the college where he was [Pembroke Hall], and after that he used to make some prayer with his pupils in his chamber; but not content with this, he then repaired to his own secret

prayer... as one that had not yet prayed to his own mind: for he was wont to say to his familiars, "I have prayed with my pupils, but I have not yet prayed with myself."[9]

Prayer, for Bradford, was a priority: "faithful prayer is the only mean(s), whereby through Christ we both obtain all things necessary... and also retain and keep still the grace of God given unto us".[10] Prayer, as we saw, was always for him a most humbling, searching, and demanding exercise of repentance. As he himself wrote:

> ... in thy prayer away with the purpose of sinning, for he that prayeth with a purpose to continue in any sin cannot be heard.... For even as in vain he that hath a wound desireth the healing of the same, so long as in the wound there remaineth the thing that is the cause of the wound, as a knife, a pellet, a dart, or a shaft-head, etc.: even so in vain is the prayer of him that retaineth still the purpose to continue in sin; for by it the soul is no less wounded than the body with a sword.... Bid adieu, when thou goest to prayer... to thy covetousness, to thy uncleanness, swearing, lying, malice, drunkenness, gluttony, idleness, pride, envy, garrulity [idle gossip], slothfulness, negligence, etc. If thou feelest thy willful and perverse will unwilling thereto, out of hand complain it (*sic*) to the Lord, and for his Christ's sake pray him to reform thy wicked will....[11]

WHY CONTINUAL REPENTANCE?

We can now clearly see why for Bradford, and for all other Christians with him, the Christian life has to be (as Luther said) an exercise of continual repentance before it is anything else. Fleshed out, the reasoning that explains this is as follows.

God is the Creator, who brought everything into being for his own pleasure, and on whom everything depends for its existence every moment. He has a right to prescribe how his rational creatures should behave. He has done this in his moral law, which requires us to be holy as he is holy—like him on our own human level in our character and our conduct, in our desires, our decisions, and our delights. We are to invest all our powers in living a life of grateful worship and loyal service—a life of fidelity, uprightness, integrity and love toward both himself and our fellow-humans—a life shaped by the purpose of glorifying him through wise and skillful obedience to his revealed will. Putting it in new covenant terms, we are to recognize that we are required in all circumstances to be honest, godly, single-minded, energetic, passionate persons who behave at all times in a Jesuslike way, with hearts aflame, heads cool, and all our wits about us. Total righteousness is called for, expressing total devotion and commitment. We are assured that nothing less will do.

The purity and uprightness of God's own character, and his judgments of value (what is good and worthwhile, and what is neither) are fixed and immutable. He cannot be other than hostile to individuals and communities that flout his law. He cannot do other than visit them sooner or later in displays of retributive judgment, so that all his rational creatures may see the glory of his moral inflexibility.

Because of God's majesty as sovereign ruler of the universe, sin (lawlessness, missing the moral mark, failing to practice righteousness with all one's heart and soul) is a major matter. Secular Western culture, which has deliberately atrophied the sense of God's majesty, finds this hard to believe, but it is so. Some sins are intrinsically greater and intrinsically worse than others—but there can be no small sins against a great God.

God's purpose in our creation, as in our new creation, is that we should be holy. Therefore, moral casualness and unconcern as to whether or not we please God is in itself supremely evil. No expressions of creativity, heroism, or nice-guy behavior can cancel God's displeasure at being disregarded in this way.

God searches our hearts as well as weighing our actions. For this reason, guilt for sin extends to deficiencies in our motives and our purposes, as well as in our performance. T.S. Eliot wrote of "… the greatest treason: To do the right deed for the wrong reason," and God observes and assesses our reasons for action as thoroughly as he does the actions themselves. In one sense, indeed, it is true to say that God focuses more attention on the heart—the thinking, reacting, desiring, decision-making core and center of our being—than he does on the deeds done, for it is by what goes on in our hearts that we are most truly known to him.

God is good and gracious to all his creatures, and has so loved the world as to give his only Son to suffer on the cross for our salvation. Active thanksgiving that expresses thankfulness of heart is the only proper response, and is in fact one of God's permanent requirements. Unthankfulness and unlove toward himself are as culpable in his sight as are any forms of untruthfulness and unrighteousness in dealing with our fellow-humans. Transgressing the first and greatest commandment has to be the first and greatest sin (see Mt 22:34-40).

God promises to pardon and restore all who repent of their sin. Because sin, both of omission and of commission, in motive, aim, thought, desire, wish, and fantasy even if not in outward action, is a daily event in Christians' lives (you know this about yourself, don't you?), regular repentance is an abiding necessity. Repentance must be thorough, coming from the heart just as did the sin. Repentance, whereby sin is confessed and forsaken in the confidence that—as the Anglican Prayer Book has been saying since Cranmer drafted it—God "pardoneth and absolveth all them that truly repent and unfeignedly believe his holy Gospel," expresses in a direct way the regenerate heart's desire to cleave to God, and to love and please him constantly. It is this desire that begets the purpose of forsaking the sin and returning contritely to the Lord.

Cherished Sin Is an Obstacle. Regenerate persons know that sin when cherished becomes an obstacle to their enjoyment of fellowship with God. It prompts God to withdraw their assurance and make them feel his displeasure through inward as well as outward chastening. Therefore, their instinct is constantly to pray with the psalmist: "Search me, O God, and know my heart; test me and know my anxious thoughts. See if there is any offensive way in me, and lead me in the way everlasting" (Ps 139:23). This has been poignantly put into verse in a hymn that starts like this:

Search me, O God, my actions try,
   And let my life appear
As seen by thine all-searching eye;
   To mine my ways make clear.

Search all my sense and know my heart,
   Who only canst make known,
And let the deep, the hidden part
   To me be fully shown.

Throw light into the darkened cells
   Where passion reigns within;
Quicken my conscience till it feels
   The loathsomeness of sin.

Search all my thoughts, the secret springs,
   The motives that control,
The chambers where polluted things
   Hold empire o'er the soul.

No regenerate person in his or her right mind wants to be found cherishing sin! As the great fish got Jonah out of its physical system by vomiting him onto dry land, so the born-again will labor to get sin out of their spiritual system by recognizing and renouncing it in repentance. Sometimes this involves dramatic public gestures, like:

* Zacchaeus announcing that half his property would go to the poor and all extorted monies would be restored four-fold (Lk 19:8); or
* the converted Ephesian wizards burning their occult library (Acts 19:19); or

- the Corinthians scurrying around to impose by congregational fiat the church discipline that they had neglected before (2 Cor 7:9-11); or
- the public confessions of sin that occur again and again in revival times. (See Matthew 3:6; Acts 19:18.)

Always, however, there will be self-search in God's presence, as a discipline of discipleship to Jesus Christ, with dependence on the help of the Holy Spirit to detect what needs to be put right. All Christians, deep down, want to repent of all that stains their lives, and to put it behind them.

Here again, there is a lesson of profound importance to be learned from Bradford. When he signed letters, as he did, as "a very [i.e., real] painted hypocrite, John Bradford," "a very hypocrite," "the most miserable, half-hearted, unthankful sinner," "the sinful John Bradford,"[12] it was not pious play-acting. He was, in fact, testifying to the intensity of his sense of present imperfection. He longed to advance further along the path of whole-hearted repentance than he had yet succeeded in doing. It is, in fact, a law of the spiritual life that the further you go, the more you are aware of the distance still to be covered. Your growing desire for God makes you increasingly conscious, not so much of where you are in your relationship with him as of where as yet you are not. What might seem exaggerated in Bradford's language is no more, just as it is no less, than an index of the ardor with which Bradford longed to become a better man in Christ than he felt he was. If only we had even half that ardor, how different we should be!

Weeding out Sin. Gardeners are constantly at war with weeds. The worst kind of weeds are those that spread below the ground by developing a cat's cradle of interlocking roots, from which shoots rise and break surface all over the place. The root system of sin produces particular sins as its shoots in similar fashion. One sin will reinforce another, being connected with it under the surface. Thus, envy and ambition will reinforce each other; so will lust, pride, and anger; greed and sloth will reinforce inclinations to cut moral corners, as they in turn will reinforce greed and sloth; and so on.

The self-knowledge that enlarges and extends as we walk with God, sit under the preaching and teaching of his Word, and live in honest fellowship with his saints, will often confront us with connections of this kind within ourselves. This forces each of us to realize again and again that, as a veteran believer once said in my hearing, "I see I have some repenting to do." (He then went off for an hour, and did it.) Unravelling the tangled roots and identifying the murky elements of our motivations proves in practice to be an endless task.

As those learning the piano must keep practicing, with a wide range of exercises designed to overcome particular weaknesses and impart new facility to the fingers, so we who are pupils in Christ's school of holiness have to keep repenting, as shortcoming after shortcoming and fault after fault in our moral and spiritual system becomes known to us. What the Anglican Prayer Book calls "hearty [meaning, heartfelt] repentance" is, as we saw, the downward dimension of growth in holiness. Growth in holiness cannot continue where repenting from the heart has stopped.

This is a way of saying that conversion must be continuous. For over three centuries, Protestants have equated conversion with what the *Westminster Shorter Catechism* calls "repentance unto life"—"a saving grace, whereby a sinner, out of a true sense of his sin, and apprehension of the mercy of God in Christ, doth, with grief and hatred of his sin, turn from it unto God, with full purpose of, and endeavour after, new obedience."[13] For many Christians there is such a moment of conscious conversion, and this experience of "sudden" conversion is a great blessing. There has to be for all of us some form of entry into the converted state, in which none of us is found by nature. It is a happy thing to be able to recall how one's own entry into that state took place.

But there is more: following on from "the hour I first believed," conversion must now become a lifelong process.

Conversion has been defined from this standpoint as a matter of giving as much as you know of yourself to as much as you know of God. This means that as our knowledge of God and ourselves grows (and the two grow together), so our conversion needs to be repeated and extended constantly.

To think in these terms is to catch up with John Calvin, who both referred explicitly to the "sudden conversion" (*subita con - versio*) by which God "subdued and made teachable" his hard heart and gave him "some foretaste and knowledge of true godliness,"[14] and also in his *Institutes of the Christian Religion* set forth a concept of conversion as the practice of lifelong active repentance, the fruit of faith, springing from a renewed heart:

> The whole of conversion to God is understood under the term "repentance.".... The Hebrew word for "repentance" is derived from conversion or return, the Greek word from mind and purpose: and the thing itself fits each derivation, for the essence of it is that departing from ourselves we turn to God, and putting off our former mind we put on a new one. So I think repentance may well be defined as a true conversion of our life to God, issuing from pure and heart-felt fear of him, and consisting in the mortification of our flesh and old man and the vivification of the Spirit.[15]

Exactly!

MODEL OF REPENTANCE

So far, we have discussed repentance in very general terms. Now, however, we should take note that repentance, by its very nature, is specific. Knowing just what one needs to turn from is part of its reality. Vague repentance is nothing, or at least next to nothing. "It is every man's duty to endeavour to repent of his particular sins, particularly."[16]

So we find that, alongside the general calls to repentance that are recorded in the Bible (see Mt 3:2, 4:17; Mk 6:12; Lk

5:32, 13:3, 5; Acts 2:38, 3:19, 17:30), there are passages naming specific lapses for which the offenders must repent. Now we look briefly at one of the most striking of these, namely the letters of the Lord Jesus Christ from his throne to five of the seven churches whom he addresses in Revelation 2-3. We should note these points:

1. Following the vision of Christ in his glory to the correspondent (1:12), the letters are the real core of the book. The visions of coming conflict and triumph for the Lord and his people (chapters 4-22) are a kind of appendix, or schedule, attached to the letters to give substance to the repeated promise that Christ will share unimaginable bliss with every believer who overcomes (see 2:7, 11, 17, 26, 3:5, 12, 21).

2. The letters address the churches, but they are actually meant for each of the individuals making up those churches. "He who has an ear" (singular) is to listen; "he who overcomes" (singular) will be rewarded. As always, the Word of God individualizes its recipients. Each hearer or reader must realize that the Word is addressed to his or her heart, for personal response.

3. The sins of the churches corporately, and of their membership individually, are specified. Ephesus has forsaken its first love (2:4); Pergamum has tolerated anti-holiness teaching (2:14); Thyatira has encouraged an immoral woman instructor (2:20); Sardis has lapsed into spiritual deadness and sub-Christian casualness of behavior (3:1); Laodicea is lukewarm, self-satisfied, and complacently half-hearted in spiritual things (3:15, 17). Putting it the other way around, these churches have failed to maintain a spirit of love for their Lord, righteousness without compromise, intolerance of the intolerable, zeal for God's glory, and willingness to exert effort for Christ. Of these specific failings—all of which have to do with the quality of their discipleship and loyalty to their King—Jesus himself now requires them to repent.

4. As it expresses Jesus' love, and his purpose of blessing, when from his glory he tells his people to face and repent of their sins, so it expresses his love when he sets himself before them for a renewal of their fellowship with him (3:20). It is to him as Lord that Christian repentance should be directed, just as it is to him as Savior that the penitent should look for their initial pardon and restoration.

Here, then, is a model for Christian repentance today.

"Confess your sins to each other and pray for each other so that you may be healed," writes James (Jas 5:16). He is talking not of the formalities of institutionalized absolution, but of the intimacies of Christian friendship in what are nowadays called "accountability relationships." In accountability relationships, one cares for another in a context of open sharing of lives: sad things like failures and falls, as well as glad things like deliverances and successes. Confession of sins within pastoral friendships of this kind is an important expression of repentance. Embarrassment should not be allowed to hold us back.

To confess one's sins to another who knows you as a peer and a friend is to commit oneself to redoubled effort not to lapse that way again. To ask one's friend to pray that one may be healed (it is moral and spiritual healing that James has in view—in other words personal healing of the most significant sort) is to make oneself accountable for maintaining that commitment on a permanent basis. Few of us, I think, really know the value of accountability relationships in the battle for honest repentance and for whole-heartedness in fighting temptations to sin.

Frank admission of one's sins to friends in Christ is part of the biblical pattern of Christian repentance.

PRACTICAL GUIDANCE ABOUT REPENTING

You have heard, no doubt, of the Irishman who, when asked the way to Dublin, scratched his head and said, "Sure, if

I was going to Dublin, I wouldn't start from here." In the same way, I must confess that when the agenda is to try to help Christians form the habit of continual repentance, I would not choose to start from here—not, that is, from the cultural milieu of the modern West at the end of the twentieth century. Everything, humanly speaking, is set against this agenda, in a way that has never, perhaps, been true before.

Culture, we know, oscillates between prideful optimism that encourages people to take themselves too seriously and trust themselves too much, and frivolous pessimism that leads them not to take themselves and their lives as seriously as they should. Buoyed up by technological triumphs, the West was in the first mood when this century opened. Deflated by wars, crises, and all sorts of public reversions to barbarism, we find ourselves in the second mood as the century draws to its close. Our sense of the dignity and glory of being human has been eroded, and nowadays life is felt to be merely trivial—which is one reason why our culture so readily smiles on abortion and euthanasia.

Christianity has totally lost its cultural leadership:

- secular relativism controls the world of education;
- consumerist materialism rules in the marketplace;
- the idea that we can know what is finally true about life is ridiculed;
- tolerance for all departures from yesterday's wisdom is demanded; and
- any appeal to absolute standards of right and wrong is viewed as bigotry.

In practice, Christianity has ceased to be the accepted basis of personal and community life in the West. It has been downgraded to a mere hobby for the minority whom it still interests.

The churches of the West, meantime, present a spectacle of confused disorder in both faith and morals. In view of the way that pluralism of belief and behavior is currently generated and applauded in centers of theological study, the confusion seems certain to continue. It is a fact, unhappy but undeniable, that repentance nowadays rarely gets mentioned in evangelism, nurture, and pastoral care, even among evangelicals and Christian traditionalists. The preoccupations of stirring congregational excitement, sustaining believers through crises, finding and honing gifts and skills, providing interest-based programs, and counseling people with relational problems, have displaced it. As a result, the churches, themselves, orthodox and heterodox together, lack spiritual reality, and their members are all too often superficial people with no hunger for the deep things of God.

No, ours is not a good time for trying to promote the discipline of constant repentance. However, this emphasis is always needed, doubly so when repenting has gone out of fashion. So I proceed.

My task now is to pull the threads together, and to sum up what we have seen about repentance in a form that yields practical guidance. As must by this time be obvious, I believe that even as we who are Christians ought to praise God, give him thanks, and make requests to him daily, so we ought to repent daily. This discipline is as basic to holiness as any. Whatever else was wrong with the old practice of penance, its requirement of regular reporting in the confessional at least kept believers aware that facing, forsaking, and fighting sins is a constant task. The further one goes in holy living, the more sin one will find in the attitudes of one's own heart, needing to be dealt with in this way. As the single-mindedness of our inward devotion is the real index of the quality of our discipleship, so the thoroughness of our daily repentance is the real index of the quality of our devotion. There is no way around that. What we need to learn, or re-learn, at this point may be summed up as follows.

Purity of God. First, only through constant and deepening repentance can we sinners *honor the purity of God.*

The God whom we claim to love and serve delights in righteousness and hates sin. Scripture is very clear about that.

You are not a God who takes pleasure in evil; with you the wicked cannot dwell. **Ps 5:4**

Your eyes are too pure to look on evil; you cannot tolerate wrong. **Heb 1:13**

The LORD detests men of perverse heart but he delights in those whose ways are blameless.... The LORD detests lying lips, but he delights in men who are truthful. **Prv 11:20, 12:22**

... the LORD hates... haughty eyes, a lying tongue, hands that shed innocent blood, a heart that devises wicked schemes, feet that are quick to rush into evil, a false witness who pours out lies and a man who stirs up dissension among brothers.

Prv 6:16-19

God's purity is just another name for this hatred. We must understand that in calling us to purity as he does (see Ps 24:4; Mt 5:8; 1 Tm 1:5, 5:22; 1 Jn 3:3), God is requiring us to cultivate the same hatred in our own hearts.

Accordingly God's Word to all his people is: "hate evil, love good" (Am 5:15). "Hate what is evil; cling to what is good" (Rom 12:9). And our appropriate response is: "Oh, that my ways were steadfast in obeying your decrees!... I hate every wrong path.... I have taken an oath... that I will follow your righteous laws.... Away from me, you evildoers, that I may keep the commands of my God!" (Ps 119:5, 104, cf. 128, 106, 115).

But how should we deal with the fact that our obedience always proves to be less than perfect?

Those who neglect the discipline of thorough repentance for their shortcomings, along with regular self-examination so as to discern those shortcomings, are behaving as if God just turns a blind eye to our moral flaws—which is actually to insult him, since such indifference would be a moral flaw in itself. But God is not morally indifferent, and we must not act toward him as if he were. The truth is that the only way to show real respect for God's real purity is by realistically setting oneself against sin. That means not only a wholehearted purpose of pleasing God by consecrated zeal in keeping his law, it also means repentance. And repentance means not mere routine words of regret as one asks for pardon without one's heart being involved, but a deliberate confessing, an explicit self-humbling, and a sensing of shame in the presence of God as one contemplates one's failures. For God's purity, as we saw, leads him to hate evil. His demand that we be like him requires us to become haters of it too, starting with the evil that we find inside ourselves.

It will help us here to look at a classic Bible passage that profiles repentance from the inside. In Psalm 51, according to tradition, David goes public by poeticizing the penitence he expressed to God after being convinced of his sin in the matter of Bathsheba and Uriah. He broke the tenth commandment by coveting his neighbor's wife, the eighth by stealing her, the seventh by committing adultery with her, the ninth indirectly, by trying to fool Uriah so that he would treat the coming child as his own, and the sixth directly, by liquidating Uriah at long range. Then, as we noted earlier, David spent a year shrugging off what he had done until Nathan acting as God's spokesman showed him God's displeasure at it (see 2 Sm 11-12). But in Psalm 51 we meet a David who has come to his senses, and is now expressing repentance very fully, in six distinct stages, thus:

1. Verses 1-2 are *a plea for mercy and forgiveness*. They show a true understanding of God's covenant. David appeals to God's "unfailing love" ("lovingkindness" and "steadfast love" in other versions), that is to God's covenant faithfulness to those to whom he has pledged himself. The covenant whereby God and human beings commit themselves to belong to each other forever is the basis of all biblical religion. When God's servants stumble and fall, God's faithfulness to the covenant to which they have been unfaithful is their only hope. This covenant relationship is emphatically a gift of grace on God's part. It is he who

initiates and sustains it, enduring all the follies and vices of his covenant partners. For God's holy ones were, are, and remain silly, sinful creatures, who can live before him only through being constantly forgiven for their constant shortcomings. To this forgiveness, however, repentance is the only road.

2. Verses 3-6 are *an acknowledgment of guilt and the punishment we deserve for our sins.* They show understanding of sin, as our inbred perversity of heart that finds its expression in sins, specific acts of evil and wrongdoing in God's sight. The deep truths here are: first, we are not sinners because we sin, but rather we sin because we are sinners (vv. 5-6); second, all our sins, our inhumanities no less than our idolatries, are sins against God (v. 4).

3. Verses 7-9 are *a heart-cry for cleansing from sin and cancella-tion of guilt.* They show understanding of salvation as a work of God restoring joy in fellowship with himself through the assurance of sins forgiven. David's "bones" (his conscious self, the person he knows himself to be) are "crushed" (rendered unable to function properly) as a result of his condemning conscience. He asks that his "bones" may be made literally to "dance" (as all the translations say, "rejoice") by the bestowing of this assurance (v. 8)—a vivid metaphor for the revitalizing of one's inner life that knowledge of one's forgiveness brings.

4. Verses 10-12 are *a petition for quickening and renewing in God.* They show an understanding of spiritual life as essentially the steady, positive response of the human spirit to God—a response that is called forth and kept in being by the regenerative ministry of the indwelling Spirit of God himself. It is God's way to remove our demerit, our defilement, and our deviancy together. He does not save us in our sins, but from our sins. Whom he justifies he also sanctifies. Where there is no sign of a pure heart (a sin-hating heart that reflects the purity of God) or of a "steadfast... willing" spirit (a disposition to

honor and obey God and resist temptations to sin), we may well doubt whether the person is in a state of grace in any sense at all. Certainly, seeking to be renewed in righteousness and kept from sin henceforth is of the essence of repentance. Without this, one lacks contrition, and is not in fact penitent at all.

5. Verses 13-17 are *a promise to proclaim God's pardoning mercy in witness and in worship.* The verses show an understanding of ministry to both God and our fellow-beings: to the holy God, by thankful praise; and to sinful humans, by proclaiming to them the grace that saves. Saints, let us note, are saved to serve—to celebrate and share what God has given them. Fresh dedication to doing this, in addition to all other good works, is one token of reality in repentance.

6. Verses 18-19 are *a prayer for the blessing of the church,* God's Jerusalem, the people on earth who bear his name. The verses show an understanding of what most delights God—saved sinners, penitents who are now pardoned and prospering spiritually, being moved by gratitude and joy to offer "righteous sacrifices" (v. 19). (The thought here is of love-gifts to God, though the slaughtered bullocks of which David speaks might not immediately suggest that to the modern mind.) David's intercession for all God's people is not really a change of theme from the penitence that he was expressing before. Intercession springs naturally from the experiences of God's pardoning love that repentance triggers. Knowledge that one is loved will call forth love for others, and love for others will lead us to pray for them.

David honored the purity of God by the way he repented of his shameful misdeeds. Humbling himself, he acknowledged the provocation he had given, sought deliverance from the power as well as the guilt of his sins, and pledged himself afresh to do God's work and advance his praise. This was true repentance, and as such is a model for us.

In their dreams and desires, even if not in their outward behavior, Christians too have their lapses into coveting, lusting, greed, malice, and deceitfulness. Christians, like others, are tempted to be self-indulgent, to abuse and exploit their fellow human beings, to treat might as right in the realm of relationships, and on occasion to wish others dead. Whether or not God in his providence keeps us from acting these things out is not the issue. The point is that the disordered desires were there, and when our hearts embraced them, our hearts were wrong. That is what we need to repent of.

Some forms of so-called holiness teaching encourage us to be insensitive to, or unconcerned about, the ungodly thoughts and motives that lurk within us, but one index of true holiness is an increasing awareness of them, a growing hatred toward them, and a deepening repentance for them, when we find ourselves harboring them in our hearts. We saw this holy hatred in John Bradford, and God wants to see it in us all, for his purity can be honored no other way.

Healthy Souls. Second, only through constant and deepening repentance can we sinners *maintain our souls in health.*

Spiritual health, like bodily health, is God's gift. But, like bodily health, it is a gift that must be carefully cherished, for careless habits can squander it. By the time we wake up to the fact that we have lost it, it may be too late to do much about it. The focus of health in the soul is humility, while the root of inward corruption is pride. In the spiritual life, nothing stands still. If we are not constantly growing downward into humility, we shall be steadily swelling up and running to seed under the influence of pride. Humility rests on self-knowledge; pride reflects self-ignorance. Humility expresses itself in self-distrust and conscious dependence on God; pride is self-confident and, though it may go through the motions of humility with some skill (for pride is a great actor), it is self-important, opinionated, tyrannical, pushy, and self-willed. "Pride goes before destruction, a haughty spirit before a fall" (Prv 16:18).

As quinine is the antidote to malaria, so humility is the antidote to pride. In the sense in which Shakespeare's Orsino in *Twelfth Night* sees music as the food of love, repentance should be seen as the food of humility. Or changing the picture, repentance should be thought as the exercise routine that maintains humility, and through humility, health in the soul. "No cross, no crown," said William Penn. "No humility, no health, and no repentance, no humility," is what I am saying now.

The self-knowledge in which a Christian's repentance is rooted comes from the law. It is a result of being made to face God's prescribed moral standards for us his creatures. In Romans 7:7-25 Paul tells us first, how in his youth the law taught him to recognize sin in himself, by stirring into action the very motives and desires that it forbade. "I would not have known what coveting really was if the law had not said, 'Do not covet.' But sin, seizing the opportunity afforded by the commandment, produced in me every kind of covetous desire" (Rom 7:7). Then he tells us how, in his present Christian life, though "in my inner being I delight in God's law... I see another law at work in the members of my body [he means, in all that he actually does] waging war against the law of my mind and making me a prisoner of the law of sin at work within my members" (Rom 7:22-23).

The "law of sin" means sin operating as a driving force, irrationally anti-God in its thrust. The words "I see" tell us how Paul perceives himself when, by the light of the law that he longs to keep, he looks at himself and measures his actual achievement—in other words, when he practices the discipline of self-examination. Each time he does so, he sees that his reach has exceeded his grasp, that nothing he said or did was as good and right as it should have been, and that his noblest, wisest, most selfless, pure-minded, God-honoring, generous acts were all flawed in some discernible way. In retrospect he always finds that his conduct could and should have been more Christ-like, and his motives less mixed. Always he finds that he could have done better than he did.

This discovery, calling as it does for the constantly renewed repentance that I advocate, is unquestionably depressing. Hence Paul's agonized cry in Romans 7:24, "What a wretched man I am! Who will rescue me from this body of death?" Yet this, we should note, is followed by the triumphant shout of Romans 7:25, as Paul looks ahead to "the redemption of our bodies" in the life beyond (Rom 8:23): "Thanks be to God [that one day he will thus rescue me] through Jesus Christ our Lord!" Partial present deliverance from the power of sin, which is the other side of his experience (see Rom 7:5-7), makes him long all the more for the total future deliverance that God has promised. Meanwhile, however, he grows downward in deepening humility as he becomes more and more aware of how sin in him still thwarts his aim of perfectly pleasing God. In this he is a model for us all.[17]

A Battle in the Church Today. A battle is being fought in the modern Christian world. It is, from one standpoint, a battle for law, and from another standpoint a battle for conscience. An educated, sensitive conscience is God's monitor. It alerts us to the moral quality of what we do or plan to do, forbids lawlessness and irresponsibility, and makes us feel guilt, shame, and fear of the future retribution that it tells us we deserve, when we have allowed ourselves to defy its restraints. Satan's strategy is to corrupt, desensitize, and if possible kill our consciences. The relativism, materialism, narcissism, secularism, and hedonism of today's Western world help him mightily toward his goal. His task is made yet simpler by the way in which the world's moral weaknesses have been taken into the contemporary church.

Church people who call themselves liberal, radical, modern or modernist, and progressive, labor on principle to baptize into Christ the thoughts and ways of each unbelieving society in which the church finds itself anchored. In the West, this means situation ethics (nothing is prescribed save the motive and mood of love), and arising out of this, safe casual sex, serial marriage through repeated divorces, abortion on demand, and legitimizing the homosexual lifestyle (because sexual self-fulfillment through whatever genital activity one favors is nowadays rated among life's highest values). Evangelicals, charismatics, and orthodox believers generally would not endorse this sexual looseness theoretically, yet they tend to fall into it practically, and in moral matters across the board they rarely do much better than their heretical opposite numbers.

Fearing heresy, misbelief, legalism, coldness, and deadness, we spend all our time teaching true doctrine, praising the Lord, defending the faith, and evangelizing the lost, and rarely get around to educating our consciences on matters of basic morality. A hundred years ago Western culture taught Christian morals through schools, the press, and the weight of public opinion, but that is no longer so. If the Christian community does not teach righteousness today, nobody will. But Western Christians today are scarcely able to teach righteousness, because they themselves have scarcely learned it. With our overall neglect of ethical education for believers, plus our constant exposure to brainwashing by expositors of positive thinking and high self-esteem who cry down all guilt feelings as unspiritual and against the mind of Jesus, it is not perhaps surprising that when it comes to uprightness, integrity, and compassion, conservative Christians are not seen to excel.

Indeed, it is worse than that. A steady flow of conservative leaders in recent years have disgraced themselves publicly by their mishandlings of sex, money, and power. No doubt conservatives themselves are partly to blame for having lionized their leaders, treating them as superstars, feeding their egos with money and applause, and thus eroding their sense of their own vulnerability. No doubt the fallen leaders are themselves directly to blame for self-deception. Someone once said, "Woe to the man (or woman) who believes all the wonderful things people say about him (or her)!" Flattery feeds pride. A flattered leader can easily come to believe not only that his experience, knowledge, and skills make him very important, not only that being the man he is, he cannot be seriously wrong about anything, but also that he is in fact above the law and can freely break the rules.

More fundamentally to blame, however, is the corporate decadence that now marks the conservative church—the decadence that concentrates exclusively on upholding the faith and ignores the biblical insistence that those who maintain the doctrines of grace must manifest in their lives the grace of those doctrines. In other words, orthodoxy (right belief) must lead on to orthopraxy (right behavior). In this era of decadent Christianity, in which niceness has replaced righteousness as the moral goal and success is valued over sanctity, the call to orthopraxy is rarely heard and rarely heeded. So we all suffer loss at this point.

The fact is that Christians today are all victims of our decadent late twentieth century ethos that wrenches public orthodoxy and personal morality apart, implying that the latter does not matter so long as one is valiant for the truth. So when leaders fall we may well reflect (Bradford-like) that there but for the grace of God go we. Were our consciences educated any better than those of the saints who sinned? Do ours work any better than theirs? Probably not. If with our own inadequate moral equipment, in a world that mocks morality anyway, we had been exposed to such temptations (first to pride and then to folly), we might well have fallen as they did. We need honestly to acknowledge that Satan has made great headway in the battle for our consciences. Unless and until it is re-established that the Christian life for everyone is a life of self-scrutiny, self-humbling, and daily repentance for daily sins, Satan will continue to score.

If it is true, as we have been saying, that holiness is an honoring of God that is health-giving to the soul, and that humility is at the heart of holiness (humility, not as a game of groveling before God, but as a frank facing of one's limitations, frailties, and failures, with dependence on God for all that is good)—if it is also true that humility is rooted in, and reinforced by, realism in repenting of our failures, and if finally it is true that realism in repentance flows from knowledge of God and of ourselves—then our first need, as disciples in Christ's school of holiness, must be to exorcise complacency from our souls.

We should not take it for granted that, because we are holding on to the faith that others have given up, God has to be pleased with us, and therefore we should be pleased with ourselves. Rather we should suspect ourselves of being like the Laodiceans, with consciences atrophied by worldliness and prosperity, and no ears for the words of the one whom we call our Savior and our Lord.

What, then, should we do? Action is required along two lines. Within the church, preaching, study, and fellowship need to be directed to raising each other's consciousness about God's hatred of sin, his requirement of righteousness, and the way we offend him by not taking his demand seriously. And in our daily pilgrimage, we must learn to listen to God for ourselves. If we dare to ask God to let us hear his word to us personally about our lives, he will.

God's word to us is normally heard out of Scripture as it is read, preached, and applied. Soaking our souls in Scripture is our wisdom, therefore, if we are seeking holiness seriously. A helpful scheme of applicatory meditation on each passage is to ask ourselves:

What Does This Passage Tell Me about God? How does it describe God's nature and power; his plan and purpose; his likes and dislikes; his works, ways, and will for his human creatures?[18]

What Does This Passage Tell Me about Living? What does it say about right conduct, wrong conduct, wise conduct, foolish conduct; different situations and relationships in which people find themselves; the way of faith with all its difficulties and delights; various emotional states and temperamental traumas; virtues to cultivate, vices to avoid, and values to hold on to; pressures from the world, the flesh, and the devil, and what to do about them? In short, what does it tell me about all the realities of belonging to a lost humanity in a spoiled world now touched by the powers of redemption, and involved in the ongoing conflict between Christ the conqueror and the defeated powers of darkness that are so desperately fighting back?

What Does All This Say to Me about My Own Life Today? What does it tell me about the tasks, problems, opportunities, pitfalls, and temptations to sin that confront me day by day? What warnings and encouragements does it give me, and what wisdom and resources does it show me?

Meditating on these things means thinking them through in the presence of God. Meditation should lead into prayer, in which we talk to God about them directly. This is always the proper conclusion of personal Bible reading.

If you practice meditating on Scripture in the manner described, with initial prayer for the Holy Spirit's light and subsequent prayer that God will write in your heart what you have seen and learned, you will certainly hear the divine voice. You will certainly encounter the enthroned Savior. Amid the assurances of grace and help with which he will delight your heart, he will again and again verify to you the truth of his word: "Those whom I love I rebuke and discipline. So be earnest, and repent" (Rv 3:19). Do not say that you were not warned about this! But do not fancy, either, that you are walking the path of holiness, growing downward as Christians are called to do, if rebuke and repentance have no place in your life.

The late Anglican Bishop Stephen Neill said many things better than anyone else. I round off this chapter by quoting some sentences from the profile of sanctity that he draws. Here Neill deftly focuses the thrust of what this chapter has tried to say:

With monotonous regularity the saints all tell us that they are the chief of sinners. To non-Christians this is sometimes extremely irritating; it seems like an affectation, a mere manner of speaking, that those who are obviously so good should condemn themselves in such extravagant fashion. But there is no doubt that, when the saints from St. Paul on have used such expressions, they did so because they could not speak in any other way.... It is paradoxical, but true, that progress in saintliness always means at the same time progress in penitence.

It is not hard to see why this is so. We have spoken of the enlightenment of the conscience by the Holy Spirit. It is only the enlightened conscience that can take sin as seriously as it needs to be taken... with increasing knowledge, there is an ever deeper sensitiveness to our failure to make the best of the opportunities that God has given. Perhaps the actual and identifiable sins are few; but, given such opportunities as have been given us, what would Jesus have made of them? For here is the heart of it all. To move forward on the road of holiness means to know Jesus better. To him we always return. The better we come to know Him, the more plainly we shall see how little like him we are....[19]

Yes, that is precisely how it is.

Growing into Christ-likeness: Healthy Christian Experience

The grace of God that brings salvation has appeared to all men. It teaches us to say "No" to ungodliness and worldly passions, and to live self-controlled, upright and godly lives in this present age, while we wait for the blessed hope—the glorious appearing of our great God and Savior, Jesus Christ, who gave himself for us to redeem us from all wickedness and to purify for himself a people that are his very own, eager to do what is good. **Ti 2:11-14**

Grow in the grace and knowledge of our Lord and Savior Jesus Christ. **2 Pt 3:18**

We, who with unveiled faces all reflect the Lord's glory, are being transformed into his likeness with ever-increasing glory, which comes from the Lord, who is the Spirit. **2 Cor 3:18**

SPIRITUAL HEALTHINESS AND GROWTH

"I hope you are well." "Keep well!" "Stay well." We constantly read and write versions of that sentiment in letters. So, too, we regularly wish people "Good health!," and get wished it ourselves, as we quaff our Coke (or whatever else we are quaffing) at parties. What are we talking about? Physical well-being, of course, in the first instance, that pain-free, elegant, and efficient bodily condition that all our jogging, workouts, health clubs, and exercise units are meant to promote. For we are a very health-conscious lot. What we are doing is generously wishing others the bodily benefit that we passionately desire for ourselves.

Is that unnatural? Not in the least, though an obsessive preoccupation with one's health is intrinsically unhealthy, just as any other obsessive preoccupation is. But wanting to be healthy is in itself just one mark of being human. Sober concern about the health of one's relatives and friends is natural and right, and it has always been thought of as good manners to express it. So the ancient Greeks and Romans would start their letters by wishing the addressee good health. The New Testament contains one example of this: "Dear friend, I pray that you may enjoy good health" is how John starts his letter to Gaius, in a sentence that ends: "even as your soul is getting along well" (3 Jn 2).

John's words alert us to the twin truths that personal health is more than physical well-being, and that health of soul (mind and heart) is ultimately more important than the well-being of the body. That is something we must never forget. Sometimes God sends us people whose physical condition effectively reminds us that this is so. Joni Eareckson, a quadriplegic with a marvelous ministry who spends her days in a wheelchair, is one such. Twice it has been my privilege to introduce Joni from a platform. Each time I have ventured to predict that her message would show her to be the healthiest person in the building—a prediction which, so far as I could judge, came true both times.

As one can be a sick person with a body that works well, so one can be a healthy person with a body that is a wreck, even a mass of pain. The secret is to accept one's lack of physical well-being as from God, to offer it back to him to make what he can of it for his own praise, and to ask him to keep you sweet, steady, and patient as you live with it.

As we noted a moment ago, it is not wrong to want to be well and able-bodied. What is wrong is to get sour and resentful about present bodily limitations—like the pretty Californian Christian with the colostomy who told me, "I hate my body," and whose face as she spoke showed me that she really did. At that moment, as it seemed to me, she was sicker mentally than she was physically. It is noteworthy that "sound" in the New Testament phrase "sound doctrine" (see 1 Tm 1:10, 6:3; 2 Tm 1:13, 4:3; Ti 1:9, 2:1), literally means "healthy," clearly in the sense of health-giving and health-sustaining. The thought is that those who internalize and digest sound doctrine will be healthy persons before the Lord, in a way that others will not be.

So while bodily wellness is important, wellness of soul is more important. Personal health has more to do with one's mindset than with the way one's limbs and organs are functioning at any particular time.

The health of children and adolescents is bound up with a growth-pattern. Part of what is meant by saying that children are healthy is that they are growing more or less as they should. It is important to realize that the same is true of Christians. As we have seen already, they are destined to be conformed at every point to the image of Christ—to be like him in outlook, aim, and attitude, and also in mode of bodily life. The transformation will be perfected beyond this world, when sin is finally rooted out of their system and they are "clothed" with resurrection bodies of the same order as Christ's own (2 Cor 5:1-4). In the meantime, here on earth, constant growth in the moral and spiritual dimensions of Christlikeness is one aspect of spiritual health. Peter writes, "Like newborn babies, crave pure spiritual milk, so that by it you may grow up in your salvation... grow in the grace and knowledge of... Jesus Christ" (1 Pt 2:2; 2 Pt 3:18). Through mutual service in the body of Christ, "we will no longer be infants... speaking the truth in love, we will in all things grow up into him who is the Head, that is, Christ," explains Paul (Eph 4:14-15).

God intends that all Christians should grow. Parents of new-borns find great joy in them, but imagine the distress they would feel if the months and years went by and their baby still remained a baby, smiling and kicking in its crib, but never growing! We should not allow ourselves to forget that God must know comparable distress when we, his born-again children, fail to grow in grace.

The general idea of growth covers change, development, enlarging, gaining strength and showing energy, advancing, deepening, ripening, and maturing. What, precisely, is the nature of growth in grace? How should we describe the growth that we are concerned with here?

In Chapter 5 we looked at one aspect of it, growth down-ward through repentance into humility, but there is far more to spiritual growth than that, just as there is far more to physical growth than regular bowel movements. Two paragraphs from the Victorian classic that we have met already, J.C. Ryle's *Holiness*, block in both negatively and positively what growth in grace involves:

> When I speak of growth in grace, I do not for a moment mean that a believer's interest in Christ can grow. I do not mean that he can grow in safety, acceptance with God or security. I do not mean that he can ever be more justified, more pardoned, more forgiven, more at peace with God, than he is the first moment that he believes. I hold firmly that the justification of a believer is a finished, perfect and complete work; and that the weakest saint, though he may not know and feel it, is as completely justified as the strongest. I hold firmly that our election, calling, and stand-ing in Christ admit of no degrees, increase or diminution....
> I would go to the stake, God helping me, for the glorious truth, that in the matter of justification before God every believer is complete in Christ (Col 2:10)....

When I speak of growth in grace I only mean increase in the degree, size, strength, vigour and power of the graces which the Holy Spirit plants in a believer's heart. I hold that every one of those graces admits of growth, progress, and increase. I hold that repentance, faith, hope, love, humility, zeal, courage and the like may be little or great, strong or weak, vigorous or feeble, and may vary greatly in the same man at different periods of his life. When I speak of a man growing in grace, I mean simply this—that his sense of sin is becoming deeper, his faith stronger, his hope brighter, his love more extensive, his spiritual-mindedness more marked. He feels more of the power of godliness in his own heart. He manifests more of it in his life. He is going on from strength to strength, from faith to faith and from grace to grace....

Ryle was apparently up against some form of the idea, falsely ascribed to Luther and Lutherans, among others, that there is no such thing in this world as character-changing sanctification. For he now takes time out to vindicate against skepticism the reality of the growth in graces that he has described. He deploys two arguments. The first is from the New Testament, where such growth appears:

- as a possibility, prescribed (1 Thes 4:1, 10; 1 Pt 2:2) and prayed for (Phil 1:9; Col 1:10; 1 Thes 3:12);
- as a reality, recognized and celebrated (2 Thes 1:3; Col 2:19); and
- as a necessity, the divinely commanded (2 Pt 3:18) and engineered (Heb 12:5-14) road that leads to final glory.

The second argument is from:

... fact and experience. I ask any honest reader of the New Testament, whether he cannot see degrees of grace in the New Testament saints whose histories are recorded, as plainly as the sun at noonday. I ask him whether he cannot see in the very same persons as great a difference between their faith and knowledge at one time and at another, as between the same man's strength when he is an infant and when he is a grown-up man. I ask him whether the Scripture does not distinctly recognize this in the language it uses, when it speaks of "weak" faith and "strong" faith, and of Christians as "new-born babes," "little children," "young men," and "fathers?" (1 Pt 2:2; 1 Jn 2:12-14). I ask him, above all, whether his own observation of believers nowadays does not bring him to the same conclusion? What true Christian would not confess that there is as much difference between the degree of his own faith and knowledge when he was first converted, and his present attainments, as there is between a sapling and a full-grown tree? His graces are the same in principle, but they have grown....[1]

Ryle is surely right in all this, and we shall treat his understanding of growth in grace as growth in graces, that is, transformation of character, as the launch-pad for everything else that the present chapter contains.

VIEWING THE GLORY OF HOLINESS

Two years ago my wife and I spent a few days near the foot of one of New Zealand's tallest mountains, Mount Egmont. There we were treated to some striking cloud effects. One day we could see only Mount Egmont's lower half, the top being completely covered with a flat-bottomed white canopy, so that what was visible looked like a huge replica of the late Buster Keaton's hat. The next day, what we saw was the top half, which seemed to be floating in space, since the clouds, flat-topped this time, were now making the bottom half invisible. Only on the third day, when all the clouds had cleared, did we see Mount Egmont whole, in its very real glory. In the same way, we are unable to appreciate the glory of holiness as the path of healthy growth for the child of God until we get beyond half-truths and incomplete briefings, and come to see it as the Christlike whole that it really is. That is the point I want to develop now.

Partial views of holiness—by which I mean, half-truths about it treated as the whole truth—have abounded. That we saw in Chapter 4. Inevitably, any lifestyle based on these half-truths ends up looking grotesque rather than glorious; one-sided human development always does, whatever form the one-sidedness takes. Now, those who long with all their heart to be holy are most certainly the salt of God's earth. I hope that you who read and I who write will always be found among their number. But such people often manifest the narrowness of tunnel vision when it comes to the specifics of sanctity, and one can see why.

Passion preempts concentration. It confines and restricts one's attention to whatever has grabbed one's heart. This happens notoriously in boy-and-girl love affairs. Since being a Christian is a love affair of a particular kind, we should not be surprised to find that it happens here too. The Christian with a passion to please God in holiness will hold tenaciously to whatever prescription for achieving a holy life he or she has been given, embracing it as subjectively precious and dismissing as unspiritual the question whether it is objectively adequate. Any set of directions for holiness may in this way become a sacred cow. But if the prescription is a half-truth only, obeying it is bound to result in a life that one way or another is lopsided and lacking, and as such odd and unimpressive (just as each half of Mount Egmont looked odd and unimpressive without the other half).

At the risk of caricature, I must illustrate this, for it is so important.

Rhapsody without Realism. Here at one extreme are those for whom holy living means what I call *rhapsody without realism.* Their heart concentrates totally on devotional exercises, experiences of divine love, ecstasies of assurance, expressions of their own love to God, and the maintaining of emotional warmth and excitement in all their approaches to him and communion with him. Of this ardor, they feel, true holiness essentially consists.

But they do not seem to think or know much about human relationships. They are not noticeably wise or patient or caring, at least when caring requires them to move beyond words to action (see Jas 2:14-16; 1 Jn 3:16-18). They are like the top half of Mount Egmont appearing without the bottom half. Their feet are, if I may put it so, firmly off the ground. Though the rhapsodic ardor of their love and adoration of God is great, they fall short when it comes to love of neighbor, sometimes even love for their own families. The problem with these people is not that they are insincere, but that their tunnel vision, born of their all-absorbing passion to know, love, and praise God, keeps them from seeing that holiness involves being a responsible realist in the life-situation in which God has placed you.

Holiness requires us to show our love for God by the quality of our love for others, whom we must assume that he loves as he loves us. Rhapsody without realism is not Christlike, and it is a failure in holiness rather than a form of it.

Rule-keeping without Relating. And here at the opposite extreme are those for whom holy living means *rule-keeping without relating*. Their heart glows with love of God's law. They see holiness as essentially a matter of keeping that law. They are meticulously honest in business; meticulously careful to observe a male-leadership pattern at home, and constitutional correctness in the church; meticulously conscientious in shunning evil and avoiding activities classed as worldly (smoking, drinking, dancing, gambling, use of make-up, etc.); meticulously insistent on maintaining God's truth and fingering error and sin in any company; and their passion to be correct by the code merits unfeigned admiration and applause. But relationally they are cool and distant people, who see rule-book rightness as the essence of holiness and who concentrate

on formal correctness of conduct rather than personal closeness either to God or to their fellow human beings. Paul distinguishes the righteous (upright, just, conscientious, correct)
person, for whom no one under ordinary circumstances
would die, from the good person (loving, caring, outgoing,
generous) for whom, out of affection, someone might even
die, were that necessary to save the good person's life (see
Rom 5:7)—and it is righteous as distinct from good persons
that I am spotlighting here.

These people are like the bottom half of Mount Egmont
appearing without the top. The correctness of what they do is
unquestionable, but they do not labor to get alongside other
people in compassion or to commune with the Father and the
Son in friendship. In other words, they fall short relationally.
Verbal orthodoxy (right belief) and formal orthopraxy (right
behavior) are there, but that is all.

Their problem is that their tunnel vision makes their passionate, grace-given commitment to law-keeping appear to
them as the whole of spiritual life. But rule-keeping without
relational closeness to God and one's fellow human beings is
not Christ-like, and is a way of missing holiness rather than a
method of achieving it.

Between these extremes you find various types of moral and
spiritual nondescripts—disciples of sorts, but not very zealous in
devotion nor very conscientious in obedience; mediocrities, in
fact, who could not in any way be described as modeling holiness, only as muddling along with the Lord. I expect that
description covers most of us. I shall not stop to diagnose the
lack of seriousness that appears here, other than to say I suspect
it springs from the folly of not viewing this life as preparation
for heaven. Focusing on extremes will teach us more than we
can hope to learn from looking at conventional half-heartedness
in any form. Therefore, that is what I shall continue to do.

The point I am trying to drive home is that holiness is the
healthy growth of morally misshapen humans toward the
moral image of Jesus Christ, the perfect man. This growth is

supernatural. It takes the sanctifying work of the indwelling Holy Spirit to effect it. Its result, as it progresses, is an all-around personal wholeness, God-centered, God-honoring, humble, loving, service-oriented, and self-denying, of a kind that we never knew before. One-sidednesses are corrected, undeveloped and underdeveloped aspects of our personhood are brought into action, and the likeness in us of the moral beauty of Christ's character begins to appear.

Moral beauty, like every other kind of beauty, is largely a matter of parts being balanced within the whole, in this case virtues and strengths of character. As the Marxist ideal is of a new person in whom mental and physical skills are developed in balance with each other, so the Christian ideal is of a re-newed person in whom love of God and neighbor; love of God's law and of his fellowship; love of the Father, the Son, and the Spirit; love of worshiping God and of working for God; love of righteousness and love of sinners, blend together in balance. Disproportion and imbalance in the formation of our spiritual identity are not a mode of holiness, but a negating of it.

"You must teach what is in accord with sound doctrine" (Ti 2:1), wrote Paul to Titus. "Sound," when applied to doctrine, means, as we saw, healthy in the sense of health-giving. These words of Paul open a chapter that is entirely concerned with the forming of Christian character, in older men (v. 2), older and younger women (vv. 3-5), young men (vv. 6-8), slaves (v. 9), and in all Christians generally (vv. 11-14). The chapter ends with the very clear apostolic directive: "These, then, are the things you should teach" (v. 15). In verse 2 the word "sound" recurs. "Teach the older men" writes Paul "to be temperate, worthy of respect, self-controlled, and sound in faith, in love, and in endurance." "Sound" in this verse means healthy in the sense of functioning in the way one was made to function, the way that is natural in terms of the ideal manhood that the pow-ers of redemption are restoring.

Such healthiness is, in fact, holiness, and such holiness is the health of the soul. In effect, Paul is saying that faith, love, and endurance, within a frame of sobriety, dignity, and self-control constitute spiritual health. Any distortion of this moral pattern would be a focus of spiritual unhealthiness, like an ulcer or a cancer in the soul.

Earlier I likened the life of Christian holiness to a three-legged stool, in which the three legs were D (doctrine: truth taken into the mind and heart to live by), E (experience: the conscientious pursuit and conscious enjoyment of fellowship with the Father and the Son), and P (practice: in the sense of the specific and habitual response of obedience to the doctrinal truth one has received). The point of the illustration was that a stool cannot stand on less than its three legs. In the absence of any one of them, the stool falls down. If one leg is larger or smaller than the other two, stability is lost, and the stool is in danger of tipping over as soon as any weight is put on it. So it is only when D, E, and P are balanced together in proper proportions that the spiritual life is solid and steady.

Unhealthy Spiritual Growth. I shall now use the same illustration to diagram three types of unhealthy Christian development, all three of which, unfortunately, I find to be common today. All three are apt to fancy themselves as holiness, but none of them has a right to that description, for in reality they are all distorted.

You probably know what proportions a diagram of a healthy human body (say, a beautiful Californian body, male or female) would have? Holiness would be pictured that way. You would draw it as head, trunk, and limbs all the right size in relation to each other, all fitted to play their part in truly godly living.

But now consider the following:

What you have here is a figure with a huge head on a matchstick body with matchstick limbs. This pictures the unnatural development of the Christian whose passion is all for doctrine, and whose discipleship revolves round the study of theology. You know the sort of person I mean—one who is always reading, always exploring questions of truth, poking half the time into esoteric aspects of typology, unfulfilled prophecy, the millennium, the symbolic chapters of Revelation, and the problems of Bible harmony. He or she is not much concerned about experience, not very active in obedience and service of others, and not distinguished for a radically changed life. But the head is always busy with theological questions, and is full to overflowing with doctrine.

In an anti-intellectual age like ours, such love of truth, and such devotion to the task of determining it, are rare and precious; and as we saw earlier, interest in the truth about God is natural to all the born-again. But is that interest, in and of itself, a token of good spiritual health? With so little E and P, no, it is not.

Now consider this:

What you see here is a figure with a pinhead and an enormous abdomen, carried on matchstick legs as before. This pictures the unnatural development of the Christian who knows very little doctrine and cares very little about doctrine (hence the pinhead), but who thinks of Christianity as a matter of constantly churned-up feelings and exciting experiences (hence, the huge abdomen). Zealous for experience, Christians of this sort are constantly running around to meetings at which they hope to be warmed up to the point where the glorious feeling of being in God's presence and overwhelmed by his love is renewed. For them, Christianity is all experience, all feeling, all thrill. The Christian I picture is not outstandingly active in trying to change the world for the Lord (hence the matchstick legs). He or she is too busy chasing experiences to have much time for that.

Now it is entirely right and natural for Christians to desire experiences of God. Joseph Hart was altogether on target when he wrote, "True religion's more than notion/Something must be known *and felt.*" But is the dominance of this desire, in and of itself, an index of good spiritual health? With so little D and P, no, it is not.

Now look at this:

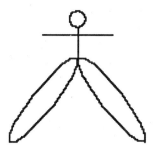

Here you have the pinhead and a matchstick body, but with them a massive pair of legs. This pictures the disproportionate development of the activist Christian: the restless do-gooder whose interest is not in doctrinal truth nor in the devotional disciplines of the spiritual life, but in programs, organizations, and world-changing tasks of one sort or another. As with the big-headed and big-bellied believers pictured above, so with the big-legged activists: the concern that they show is in itself fully Christian. But is it, in and of itself, a sign of good spiritual health? With so little D and E, no, it is not.

My point is simply that the life of Christ-like consecration to God which is holiness, the health of the human soul, requires of each of us a balanced threefold concern, for truth, for experience, and for action. Where this proportioning of zeal has not yet become habitual, personal spiritual development is lopsided, just as when one's Christian life is a matter of rhapsody without realism, or rule-keeping without relating. When that is the case, however ardent one's heart for that for which one so much cares, neither authentic Christian holiness nor personal spiritual health is being achieved to any significant degree. This is an issue, not of temperament or natural aptitude, but of will. Not to be concerned about the things that concerned Jesus is real moral failure. The only way to get beyond it is to look harder at him, the faithful witness, the man of prayer, the doer of good, and as such, in the conjunction of the D, E, and P interests, the model of holy humanity.

Our calling is to imitate Christ, both in the humble love with which he related to his Father and his fellow human beings and in the range of his aims and concerns. As in golf they say, "keep your eye on the ball," so in Christianity we must say, "keep your eye on the Savior." Any unlikeness to him, whether by being what he was not, or by not being what he was, or by lack of concern about something that concerned him, is not holiness, but lack of it. The point is, I trust, now clear enough, so I move on.

HOLINESS AND SANCTIFICATION

We just completed an exposition which sought to draw verbally a wide-angled picture of holiness that would keep us from taking up with too narrow a notion of what it is. The next task is to frame our picture, so to speak, in theology, by redefining and circumscribing the grace that induces growth in holiness through the Holy Spirit's work of sanctification. The doctrine of this grace is expressed in seven propositions which I have cited already,[2] and which I discussed in detail in my book, *Keep in Step with the Spirit* (see chapter 3 especially). Here I shall reproduce these propositions with comments as brief as I can make them in light of the line of thought we are pursuing.

The Nature of Holiness Is Transformation through Consecration. This is the formula, so to speak, from the inside.

What is this consecration? It is the flip side of repentance. In repentance one turns away to God from what is wrong; in consecration one gives oneself to God for what is right. Both terms express the same "no" to the siren-songs of sin and the same "yes" to the saving call of Christ.

What is this transformation? It is the change into Christ-likeness of which Paul speaks in 2 Corinthians 3:18. The New American Standard Version (NASV) renders very accurately thus: "All of us, with unveiled faces, seeing the glory of the Lord as though reflected in a mirror, are being transformed into the same image from one degree of glory to another." Through the Holy Spirit's agency, we become like the One we look at as we absorb the gospel word. Each step in this character-change (for conformity of character is what Paul is talking about) is a new degree of glory, that is, of God's self-display in our human lives.

How are the consecration and the transformation linked? Paul explains this in Romans 12:1-2, which the New International Version (NIV) renders well:

> Therefore [as your way of glorifying God for his grace: see Rom 11:36], I urge you, brothers, in view of God's mercy [which has laid the groundwork for the gratitude we must now show], to offer your bodies [not bodies as opposed to souls, but your entire selves, body and soul, as in Phil 1:20] as living sacrifices, holy [consecrated] and pleasing [a delight] to God—this is your spiritual act of worship. Do not conform any longer to the pattern of this world, but be transformed by the renewing of your mind [your heart, your desires, your thoughts and purposes, your entire inner life].

Paul's thought is that by our self-offering, we open ourself to God, and thereby bring to an end any resistance to the indwelling Holy Spirit that may have been in us before. As a result the planned and promised supernaturalizing of our inner life through our sharing in Christ's risen life will proceed unhindered. "Then you will be able to test and approve [in each situation] what God's will is—his good, pleasing and perfect will" (v. 2). "Test and approve" renders a single Greek verb that means discern through examining alternatives. The renewed mind, enlightened by the Spirit, and tuned by regeneration to seek God's glory, will compare the options and thereby perceive what course of action will best please God.

The Context of Holiness Is Justification through Faith in Christ. Sanctification is in no sense the ground of justification; on the contrary, holy living presupposes justification, being the response of grateful love to it.

All we need do to establish this point is remind ourselves of the order of things in Romans, where the justification of sinners through faith in Christ, apart from works, fills Romans 3, 4 and 5, and the gift of new life in Christ to the justified precedes the summons to consecrated living. (See Romans 6, especially verses 12-14, 19-22, and 12:1, just quoted.)

The Root of Holiness Is Co-Crucifixion and Co-Resurrection with Christ. Heart-hostility to God, which is natural to all the unregenerate, makes holiness impossible for them (Rom 8:7-8). The taproot of holiness is love for God and his law, which the Holy Spirit imparts by uniting us to Christ in his death and resurrection.

That is a momentous transaction that changes our heart forever and ends sin's rule over us for good, so that we do not, and in fact cannot, go on living under sin's sway as we did before (Rom 6:1-10, 17; Eph 2:1-10). After this has occurred—after our regeneration and the birth of our personal faith—the Spirit permanently indwells us (1 Cor 6:19; 2 Cor 1:22, 5:5; Eph 1:13) to help us do what now we will and plan to do, namely to give God pleasure (Phil 2:13).

The Agent of Holiness Is the Indwelling Holy Spirit. The Puritans, following Calvin, as we saw, analyzed holiness as the mortifying of sin (killing it in all its many forms) and the vivifying of graces (strengthening holy habits). Paul tells us that we mortify sin "by the Spirit" (Rom 8:13), and that our holy habits are the "fruit" of the Spirit (Gal 5:22).

Think of a child who wants to help his father paint the fence. The father holds and guides the hand in which the child holds the brush, and both are active in each stroke. When we labor, carefully and prayerfully, to mortify sins and practice virtues, the Spirit works with us, guiding our hand as it were. All actual achievement must be ascribed to him, however much self-denial and sweat it may have cost us. Without his controlling and empowering activity we would never be able to achieve any conquests of sin, or any reshaping of our lives in righteousness.

A classic statement on the Spirit's agency in our holiness, drawn up almost three and a half centuries ago, is *The Westminster Confession*, chapter 13, "Of Sanctification."

I. They, who are once effectually called, and regenerated, having a new heart, and a new spirit created in them, are further sanctified, really and personally, through the virtue of Christ's death and resurrection, by his Word and Spirit dwelling in them: the dominion of the whole body of sin is destroyed, and the several lusts thereof are more and more weakened and mortified; and they more and more quickened and strengthened in all saving graces, to the practice of true holiness, without which no man shall see the Lord.

II. This sanctification is throughout, in the whole man; yet imperfect in this life, there abiding still some remnants of corruption in every part; whence ariseth a continual and irreconcilable war, the flesh lusting against the Spirit, and the Spirit against the flesh.

III. In which war, although the remaining corruption, for a time, may much prevail, yet, through the continual supply of strength from the sanctifying Spirit of Christ, the regenerate part doth overcome; and so the saints grow in grace, perfecting holiness in the fear of God.

The Experience of Holiness Requires Effort and Conflict. Holiness means, among other things, forming good habits, breaking bad habits, resisting temptations to sin, and controlling yourself when provoked. No one ever managed to do any of these things without effort and conflict.

How do we form the Christ-like habits which Paul calls the fruit of the Spirit? By setting ourselves, deliberately, to do the Christ-like thing in each situation. "Sow an act, reap a habit; sow a habit, reap a character." That might sound very simple and straightforward, but in practice it does not prove so. The test, of course, comes when the situation provokes us to cut loose with some form of ungodly tit-for-tat.

We should think out our behavioral strategy with such situations directly in view. Thus, we should think of:

- *love* as the Christ-like reaction to people's malice;
- *joy* as the Christ-like reaction to depressing circumstances;
- *peace* as the Christ-like reaction to troubles, threats, and invitations to anxiety;
- *patience* as the Christ-like reaction to all that is maddening;
- *kindness* as the Christ-like reaction to all who are unkind;
- *goodness* as the Christ-like reaction to bad people and bad behavior;
- *faithfulness* and *gentleness* as the Christ-like reaction to lies and fury; and
- *self-control* as the Christ-like reaction to every situation that goads you to lose your cool and hit out.

The principle is clear, the Spirit is with us to empower us, and we know that Christ-like behavior is now in the profoundest sense natural to us. But still, maintaining Christ-likeness under the kind of pressures I have described is hard.

How do we "by the Spirit... put to death the misdeeds of the body" (Rom 8:13)? This too is hard. It is a matter of negating, wishing dead, and laboring to thwart, inclinations, cravings, and habits that have been in you (if I may put it so) for a long time. Pain and grief, moans and groans, will certainly be involved, for your sin does not want to die, nor will it enjoy the killing process. Jesus told us, very vividly, that mortifying a sin could well feel like plucking out an eye or cutting off a hand or foot, in other words, self-mutilation. You will feel you are saying good-bye to something that is so much part of you that without it you cannot live.

Both Paul and Jesus assure us that the exercise, however painful, is a necessity for life, so we must go to it (Mt 5:29, 18:8; Rom 8:13). How? Outward acts of sin come from inner sinful urges, so we must learn to starve these urges of what stimulates them (porn magazines, for instance, if the urge is lust; visits to smorgasbords, if the urge is gluttony; gamblings and lotteries, if the urge is greed; and so on). And when the urge is upon us, we must learn, as it were, to run to our Lord and cry for help, asking him to deepen our sense of his own holy presence and redeeming love, to give us the strength to say "no" to that which can only displease him. It is the Spirit who moves us to act this way, who makes our sense of the holy love of Christ vivid, who imparts the strength for which we pray, and who actually drains the life out of the sins we starve.

Thus habits of self-indulgence, spiritual idolatry, and abuse of others can be broken. But while surrendering sins into which you drifted casually is not so hard, mortifying what the Puritans called "besetting" sins—dispositional sins to which your temperament inclines you, like cowardice or thoughtlessness, and habitual sins that have become addictive and defiant—is regularly a long-drawn-out, bruising struggle. No one who is a spiritual realist will ever pretend otherwise.

The Rule of Holiness Is the Law of God. Holiness sets its sights on absolute moral standards and unchanging moral ideals, established by God himself. God's law defines the righteousness he requires of believers.

What is God's law? The Hebrew word *torah*, which is the basic term, means not legislated regulations as such (which is what "law" means in the modern state), but family instruction, which a father—in this case, the heavenly Father—gives to his children. All the directives for right living that God gave through his spokesmen in Old Testament times, the maxims of the wisdom books no less than the sociopolitical and liturgical legalities laid down through Moses and the diagnostic exhortations to righteousness voiced by the prophets, were in essence the Father's admonitions to his family (which is what Israel was: see Ex 4:22) and were centered on the Ten Commandments.

The sociopolitical and liturgical laws, which were for Old Testament Israel exclusively, have lapsed. But the Decalogue, as interpreted by Jesus' two-commandment summary ("love God" and "love your neighbor"; see Mt 22:37-40), stands as the all-time expression of God's moral will for his people.

What then is the kingdom edition of the law? The kingdom of God (the new life of heaven on earth through the Holy Spirit) came into the world with Jesus, and now releases new moral power and energy in the lives of believers, whom Jesus called "sons of the kingdom" (Mt 13:38). What I mean by the kingdom edition of the law is the exposition that Jesus and the apostles give of the breadth and depth of God's requirements.

Their exposition stresses the motives, attitudes, and virtues proper to one who is consciously enjoying God's salvation. Also, it reflects their expectation that the Holy Spirit will change people into law-keepers from the heart, so that their "good works" will no longer be role-play, but an eager doing of what they now really want to do. So it focuses on moral character in a way that goes beyond the Old Testament.

Thus the law of God—the "royal law" as James calls it (Jas 2:8), meaning the King's law for his household and realm—is first and foremost a family code. God's born-again children, who make up the royal family, are required to live up to his standards.

Human royal families nowadays live in goldfish bowls, constantly watched by media people poised to headline their lapses. In the same way God's children live under the eye of a watching world that licks its lips over lapses among the supposedly godly. As it is no credit to Britain's Queen if her children run wild, so Christians who flout God's family code dishonor him. They fail him, and let him down. We never dare forget that while holiness honors and glorifies God, unholiness does the opposite.

The Heart of Holiness Is the Spirit of Love. The Bible views love, whether moved by affinity, gratitude, or both, as a purpose of making the loved one great in some way. Affectionate feeling that indulges its human objects, like parental spoiling of children, is precisely not love in the biblical sense, though the world insists on giving it that name. Love, whether to God or to others, is a responsible commitment to persistent, intelligent, self-denying service, according to the terms of God's own Word. Love knows itself to be blind and to need the law as its eyes. Jesus embodies love to God and others. He was, we might say, love incarnate. The nature of love may be learned by watching him.

Law-keeping love is the epitome of holiness, though love in any other sense negates it. Law-keeping love is God's prescription for the fulfilling of our humanity. Any alternative to it pulls us, more or less, out of our proper human shape. Grace restores and perfects nature by teaching us truly to love. Let us not permit ourselves any vagueness or confusion about that.

The New Testament regularly portrays holy living as the practice of "good works." What makes good works good? Two things: they are works of obedience to God's law; and they are works of love, aimed at exalting the God whom one loves out of affinity and gratitude, and enriching human beings whom one loves out of compassion and fellow-feeling. Love to one's neighbor, and love to the Father and the Son, do in fact blend, for the first is the required expression of the second (see Jn 13:34, 14:15, 23, 15:10-14, 17; 1 Jn 3:11, 16-18, 23, 4:7-11; cf. Mt 5:43-48; Lk 10:25-37).

Outwardly, holiness is obedience; inwardly, holiness is love in action. The love for God that prompts the obedience that expresses love for fellow human beings is holiness' true heart and heartbeat: heart in the sense of essence and core and fount, and heartbeat in the sense of energy-center and driving force. As it is God's love that makes the world go round (yes, it is!), so it is love for God that makes the holy person tick, and care, and serve. Gospel-taught, God-wrought, grace-given love is what holiness in the final analysis is all about.

ONGOING GROWTH IN GRACE

This chapter is exploring holiness as an ongoing process of growth in graces that constitutes a condition of personal spiritual health. We have framed our picture of healthy growth with some of the larger truths about God's grace in action to show us how the process of growth in graces takes place. The next step is, so to speak, to get the lighting right: to shield our picture from false lights, whose dazzle imposes distracting patterns on it and obscures features of it that are really there, and to arrange illumination that will help us to see what we are looking at as we fix our gaze on it. So this section will be devoted to detecting some common mistakes about spiritual growth.

Growth in Grace Is Visible. The first mistake is *to think that growth in grace is always clear to see.*

Bodily growth, as we noted earlier, can be measured very straightforwardly. There is no problem involved in checking the height and weight that a person has gained. Spiritual growth, however, is a mystery in the theologians' sense of the

word—a reality that has in it more than we can ever understand or monitor. In this sense such realities as the Trinity,
creation, providence, the Son's incarnation, and our regeneration, are all mysteries. Indeed, everything involving God's
interaction with his world is mystery as defined, and growth in
grace is a case in point.

Through God's own teaching in Scripture we know a good
deal about all these mysteries, but it is only the sort of knowledge that enables us to identify, conceive, and circumscribe
them. It is not exhaustive knowledge, nor is it the sort of
knowledge that enables us to control them. However fully we
master the biblical revelation of divine truth, the mysteries of
God to which that truth testifies remain mysteries still.

Growth in grace is a process wrought by the Holy Spirit that
centers on the human heart, in the non-physiological sense
of that word. The heart, as we have seen, is the dispositional
and dynamic core of our selfhood. It is the source from which
our thoughts and words, our desires, decisions, and deeds, all
spring. We can guess the state of the heart, our own or another's,
by noting what comes out of it, but we cannot inspect it directly
to see what is happening in it.

Scripture highlights the inaccessibility of the heart to everyone except God himself. "The heart is deceitful above all
things and beyond cure. Who can understand it? I the LORD
search the heart" (Jer 17:9-10). "You alone know the hearts of
all men" (1 Kgs 8:39). Processes in the heart are beyond
human power to track.

This does not mean, however, that it is impossible ever to
tell when spiritual growth has been taking place. The quality
of a person's responses to a crisis, a shock, or the demands of
any new situation, may tell us all sorts of things about them
that we did not know before—and one of those things may
well be their spiritual stature.

Thus it was (to take just one example) with the unnamed
lady whom we call Mrs. Manoah, whose story we read in
Judges 13. The angel of the Lord (God acting as his own mes-

senger: a pre-incarnate manifestation, apparently, of God the Son) had told her she was to have a special child (Samson), who would become Israel's deliverer. The angel messenger gave her special instructions on how to prepare for the birth. When she told Manoah, he (a pompously pious male chauvinist, as it seems) prayed that the messenger might return and give them both further instructions. Clearly he was very conscious of his spiritual leadership role. Equally clearly he did not trust his wife to have gotten the message right. The messenger graciously reappeared and repeated the instructions. Then came the traumatic moment when Manoah realized that their visitor had been the Lord himself. Pomposity gave way to panic. The man who had hitherto assumed his own spiritual superiority totally lost his head. "We are doomed to die!" he gibbered to his wife. "We have seen God!" (v. 22). He knew, in a general way, that no one is fit for God's fellowship, and hence he nose-dived in despair.

Happily, his wife, who thus far in the story seems a very low-key person, now emerged as a woman of wisdom, faithfully ministering to her husband with some good straight thinking about God's faithfulness to his own purposes. "If the LORD had meant to kill us, he would not have accepted a burnt offering and grain offering from our hands, nor shown us all these things or now told us this" (Jgs 13:23). "If you can keep your head when all around you/Are losing theirs and blaming it on you… you'll be a Man, my son!" wrote Kipling. Humanly and spiritually, Mrs. Manoah appears here as a "Man" in Kipling's sense, while her husband behaved like his own idea of an irrational woman—in fact, like a frightened child. Thus Mrs. Manoah's reaction to the shock revealed her as a woman who had been growing spiritually, in a way that her spouse, for all his careful and laborious religiosity, had not. God's children are not born with stature, but gain stature through growth. The lady has the stature in this story.

Again, a critical moment of testing may evoke a response which shows that a person has grown spiritually in a particular way since a previous testing. So it was with Abraham, whom God purposed to exhibit as a model man of faith for all time (see Rom 4; especially Rom 4:11, 16-25; Gal 3:6-9, 14; Heb 6:13-15). Faith, which brings justification, fellowship with God, and inheritance of promised benefits, is a matter of obedient trust and trustful obedience. God keeps both our trust and our obedience under constant scrutiny, and in this case both were challenged together.

God put Abraham's faith to its supreme test by telling him to kill teenage Isaac, child of God's promise and heir of God's promises, as a human sacrifice. One can hardly imagine the turmoil of bewilderment, agony, and despair in Abraham's mind as he plodded up Mount Moriah with Isaac at his side and his knife at the ready. But Abraham passed the test magnificently, so that when at the last minute the angel of the Lord (again, God acting as his own messenger) intervened to halt the sacrifice, he was able to declare: "Now I know that you fear God, because you have not withheld from me your son, your only son" (Gn 22:12).

Three decades before, however, it had been a different story. Promised a son when he was seventy-five, Abraham at eighty-six had fathered Ishmael upon Hagar, evidently believing, with Sarah, that there was now no hope that Sarah herself would ever be pregnant—whatever God might have said eleven years before (Gn 16). That was a very obvious failure of faith.

What then had happened during the years between the birth of Ishmael and the sacrifice of Isaac? In a word, Abraham had grown. When, thirteen years after Ishmael's birth, God renewed to Abraham and Sarah the promise of a son (Gn 17:15-19), Abraham was a different man. This time he trusted God's word absolutely. Paul waxes eloquent about the way in which "without weakening in his faith, he faced the fact that his body was as good as dead—since he was about a hundred years old—and that Sarah's womb was also dead. Yet he did not waver through unbelief regarding the promise of God, but was strengthened in his faith and gave glory to God, being fully persuaded that God had power to do what he had promised" (Rom 4:19-21). Over those thirteen years, Abraham had grown in faith.

Doubtless it was the memory of Isaac's miraculous birth that sustained Abraham at Mount Moriah, so that it could be said of him: "By faith Abraham, when God tested him, offered Isaac as a sacrifice. He who had received the promises was about to sacrifice his one and only son, even though God had said to him, 'It is through Isaac that your offspring will be reckoned.' Abraham reasoned that God could raise the dead, and figuratively speaking, he did receive Isaac back from death" (Heb 11:17-19).

Abraham's actions under successive tests reveal his growth in the specific grace of faith. In a similar way, the contrast between Peter's craven cowardice when he denied Christ and his later defiant courage in refusing to keep quiet about him (see Mt 26:69-75; also Acts 4:13-20, 29, 5:17-32) shows growth after Pentecost in the specific grace of boldness (which, says J.C. Ryle, is just "faith honestly doing its duty"[3]).

The inward work of God that induces growth remains hidden from us, but testing times evoke responses that show growth to be a fact. This, however, is all that can be said about tracking the growth process. It does not really get us very far. Moments of pressure and decision will bring out of persons what is in them spiritually, as well as in other respects. But at other times their growth in grace, if any, the intensity of their zeal, and their current gift and ministry potential, which ordinarily grow out of their growth in grace and their increase of zeal, are far from plain to see. It is a mistake to expect that they would be. Our judgments as to who has and has not grown in grace, and how much growth there has been in those who have thus grown, can only be provisional. All such judgments are hazardous, and may easily be falsified by the next round of events, so that it would really be better and wiser not to pass them at all.

Growth in Grace Is Uniform. A second mistake is *to think that growth in grace is always a uniform process,* either in itself throughout the stages of a believer's life, or in comparison with what God is doing in the lives of others. Growth in grace is not uniform in either sense.

This mistake is linked with the first one, but I treat it separately because it is so common and so easy to make. Superficiality betrays us. We think of physical growth as a steady process, and of human beings as all the same. We then simplistically project these ideas into the realm of grace. The truth is however, that as physical growth is really a somewhat irregular business, and as people are really quite different from each other, so the changes and developments in individuals that sanctifying growth involves vary from one to another in speed, in degree, and in what we may call internal proportioning.

Bluff, impetuous, warm-hearted, unthinking, unstable Simon passed through Pentecost and suddenly became clear-headed, solid, resolute, discerning, leaderlike Peter, the early church's anchor-man—Cephas, the rock that Jesus had said that Simon would be (Jn 1:42). Ardent, raw, fire-eating John, whom Jesus had nicknamed Son of Thunder (Mk 3:17; for his fire-eating rawness, see Lk 9:49, 54), also passed through Pentecost. There is, however, no indication of equal suddenness in the process that turned him, without in the least blunting his black-and-white, for-or-against, adversarial quality of mind, into the apostle of thoughtful love, deep simplicity, and patient restraint whom we meet in his letters. But if Simon was changed quickly while John was changed slowly, what of it? They were different men. Sanctifying grace worked differently in them, maximizing their individuality (God likes variety; cloning is not his way), and giving prominence in the developed product to different facets of the glorious likeness of Christ, which no single person, not even an apostle, can ever embody in its entirety.

The precise quality of change involved in people's growth in grace is always conditioned by their natural make-up. It is easy to underestimate the Holy Spirit's achievement in the lives of those who, in addition to the God-opposing, self-deifying twist of original sin, suffer from badly flawed temperaments and characters. The trembling, quickly daunted faith of Bunyan's clutch of memorable depressives in *Pilgrim's Progress*: Mr. Fearing, Mr. Feeble-mind, Mr. Ready-to-Halt, Mr. Dispondency and his daughter Much-Afraid, who kept struggling on as Christians though tormented by the grisly feeling that they would never reach heaven, reflects a deeper work of grace than does the steadier faith and fortitude of a naturally equable person.

The partial moderating of some choleric's furious temper, or the partial melting of some phlegmatic's chilly aloofness, or the partial curing of some sanguine's zany irresponsibility, or the partial deliverance of some melancholic from the paralyzing obsession of despair, may well argue a greater measure of growth in grace—growth in graces through God's grace in Christ, as we are now analyzing it—than is present in more sturdy, forthcoming, realistic, energetic saints who never had to cope with these particular flaws in themselves. Having to fight your temperament for your Christian virtues makes you feel your progress is much slower than that of others, but that may not be so.

Christ finds us in different places in terms of our character and personal story, and he works on us by his Spirit in the place where he finds us. Though one of us may be naturally nice in a way that another is not, we are all at deepest level wrecked vessels spiritually, each needing a divine salvage operation geared to the specifics of our condition. No wonder, then, if God's health-giving, growth-producing work of sanctification is differently shaped in detail, and appears to proceed at different speeds, in different lives.

Since so much of this work, in others and in ourselves, goes on in the heart, below the level of consciousness, we can never measure how far it has gotten, or how far it still has to go, in any single case. Any comparisons we make between its progress in one and in another are bound to be ignorant and fallacious, so we had better learn not to make them. The only generalizations it is safe to make are:

- moral and spiritual Christ-likeness is the goal in every case;
- all Christians can testify that knowing God through Jesus Christ enables them now to live and act in ways that were simply beyond them before; and
- a professed Christian with no such testimony can hardly be genuine, and is certainly not growing in grace.

Growth in Grace Is Automatic. A third mistake is *to think that growth in grace is automatic if you are a religious professional,* whether minister, missionary, full-time Christian worker, tele-vangelist, monk, or nun. In reality, growth in graces is never automatic. Being a Christian professional makes it harder to grow spiritually rather than easier.

Why is this? The reason is that since professionals are expected, as we may say, to perform—to fulfill roles, that and no more—the temptation to a professional to settle for an appropriate form of mask-wearing role-play, in which one's own personhood is kept out of sight, is very strong. Professional identity then eats up personal identity, so that one is no longer closely related to anyone, neither to people nor to God. So one is lonely. Even worse, since life is relationships, and behind one's mask one has distanced oneself from relationships, one is shrinking rather than growing as a person. And one cannot grow in grace while one is shrinking overall.

When my wife used to say to me, "I don't want your ministry, I want you," she was telling me that she feared this temptation was engulfing me. When that role-player extraordinary, the late great film actor Peter Sellers, declined an invitation to have records made of him reading the Bible, the reason he gave was that you can only read the Bible aloud convincingly if you know who you are—and he did not know who he was. All Christians need God's help to know who they are, and to live with him and with their own human intimates in honesty, integrity, and vulnerability. But Christian professionals need this help most of all.

Growth in Grace Is Protection. A fourth mistake: *to think that growth in grace shields one from strains, pains, and pressures in one's Christian life.* The fancy persists that growth in grace brings a kind of inner peace that insulates you emotionally against being torn the way others are torn. But, in fact, it does the exact opposite.

There are, to be sure, zombie states of mind in which people numb themselves, one way or another, to feelings of personal pain and grief. There are self-absorbed states of mind in which people muzzle all concern for those around them, so that they are unmoved by others' misery. But there is nothing of God's grace about these states of mind, even when the escapism and hard-heartedness that they express wear religious clothes.

The truth can be stated in two propositions. First, Christians have no more exemption from strains, pains, and pressures than did Jesus or Paul. (Think of Jesus in Gethsemane and on the cross, and of Paul with his thorn in the flesh—some painful disability, we do not know what—and his life in and out of persecutions, prisons, and shipwrecks.) Second, Christians can and do cope with personal pain in God's strength, rejoicing like Paul in the way that that strength is made perfect in their weakness (2 Cor 12:10). But as they grow in grace they become increasingly distressed at the sorrows and follies of others (think of Jesus weeping over Jerusalem [Lk 19:41-44], and Paul agonizing over the unbelief of the Jews [Rom 9:1-4, 10:1]). Compassion generates more distress for growing Christians than other human beings ever know.

That growing Christians enjoy God's gift of peace more and more is true, but the peace in question is relational:

- peace with God himself through the peace-making blood of Christ;
- peace with circumstances, which, however harrowing, God has promised to order for our good (that is, our growth in grace);

- peace with themselves, for Christ's forgiving and accepting them requires them to forgive and accept themselves, hard though this might at first seem; and
- peace with those around them, to whom at Jesus' bidding they go as peacemakers (Mt 5:9).

It is not the peace of unfeeling Olympian tranquility, gained and maintained by ignoring other people's agony.

Growing Christians grow in peace, but their growing in grace often has them groaning in grace as Christlike compassion comes more and more to possess their hearts. God does not mean the lives of his children in his tragically spoiled world to be sorrow-free, and we may confidently say that any who are sorrow-free, whatever else may be true of them, are certainly not growing in grace.

Growth in Grace Is a Retreat. A fifth and last mistake is *to think that growth in grace may be furthered by retreating from life's hard places, heavy burdens, and hurtful relationships.* Centuries ago, people left the rough-and-tumble of the wider world for the sheltered life of the monastery in order to save their souls. One still meets the idea that for true spiritual development, this is the way to go. But that is not the case. There may be good reasons why some Christians should choose to live relatively withdrawn lives, but the belief that only so can they grow is not one of them.

A middle-aged Christian woman, distinguished in her profession, lived with her parents. They treated her still as their little girl, whose first task was to look after them. Feeling she could not survive, let alone grow spiritually, in that situation, she planned to leave. Ministry centered on the fifth commandment and Romans 8:28 transformed her viewpoint. She returned in peace to a galling relationship, knowing that that was where she ought to be. Thus she grew in grace.

Christians grow as they accept their destiny of self-denial and cross-bearing (Lk 9:23). Unlike orchids, they do not grow as hothouse plants. Jesus did not live the life of a hothouse plant, evading life's abrasiveness, and he does not intend that his disciples should either.

Wisdom, then, directs us to avert our eyes from the unhelpful dazzle of these five false lights, and to look for better illumination to show up all that our picture of growth in grace contains. Here, now, are five true lights to replace the false ones.

When spiritual growth—growth in the graces of Christian character, and in intimacy with God—is taking place, one may expect to see at least these signs of it:

1. *Sign one* is a growing delight in praising God, with an increasing distaste for being praised oneself. A purpose of praise runs throughout the Bible. It roots itself in every Christian heart and becomes, not necessarily more exuberant, but certainly more emphatic, as the saint matures. And the higher one goes in praising God, the lower one will go in one's own eyes, and the more passionately one's heart will cry, with the psalmist: "Not to us, O LORD, not to us but to your name be the glory, because of your love and faithfulness" (Ps 115:1). When Christians feel this way more and more strongly, it would seem that they are growing in grace.

2. *Sign two* is a growing instinct for caring and giving, with a more pronounced dislike of the self-absorption that constantly takes without either caring or giving. Love, we have seen, is of the essence of Christ-likeness; and love is entirely a matter of caring and giving. Jesus cared and gave without stint all through his ministry. Even in the agony of his crucifixion we find him caring and praying for his executioners, that they might be forgiven (Lk 23:34); caring for his mother, and charging John to look after her (Jn 19:26-27); and caring for the penitent thief, to whom he promised salvation (Lk 23:43). When Christians become more committed to love, and more abhor-

rent of unlove in its various forms, it would seem that they are growing in grace.

3. *Sign three* is a growing passion for personal righteousness, with more acute distress at the godlessness and immorality of the world around, and a keener discernment of Satan's strategy of opposition, distraction, and deception for ensuring that people neither believe nor live right. "We are not unaware of his schemes," said Paul, with some grimness (2 Cor 2:11). Every Christian needs to be able to say the same. When Christians show more grief that God is being dishonored and provoked by behavior that he hates, and more realism about the spiritual warfare involved in rolling back the evil tide, and more care lest they be drawn into sin themselves, it would seem that they are growing in grace.

4. *Sign four* is a growing zeal for God's cause, with more willingness to take unpopular action to further it. This is not to defend foolish gestures, which will certainly be unpopular and deservedly so. Strategic and tactical wisdom, and mature understanding of the issues involved, are called for in any public action. "Praise be to the LORD my Rock, who trains my hands for war," wrote David (Ps 144:1). Similarly, Christians preparing to fight the Lord's battles for truth and life need God to train, in this case, their minds. When Christians humbly allow wisdom to temper their zeal and yet remain ready (more so than at one time) to lay themselves on the line in what is unmistakably God's cause, it would seem that they are growing in grace.

5. *Sign five* is a greater patience and willingness to wait for God and bow to his will, with a deeper abhorrence of what masquerades as the bold faith, but is really the childish immaturity, that tries to force God's hand. It is the way of children to want things now, and to say and feel most passionately that they cannot wait for them or do without them. But the adult way of petitioning is the

way of submission, modeled by Jesus in Gethsemane—
"My Father, if it is possible... Yet not as I will, but as you
will" (Mt 26:39). It is right to tell God what we long for
and would like him to do, but it is also right to remind
ourselves and acknowledge to him that he knows best.
When Christians are learning to submit to God's ordering of events with undaunted realism and humility, it
would seem that they are growing in grace.

APPLYING THESE PRINCIPLES PERSONALLY

It remains now only to pull the threads together and indicate how all this applies to the individual Christian. Since
God's teaching in Scripture on holy growth has been given to
measure, guide, and direct me as much as anyone, it will once
more be fitting (as well as straightforward) for me to formulate the application in personal terms.

First, then: is my concern about growing in grace all that it
should be?

Am I Concerned about Growth? In 2 Peter 3:18, growing in
grace is put forward not as an option, but as a necessity; not
suggested, but commanded. Peter's verb is in the imperative:
"Grow in the grace and knowledge of our Lord and Savior
Jesus Christ." This is the apostle's last injunction, set forth in
the last verse of his last letter, at a time when he knew that his
death was imminent (2 Pt 1:14). So it has the special weight
and solemnity that last words always carry. It is as if Peter is
telling us: "Whatever else you forget of what I have said to you,
remember this, for this is the most important thing of all." So
indeed it is; for the thought Peter was expressing was in truth
bigger and richer than we have yet seen.

With Ryle, who on this point was following the Puritans, we
have so far taken the phrase "grow in grace" to signify "grow in
graces (virtues, facets of Christian character)." While this is

certainly part of Peter's meaning, there is much more to it than that.

To grow in the grace and knowledge of Christ means:

- to strengthen one's grasp on the whole doctrine of grace that we reviewed in Chapters 2 and 3;
- to deepen one's faith-relationship with Christ, and through him with the Father and the Spirit, by involving the holy Three consciously and directly in the living of one's life; and
- to become more Christ-like as the Spirit assimilates us to the One we contemplate, leading us to pray for conformity to him, to act in imitation of him, and to manifest our progressive transformation into his moral image.

To obey this command on an ongoing basis (which is what Peter intends; "grow" is in the present tense, and means "keep growing") is a matter of being consciously Christian, and trying all the time to be more Christian, in every department of our living. Thus, growing in grace is our true life's work, a huge and never-ending task. Since it is a matter of command, we are bound to tackle it, and to labor to get as far in it as we can. This is real discipleship. This is how we show ourselves to be believers. Growth in grace is thus the acid test of us all.

Many Christians, however, seem not to grow in grace, nor to be concerned to grow in grace. Apparently they are content to mark time spiritually, or even to slip backward. That is tragic. Why is it so? There are various possible reasons. Perhaps they have never read Peter's words, nor been told that God requires them to grow in grace. People do not have a conscience about that of which they are ignorant. Or perhaps they are held back by fear that a serious commitment to grow in grace would bring major disruption and upheaval into their lives— as it probably would. W.H. Auden testified to the paralyzing effect of such fear in his chilling line, "We would rather be ruined than changed."

Or perhaps they are taking their cue from Christians around

them who also have no concern to grow in grace. They may have concluded from this that they need not be concerned about it either, never mind what the Bible says. Or perhaps they have lost their first love for Christ and their appetite for divine things and are, like Paul's one-time colleague Demas, "in love with this present world" (2 Tm 4:10, RSV). But whatever the reason, their unconcern is disobedient, wrong, irresponsible, and indefensible. All Christians are charged to grow in the grace and knowledge of Christ.

At the start of his letter Peter had spelled out, in a vivid if wire-drawn way, the down-to-earth specifics of commitment to grow in grace. "Make every effort to add to your faith goodness; and to goodness, knowledge; and to knowledge, self-control; and to self-control, perseverance; and to perseverance, godliness; and to godliness, brotherly kindness; and to brotherly kindness, love. For if you possess these qualities in increasing measure, they will keep you from being ineffective and unproductive in your knowledge of our Lord Jesus Christ" (2 Pt 1:5-8). Note how neatly D, E, and P dovetail here! This is a formula that applies to all. I must, therefore, face the fact that this is the way of living I am called to, and that I lapse into an unholy, unhealthy state of heart the moment I cease to labor thus to grow. And what is true of me is true of each of my readers, too.

Do I Practice These Principles? Second, then: *is my practice of the principles of growing in grace all that it should be?*

What, we ask, are those principles? If one simply said: make use of the means of grace (Bible reading, prayer, church worship, and Christian fellowship, to cite the classic four), one would not be wrong. But it is helpful to say more than this. So here now are three maxims (principles for fulfilling the principle of required growth; middle axioms, ethicists would call them), plus four disciplines, all set forth for my guidance as well as for yours.

1. Work Out Your Salvation. This phrase, from Philippians 2:12, is Paul's explanation of what his readers' obedience to the call to demonstrate the mind (attitude) of Christ (Phil 2:5-11) will really amount to. It will be an expressing in action, and so a perfecting and completing (all these ideas seem to be present), of the salvation that is theirs now. And they should work out their salvation "with fear and trembling"—that is to say, with awe and reverence for God's work in them. For the ability that their obedience actualizes is not natural, it is the fruit of divine enabling. It is awesome to realize that "it is God who works in you to will and to act" (Phil 2:13), yet that is the sober truth. As we express our salvation by divinely empowered obedience, so God the Holy Spirit transforms our moral nature to make us more like the Christ on whom we model ourselves.

This suggests the proper procedure every time a new act of obedience is called for. First, take it to God in prayer, acknowledging your own lack of strength for it and asking to be enabled from on high. Then go into action, expecting to be helped, and you will find that you are. Then thank God for the help you received. It is by this pattern of humble, dependent activity that our salvation is worked out. It is thus that we shall grow in grace.

2. Remain (Abide, Stay Put) in Christ. This maxim reinforces the first. It comes from Christ's own lips. "No branch can bear fruit by itself; it must remain in the vine. Neither can you bear fruit unless you remain in me. I am the vine; you are the branches. If a man remains in me and I in him, he will bear much fruit; apart from me you can do nothing.... Now remain in my love. If you obey my commands, you will remain in my love" (Jn 15:4-5, 9-10). Jesus' point is that he himself must be the focus of his followers' lives. By faith in him they are already united with him in such a way that his life really, although mysteriously, flows through them (they are branches in him, the vine). Now they are to look to him as their source of power to serve, listen to him to find what form that service should take, cultivate his company as they go about his business, and bask in the certainty of his ongoing love.

In this all-encompassing relationship to him they are to

"remain" (stay put, and stay steady). This is their secret of fruitfulness. The fruit that they will then bear—"fruit that will last" (Jn 15:16)—will consist of righteousness in their own changed lives, and spiritual influence changing the lives of others. For such fruitfulness, which embraces holiness, health, and growth as we have been defining them, Christ-centered living of the kind described is absolutely essential. It was so for the apostles to whom Jesus gave this teaching, and it remains so for us to whom John in his Gospel relays it.

Well, then, might the hymn-writer say to the Lord:

O Jesus Christ, grow thou in me,
And all things else recede;
My heart be daily nearer thee,
From sin be daily freed.

Each day let thy supporting might
My weakness still embrace;
My darkness vanish in thy light,
Thy life my death efface.

In thy bright beams which on me fall
Fade every evil thought;
That I am nothing, thou art all,
I would be daily taught.

More of thy glory let me see,
Thou holy, wise, and true;
I would thy living image be
In joy and sorrow too.

Fill me with gladness from above,
Hold me by strength divine:
Lord, let the glow of thy great love
Through my whole being shine.

Make this poor self grow less and less,
Be thou my life and aim;
O make me daily, through thy grace,
More meet to bear thy name!

It is thus, through our decrease and his increase as described, that we shall grow in grace.

3. Watch and Pray. These are words of Jesus, spoken as warning to the three disciples whom he had asked to watch with him (stay awake and alert, supporting him by their presence and concern) while he prayed in Gethsemane. The full warning was: "Watch and pray so that you will not fall into temptation. The spirit is willing, but the body is weak" (Mt 26:41).

The point of the warning was that Satan, the enemy of souls, is endlessly malicious and deceptive. All who serve God have to run the gauntlet of Satan's unwelcome attentions for the whole of their lives. If Satan cannot keep us from being believers, he will certainly draw on all his resources to keep us from growing in grace and to ensure that God is dishonored, one way or another, by the way we live. "Fall" (literally "enter") "into temptation" means becoming a victim of one of Satan's schemes for dishonoring God by doing damage to one who is his. Inducements to "fall" in this way are constant in the Christian life.

Peter, to whom Jesus' warning was first spoken (and whom within the next few hours Satan trapped into publicly denying Jesus three times), was later to write a poignant exposition of what it means to watch: "Be self-controlled and alert. Your enemy the devil prowls around like a roaring lion looking for someone to devour. Resist him, standing firm in the faith" (1 Pt 5:8-9).

As for praying, Jesus' own struggle in Gethsemane to pray "thy will be done" from his heart shows us what we need to know about the prayer that will repel satanic allurements. As long as our hearts echo Jesus' prayer, "Not my will but thy will be done," and avail themselves of the precious truth that "because he (Jesus) himself suffered when he was tempted, he is able to help those who are being tempted" (Heb 2:18, cf. 4:15), we shall be victorious. The essence of the spiritual warfare in which Christians are involved is battling to say "no" when the world, the flesh, and the devil urge you to say "yes," and to say "yes" when weariness, dead-heartedness, and unbelief prompt you to say "no." In these battles, those who have learned to watch, to pray, to fight, and to win grow in grace. It is through just such experiences that we, too, shall grow in grace.

Wrote Eric Liddell, the legendary Flying Scotsman of the film *Chariots of Fire:* "The Christian life should be a life of growth. I believe the secret of growth is to develop the devotional life."[4] Surely he was right. But the devotional life can be undermined by folly and neglect, and thus kept from developing in a truly healthy way. So I close this chapter by calling attention to four disciplines that have to do with clearing the path to healthy growth. All were suggested by the contents of 2 Peter, and particularly of 2 Peter 3, the chapter that has God's call to grow in grace as its climactic conclusion.

First Discipline: Acceptance of Facts. Realism is a Christian virtue that acknowledges God's sovereignty over his world. It interprets unexpected disappointments and deferrings of hope as acts of God's wisdom and goodness, according to his promise. No discouragement, bitterness, or cynicism (the wasting diseases of the soul) find any foothold in realistic hearts. Peter tells his readers, who were seemingly daunted and perplexed because the Lord had not yet returned, that Christ's apparent slowness to end history was really patient mercy, making for the salvation of some who would otherwise be lost (2 Pt 3:3-9, 15). Acceptance of this, in the confidence that God does all things well, was necessary for their continued devotional growth. To hold a grudge against God, for this or any other fact, would block growth completely.

Second Discipline: Avoidance of Folly. Righteousness is a Christian obligation, and what Peter calls "the error of lawless men" (2 Pt 3:17)—namely, the immoralism and proud unconcern about holiness described in 2 Peter 2—is folly flying in the face of God's requirement and provoking judgment. Rejecting such folly is necessary for continued devotional growth. Yielding to it, settling for some form of moral slackness, and thereby displeasing God, would block growth completely.

Third Discipline: Assimilation of Food. Bible truth, the Word of God, is the true soul food. In his first letter, Peter told his readers to long for it (2:2). In this second letter, he tells them to pay heed to the Scriptures written by the prophets (1:19-21, 3:2) and to make sure they do not misunderstand the letters of St. Paul (3:15). Confidence in the divine truth of Bible teaching, and constant thoughtful absorption of it, are necessary for continued growth in grace. Doubt about the Scriptures, however, would block growth completely.

Fourth Discipline: Affirmation of Fellowship. God did not create, nor does he redeem, anyone to be a lone wolf in his world. We are made, and we are saved, for affectionate togetherness and mutual help. Peter models this: first, he calls his readers his "brothers" (2 Pt 1:10, cf. 2 Pt 1:7) and then, four times in 2 Peter 3, he addresses them as his "dear friends" (literally, "beloved ones"), just as he refers to Paul as his "dear (beloved) brother" (2 Pt 3:1, 8, 14, 15, 17). The uniqueness of the apostles' role and authority never restricts or inhibits their fellowship with their converts as brothers who love and are loved in God's family. Taking our place in the interdependent brotherhood of the Christian fellowship is necessary for continued growth in grace. Voluntary isolation from it, however motivated, would block growth completely.

AVOIDING THE PETER PAN SYNDROME

A haunting twentieth-century literary creation, haunting because he mirrors so much uncomfortable truth about us, is J.M. Barrie's *Peter Pan*, "the boy who would not grow up" as Barrie's subtitle for the play puts it. For two generations *Peter Pan* has been celebrated and enjoyed as quality entertainment for children. Generations have perceived it simply as the story of Peter and the pirates, with Wendy in tow, and have loved it as such. I read the play often when I was a child; it was, indeed, a favorite book of mine, and that was what I got out of it. No doubt Steven Spielberg's movie *Hook* will give the pirate part of the story a new lease on life. No doubt *Peter Pan* will still be rated a children's classic in the twenty-first century.

Yet Peter is not a person with whom any wise child, or wise adult for that matter, will identify. His twice-repeated declaration, "I just want always to be a little boy and to have fun,"[5] is really bad news. Peter represents the fixation of a phase that a boy goes through and, if all is well, grows out of. His choice (for such it is) to arrest his own development leaves him so flawed that we have to describe him as an anti-hero, a character significantly unsympathetic and even repellent. Though brave, clever, and leaderlike, he is also a conceited show-off, self-absorbed, heartless, and unable either to love or to accept love from others. Through thick layers of the sentimental ambivalence (joking and sad by turns, for that was Barrie's speciality), the play makes clear that, after their sojourn in the Never Land, Wendy and her brothers are well off to be back in a family committed to adulthood as childhood's normal destination. For Peter to turn his back on the world of relationships and work, in order endlessly to play his Pan-pipes among the fairies, is a small-scale tragedy. Grown-ups in the audience are meant to feel it as such.

The Western world's current drift from its Christian moorings into secular materialism has generated what can only be called a Peter Pan culture. Here all the facets of Peter's childish egoism are encouraged to emerge and entrench themselves, and are treated as virtues when they do. In such a culture it is hard to become a responsible adult, particularly in the realm of the emotions. It has been truly said that the greatest social problem of the modern world is extreme emotional immaturity masquerading as an adult lifestyle. In God's ordering of things, the human family is meant to function as a relational network in which the lesson of responsible love and life-strategy will be thoroughly learned. But with the weakening of family life almost everywhere this is not happening. Today's world is full of people with adult bodies housing a juvenile, even infantile, emotional make-up—people, in other words, who just always want to be little boys or girls and to have fun. Affluence allows childish self-indulgence to become a lifestyle from one's teens onward, and the results in later life are painful.

Christians, no less than others, are conditioned and shaped by the culture of which they are part. They also get infected by this Peter Pan syndrome. Maxims and disciplines of devotion cannot help us if we are not prepared to be changed at this point. Am I willing to learn whether I need to grow up emotionally? Are you?

Once more, it is Jesus, "the author and perfecter of our faith" (Heb 12:2), who stands before us as the model of that emotional and attitudinal maturity to which our growth in grace is meant to bring us. It is supremely through measuring ourselves by him, as we meet him in the pages of the Gospels, that we shall come to see what our true needs in this area are, and what growth towards his stature will require of us.

May you and I be enabled to grow in grace at this present time, "perfecting holiness out of reverence for God" (2 Cor 7:1).

CHAPTER 7

Growing Strong: The Empowered Christian Life

I kneel before the Father.... I pray that out of his glo-rious riches he may strengthen you with power through his Spirit in your inner being, so that Christ may dwell in your hearts through faith. And I pray that you, being rooted and established in love, may have power, together with all the saints, to grasp how wide and long and high and deep is the love of Christ, and to know this love that surpasses knowl-edge—that you may be filled to the measure of all the fullness of God.

Now to him who is able to do immeasurably more than all we ask or imagine, according to his power that is at work within us, to him be glory in the church and in Christ Jesus throughout all genera-tions, for ever and ever! Amen. **Eph 3:14-21**

As servants of God we commend ourselves in every way: in great endurance; in troubles, hardships, and distresses; in beatings, imprisonments and riots; in hard work, sleepless nights and hunger; in purity, understanding, patience and kindness; in the Holy Spirit and in sincere love; in truthful speech and in the power of God; with weapons of righteousness in the right hand and in the left. **2 Cor 6:4-7**

POWER: AN OVERUSED WORD?

At the turn of each year *Time* magazine looks back, looks ahead, and makes whatever comments it thinks fit. The first issue for 1990 contained a list of "Buzzwords Most Ready for Early Retirement," in which, after "upside potential, upscale marketing, fast-tracker, bottom line, synergy, networking, streamlining, interfacing, prioritizing quality time, soft landing, hands-on manager" came "power player, power breakfast, power tie, power anything."

As I look at my bookshelves today, I see there items titled *Power Healing, Power Evangelism, Healing Power, Power Encounters, When the Spirit Comes with Power, Christianity with Power,* all published since 1985. Round go the wheels of the mind. Buzzword, eh? Fluffy, tiresome jargon, right? Overused among Christians, just as it is in the commercial world? Ripe for retirement? First thoughts might prompt us to say so, but second thoughts should give us pause.

For "power" is a very significant New Testament word. Where would I be if I imposed a self-denying ordinance on myself and declined to use it any longer? Where would the church be if we all acted that way? If we stopped talking about power we should soon stop thinking about it. If that happened we should be impoverished indeed. Hey, then, put on the brakes; stop being snide. For Christianity, at least, the word "power" is precious. Buzzword it may be, but we need it, so that we can focus on what it refers to. This chapter will, I hope, make clear the importance of doing that.

The Power of God. The power that now concerns us is God's power—the energy exercised by him in creation, providence, and grace. The usual word for it in the Greek New Testament is *dunamis,* from which comes our word "dynamite." Here we shall deal with just one segment of this tremendous topic, namely the power of God regenerating, sanctifying, and operating through us sinners.

To deal with this, however, means facing up to a problem, the recurring buzzword problem of passionately committed short sight. We may analyze the problem thus: a word presses buttons of interest, excitement, and desire to be in the swim and not be left behind. So people pick up the word and flash it as a kind of verbal badge, in order to show that they are fully up-to-date and know about the latest significant thing. But such use reflects little or no thought about this latest thing in itself. So the more the word is used this way, the woollier grows its meaning and the shorter the sight of its zealous users.

At the present time, more and more people are anxiously asking themselves and each other whether they have the power of God in their lives, with less and less certainty in their minds as to what that might mean. All they are sure of is that they want to identify with the folk who claim acquaintance with that power, since they do not want to be left out of any good thing that is happening. As in other instances, the buzzword problem thus opens out into a flock-of-sheep neurosis, an inclination to follow fashions blindly so long as one is part of a confident crowd. Where buzzwords buzz, you get notional fuzz! If we are to talk meaningfully about the power of God, we shall have to cut through some of that.

As a first step towards proper clarity on our theme, we need to see right at the outset that God does not give us his power as a possession of our own, a resource to use at our discretion. It should not be necessary to say that, but the amount of talk today about using the power of God shows that this misconception is common. God uses us, calling into play the powers he has given us, as channels through which his own power flows. But we are not storage units like batteries, or receptacles like buckets, in which the potential for power in action can be kept until needed. And we do not use God, or God's power, as we use electricity, switching it on or off as we like.

Wanting to possess divine power to use at his own discretion was the sin of Simon the sorcerer (Acts 8:18-24). His sin is recorded as a warning, not as an example to follow. The right desire at all times is to be "an instrument for noble purposes, made holy, useful to the Master and prepared to do any good work" (2 Tm 2:21). The King James Version (KJV) reads "a vessel unto honor, sanctified, and meet for the master's use," which is stronger and clearer.

Should Christians speak to us of using the power of God, red lights should flash before our mind. If however, the talk is of how to be usable and useful to God, we should be nodding our heads. Let us see to it that we do not go wrong here.

GOD'S SUPERNATURAL POWER

During the past century, evangelical Christians (and some others with them) have been very concerned about power in the Christian life. Was that wrong? Not at all. A journal founded in the 1870s was called *The Christian's Pathway of Power*. Its theme was God's enablement of us to do our duty, to perform the tasks that life sets us, and to overcome the temptations that would keep us from thus pleasing God. During the years of my nurture by an evangelical student movement, a whole regiment of devotional speakers knitted their brows and pressed on us the question, "Do you have power in your life?"—meaning the same thing. Was it wrong to want greater self-control and a more thorough, fruitful practice of righteousness through God's power? Of course not.

At the same time, and among the same people, concern focused too on being able, through God's power, to influence others for God through one's witnessing (and, if one was a preacher, through one's preaching). A great deal was said about the difference between Christians whose witness had "power" and those whose witness did not have "power." Was it right to be concerned that one's witness have power? Was it right to be fearful lest one's witness prove to be power*less*? Of course it was right. These should be our concerns as well.

More recently, Christians who have been touched by the

movements known as Pentecostalism, the charismatic renewal, and the Third Wave, have begun to seek (and some claim to have found) the ability through prayer to channel supernatural demonstrations of God's power in all sorts of healings: healings of the body, inner healing of the heart, and exorcisms where there appears to be something demonic acting in a person's life.

Again I ask myself, is it wrong that Christians are concerned about these things? Though I see some dangerous pitfalls,[1] I cannot find it in my heart to say this is wrong. In my New Testament, I read a great deal about such manifestations of the power of God, understood as "powers of the coming age" (Heb 6:5)—in other words, the Holy Spirit in action.

It is true that the New Testament regularly views the "signs and wonders" as the Father's authentication of the ministry of Jesus and his apostles (Acts 2:43, 5:12, 14:3, cf. 10:38, 19:11; Rom 15:19; 2 Cor 12:12; Heb 2:3). There is no clear promise that these manifestations will continue after the apostles' ministry is over.[2] But there is no denial that they will either. The New Testament leaves open the possibility.

In any case, it is said most emphatically that all Christians, as new creations in Christ, have already been touched by the supernatural (2 Cor 5:17; Eph 2:4-10; 1 Jn 3:9). The consistent expectation is that now they will live differently, and will be seen to be living differently, from the rest of the world. The supreme sign and wonder, giving the fullest credibility to Christianity, will thus always be the changed life of the believer. Two conclusions seem to follow. First, a Christianity that is prepared to go on cheerfully without any signs of God's supernatural transforming power in people's lives shows a very unbiblical spirit. Second, this expectation of overall moral change is the frame into which all hopes and quests for supernatural healing properly fit.

Miracles of the New Creation. The coming of Christ the Savior has led to the outpouring of the Spirit on the church and on the world. And the Holy Spirit comes with power. In the New Testament, we see this power manifested in all the modes of which I have spoken so far: the ability to perform tasks of devotion and service, and to overcome temptation; the ability to influence others through preaching and witness; and the ability to act as a channel for God's power in miracles, healings, and the like. Let us consider each of these three modes, in reverse order.

Signs and Wonders. First, in the Gospels and in Acts, we encounter works of power in the physical realm, including miracles of nature and healings of all sorts. The phrase "signs and wonders" is used for them by Jesus himself in John 4:48. These are, to use C.S. Lewis' apt phrase, "miracles of the new creation,"[3] in which the power of God that made the world works again to bring something out of nothing—to bring about a state of affairs for which no explanation can be given in terms of what was there before. Everyone knows you cannot get enough food for five thousand out of five loaves and two fishes, but enough food for five thousand was produced. Everyone knows you cannot bring the dead back to life, but on three occasions Jesus brought the dead back to life: Jairus' daughter, the widow's son at Nain, and Lazarus (see Lk 7:11-17, 8:49-55; Jn 11).

To be sure, these three incidents were not the same as the greater miracle of new creation that occurred when Christ himself was raised from the dead. They were only resuscitations. In each case, the person died again a little further down the road. The same was true of Dorcas, whom Peter raised (Acts 9:36-41), and of Eutychus, whom Paul raised (Acts 20:9-12), just as it had been true of the dead children whom God restored to life through Elijah and Elisha (1 Kgs 17:17-23; 2 Kgs 4:18-37). Jesus, however, rose from the dead never to die again. His resurrection is an even more remarkable miracle of new creation—indeed, it is the normative one. Christ is the first-fruits, the beginning of the new creation of God, as the New Testament itself says (see 1 Cor 15:20, 23; Col 1:18; Rv 1:5).

Nevertheless, all these are instances in which the power that created the world out of nothing produces effects for which no cause can be cited, except that God the Creator has been showing his power again.

Words of Power. Second, one reads on in the New Testament and finds that words of power in Christian communication are very much a part of the gospel story and of the story of the new church. Luke is particularly interested in the power of God, and there are several texts in Luke that are significant here. Let us look at some of them.

In Luke 4:14 we read that, following the wilderness temptation, "Jesus returned to Galilee in the *power* of the Spirit." This text introduces not only his works of power but also the words of power that came from his lips. Then, after his resurrection, Jesus told the disciples to wait in Jerusalem until they were endued with "*power* from on high" for the ministry of worldwide evangelism to which he was committing them (see Lk 24:49).

At the beginning of Acts, Luke picks up the same theme. Jesus tells his followers, "You will receive *power* when the Holy Spirit comes on you; and you will be my witnesses... to the ends of the earth" (Acts 1:8). Later we read, "With great *power* the apostles continued to testify to the resurrection of the Lord Jesus, and much grace was upon them all" (Acts 4:33).

Paul likewise has tremendous things to say about the power of God working through the gospel and through its messengers. "I am not ashamed of the gospel, because it is the *power* of God for the salvation of everyone who believes" (Rom 1:16). At the end of the lengthy argument that makes up the letter to the Romans, and speaking of his own ministry, Paul says, "I will not venture to speak of anything except what Christ has accomplished through me in leading the Gentiles to obey God by what I have said and done—by the *power* of signs and miracles, through the *power* of the Spirit" (Rom 15:18-19). Again, in his first letter to the Corinthians, he says: "For Christ did not send me to baptize, but to preach the gospel—not with words of human wisdom, lest the cross of Christ be emptied of its *power*. For the message of the cross is foolishness to those who are perishing, but to us who are being saved it is the *power* of God" (1 Cor 1:17-18).

"Words of human wisdom" is a phrase Paul uses to indicate the endeavor to swap philosophy with the philosophers. The people in the Greek cities where Paul went to evangelize expected him to parade his own cleverness when he spoke in public. Wandering lecturers who showed off in this way were familiar figures in Greek cities, and they were appreciated as good entertainment. But Paul would not behave as they expected. He adopted a plain, straightforward, matter-of-fact style of presentation which made him seem foolish to those who were expecting the sort of self-display they got from other traveling teachers.

"I knew what you wanted," Paul tells them, "and I was resolved not to give it to you. You wanted me to show off as a philosopher, with dazzling arguments, and to put on a performance that pandered to your sophistication, but I wouldn't do it. I was with you as a messenger, not a philosopher or an orator or an entertainer; I came to testify to God and Jesus Christ and his cross, and to tell you how to be saved from sin and hell (cf. 1 Cor 2:1), and that was all I was willing to do. And so you thought me a fool."

But, says Paul, they should by now have come to appreciate his strategy. "My message and my preaching were not with wise and persuasive words [wise, by the world's standards], but with a demonstration of the Spirit's *power*, so that your faith might not rest on men's wisdom, but on God's *power*" (1 Cor 2:4-5). It was to make way for God's power that he spoke as he did.

Jesus himself had predicted that through the apostles' witness, the Spirit would convince people of the truth about Jesus and their need of him. Paul had trusted the Holy Spirit to do just this, and he had not been disappointed.

Transformed Lives. Third, the New Testament speaks not only of God's power in the miraculous and in the communication of the gospel, but also of God's power at work *in us*, enabling us to understand and do what we otherwise could not.

In Ephesians 1:17-19, Paul tells the Christians what he prays that God will give them: "I keep asking that the God of our Lord Jesus Christ, the glorious Father, may give you the Spirit of wisdom and revelation, so that you may know him better. I pray also that the eyes of your heart may be enlightened in order that you may know the hope to which he has called you, the riches of his glorious inheritance in the saints, and his incomparably great *power* for us [other translations say, "*in us*"] who believe."

The power of which Paul speaks is not just power in the *message*. It is not just power through the *messenger*. It is power *in and upon those who believe*, opening their formerly shuttered hearts wider and wider so that they understand gospel truth better and better, thereby making their life utterly different from what it was before. It is resurrection power—a matter of God raising with Christ those who have become willing to die with Christ. Clearly Paul is expecting tremendous changes in the lives of those who now belong to Christ.

He comes back to this theme at the end of Ephesians 3: "I pray that out of [God's] glorious riches he may strengthen you with *power* through his Spirit in your inner being, so that Christ may dwell in your hearts through faith. And I pray that you, being rooted and established in love, may have *power*, together with all the saints, to grasp how wide and long and high and deep is the love of Christ, and to know this love that surpasses knowledge—that you may be filled to the measure of all the fullness of God" (v. 16-19).

Again we see that Paul is talking about something radical, in the fullest sense of that word: something that produces a total change. He is praying that through this marvelous inner transformation and enrichment of which he speaks, the Ephesians will become utterly different from folk around them—utterly different, indeed, from what they have been so far. This becomes obvious when he moves into the closing doxology of his prayer and gives praise to "him who is able to do immeasurably more than all we ask or imagine, according to his *power* that is at work within us" (Eph 3:20). Paul speaks as if for him the sky is the limit so far as the transforming agency of the Holy Spirit is concerned, and his expectations of change are accordingly high.

These are samples of the many precious texts in the New Testament about the power of God. Each was an example of God's power working through Christ and through the apostles, manifested in works of power in the physical realm, in giving power to Christian communications so that they would have a significant impact, and also in enabling Christians to understand and do what otherwise they could neither understand nor do.

Thus, reflecting on the matter in light of the New Testament, I am compelled to correct my initial feeling about *Time* magazine's wish to retire the word "power." It remains a word in season for Christian people. Power is a theme that Christians must ever hold on to. It is very clear from the New Testament that the power of God is meant to accompany the gospel, and to find expression through its messengers and in the lives of those to whom the message comes.

MANIFESTING GOD'S POWER

This book is about holiness. Our review of the power of God as seen in the New Testament has led us to look at ministries of various kinds. Was that relevant? Are we not ranging too widely, and going beyond our subject? I do not think so. It is artificial and unscriptural to draw a hard and fast dividing line between God's work of transforming a person's character, which is what we have discussed so far, and his work of thrusting that person into ministry—into active service of others, accepted as a task that God has given. I am not speaking here of ordained or salaried ministry only, or even primarily.

Ministry means any form of service, and there are many such forms. Thus,

- being a faithful spouse and a conscientious parent is the form of ministry at home;
- discharging an office, fulfilling a role, and carrying a defined responsibility is the form of ministry (both ordained and lay) in the organized church;
- sustaining pastoral friendships that involve advising, interceding, and supporting is a further form of ministry in Christ; and
- loving care for people at any level of need—physical or mental, material or spiritual—is the true form of ministry in the world.

Holiness, as we have seen, is neither static nor passive. It is a state of increasing love to God and one's neighbor, and love is precisely a matter of doing what honors and benefits the loved one, out of a wish to raise that loved one high. Holy persons, therefore, show themselves such by praising God and helping others. They know they should, and in fact, they want to. God himself has made them want to, however self-absorbed they may have been before.

As their Christlikeness adds to their impact, credibility, and effectiveness for God when they serve their neighbors, so God uses their experiences in such ministry (success, failure, delight, frustration, learning patience and persistence, going the second mile, staying humble when appreciated, staying kind when attacked, holding steady under pressure, and so on) to advance the change "from glory to glory" in their own lives (2 Cor 3:18). He continues to make them more like Jesus than they were before.

It is noteworthy that most speakers and books on holiness say little about ministry, while most speakers and books on ministry say little about holiness. It has been this way for over a century. But to treat holiness and ministry as separate themes is an error. God has linked them, and what God joins man must not put asunder.

One regular result of ongoing sanctification is that concern for others, with recognition of what they lack, and wisdom that sees how to help them, is increased. Ministry blossoms naturally in holy lives. In effective ministry, God's power is channeled through God's servants into areas of human need. A saintly person of limited gifts is always likely to channel more of it than would a person who was more gifted but less godly. So God wants us all to seek holiness and usefulness together, and the former partly at least for the sake of the latter.

Out of this awareness I now venture to formulate five theses that bear on the manifesting of the power of God among his people today. My aim in putting them forward is to make us readier to receive and show forth this power in its various forms. I must frankly say that I think there are unhelpful cross-currents in today's discussions about the power of God in Christians and in the church. Thus I offer some aspects of these five theses for corrective purposes. I want the power of God to be manifested to God's glory in your life, in my life, and in our churches. That is why I write as I do.

1. Heightened Expectations. *It is right to bring the supernatural into prominence and to raise Christians' expectations with regard to it.*

Generally speaking, our expectations with regard to seeing the power of God transforming people's lives are not as high as they should be.

It is a fact of history that in the years before the Reformation broke in on the church in the sixteenth century, there was a tremendous amount of superstition regarding the working of miracles. I do not deny that God may have worked many miracles through many saints before the Reformation (as it seems he has worked some miracles through some of his saints since the Reformation). But the Reformers saw a great deal of the supposedly supernatural which seemed to them unmistakably superstitious, and they reacted violently against it.

Packer's proverb, however, if I may so speak, is that the reaction of man worketh not the righteousness of God. This is surely obvious. If you are walking backward away from something that you think is a mistake, you may be right in supposing it is a mistake, but for you to be walking backward is never right. Sooner or later people who walk backward in the physical sense stumble over some obstacle behind them which they never saw, because their minds and their eyes were fixed on what they were trying to get away from, and then they fall. We are meant to walk forward, not backward. Reaction is always a matter of walking backward, and thus it brings its own nemesis.

The Reformers, being Bible-based, believed in a Creator God who controls his world absolutely, who worked many miracles in biblical times, and who still takes special action in response to prayer. So, when Luther thought that Melanchthon, his right-hand man, was dying, he stood at the sickroom window looking at the sky and prayed aloud for some hours for the young man's recovery. At the end of this time Melanchthon's temperature was down, and he was visibly getting better.[4]

Praying for the sick, and looking for special providences of recovery, was in fact standard evangelical practice from the sixteenth to the nineteenth century, though with a clear understanding that continued illness and early death might well be God's gracious will in any particular case—an understanding, let it be said, that is often (and very unfortunately) less clear among those who pray for the sick today. But because belief in the saints' miracles was bound up with the supposedly meritorious relic-cult of the Middle Ages, the Reformers spent time ridiculing it, just as they ridiculed claims to supernatural revelations and miraculous providences on their own left wing. Thus they left the impression that in their view, supernatural providences should not be expected at all now that the apostolic age was over.

This negativism, the legacy of a defensive reaction, as we can now see, was later reinforced by the Newtonian notion of the material universe as a closed box of forces and processes. This makes it appear at least unseemly, and perhaps impossible, for God to break into the world which he has created—a notion that came to pervade Protestant culture and seems to have led directly to the still widespread assumption that God in grace touches only the soul, not the body at all. It is clear that such an assumption drastically dampens one dimension of biblical faith.

At the beginning of this century, the new Pentecostal denominations challenged this assumption, and Christians touched by the charismatic movement have maintained the challenge. During the past thirty years openness to the supernatural in the physical realm has been recovered by many who had lost it. Expectations of direct divine healing and other startling providences in answer to prayer have risen throughout the Christian world. For this we should be thankful. Twentieth-century hostility to the idea that God might heal or shape events today in a way that would call attention to his presence in power was always unjustified and unbalanced. Its motives do not bear examination. We should be glad that it is melting away.

But a caution is now in order, for an opposite error, no less unjustified and unbalanced, now threatens. The corrective pendulum-swing away from one extreme of reaction was itself a reaction. This has led to another extreme, just as false as the first. The immaturity and childish egoism that infect our culture claim their victims among Christians too. Symptoms of these defects appear in the all-too-common tendency of modern Christians to undervalue the natural and the ordinary. There are just too many people who want every problem to be solved by an immediate miracle, a display of the supernatural, a wonderful providence that will change everything. I think that is a sign not of great faith, but of great immaturity. Let me explain.

Again and again our Lord leads us into situations that are painful and difficult, and we pray—as Paul prayed regarding his thorn in the flesh—that the situation will change. We want a miracle! But instead the Lord chooses to leave things as they are and to strengthen us to cope with them, as he did with

Paul, making his strength perfect in continuing human weakness. (See 2 Corinthians 12:7-10.)

Think of it in terms of the training of children, and you will see my point at once. If there are never any difficult situations that demand self-denial and discipline, if there are never any sustained pressures to cope with, if there are never any long-term strategies where the child must stick with an educational process, or an apprenticeship, or the practice of a skill, for many years in order to advance, there will never be any maturity of character. The children (who, of course, want life to be easy and full of fun, as children always do) will remain spoiled all their lives, because everything has been made too easy for them. The Lord does not allow that to happen in the lives of his children.

It is extraordinary how little the New Testament says about God's interest in our success, by comparison with the enormous amount that it says about God's interest in our holiness, our maturity in Christ, and our growth into the fullness of his image. Typical of his revealed interest is his message through the writer of Hebrews to a group of converted Jews who were being harassed, apparently by unconverted Jews, because of their Christian faith. He does not promise to shield them from trouble, either by natural or by supernatural means. Instead, he tells them (and thereby tells us) that, like Jesus, Christians must focus their thoughts on the joy set before them. They must be ready to shed their blood rather than yield to pressure and renounce their faith. Moreover, they must understand that hardship is the discipline by means of which their heavenly Father hammers them into shape for a harvest of holiness, which is what he is resolved to see in their lives. If they were not being thus hammered, one way or another, they would have a reason to doubt whether they were his children at all (Heb 12:2-14). Strong stuff!—but it makes crystal clear what we need to know: God's priority in all his dealings with us is to make us holy. It would be ruinous to twist today's healthy openness to the supernatural in a self-serving direction.

2. Empowered Ministry. *It is right to aspire to use one's God-given gifts in powerful and useful ministry.*

It is right to want to know what gifts for ministry God has given us. It is right to want to harness them and see them used for the blessing of others as widely as possible. Sanctified persons (as we saw) want to serve. Therefore, they both want and need to know what resources God has given them for this purpose.

But there is always a danger that the person who sees that God has given him or her a good sprinkling of gifts will be betrayed by that old enemy, self-importance—which is another name for pride. God does not value us according to the number of gifts we have, or by their spectacular quality. God does not value us primarily in terms of what we can do— even what we can do in his strength. He values us primarily in terms of what he makes us, character-wise, as he conforms us to Christ by his grace. We dare not forget that.

Jesus was already sounding the warning note when his disciples came back from a preaching tour all gung-ho, as we would say, and excited. "Lord," they cried, "even the demons are subject to us in your name!"

"Very good," says Jesus. "But do not rejoice that the demons are subject to you. That is not the truly important thing. Rejoice, rather, that your names are written in heaven. Rejoice in your salvation. Rejoice in what you *are* by the grace of God, rather than in the way God uses you. Rejoice in being his children, and in entering upon your destiny of being transformed into my image." (See Luke 10:17-20.)

Gifts are secondary. Sanctity is primary. Never let anything divert you from holding that truth before your mind and heart.

3. Meeting Needs. *It is right to want to be a channel of divine power into other people's lives at their points of need.*

Neighbor-love, as we have seen, seeks the good of the loved ones. For strong neighbor-love to be active in our hearts is a sign of spiritual health. But be careful lest you become one of those people who suffers from the neurosis of needing to be needed—the state of not feeling that you are anything or anybody unless you are able to feel that others cannot get on without you! That is not true neighbor-love, nor is it spiritual health. That is *lack* of spiritual health; it is in fact another form of pride. Our sense of personal worth is to flow, not from our Christian activities, nor from having others depending on us, but from our knowledge that God loved us enough to redeem us at the cost of Calvary.

Redeeming love imparts worth to the otherwise worthless creatures in whom it is invested, making it needless to seek a sense of worth from any other source. And if I am using my neighbors to bolster my sense of self-worth, I am *using* them, which is something different from loving them. My attitude is likely to make me keep them dependent on me when I ought to be setting them free, and that will be harmful both to them and to me.

One of the disciplines to which the Lord calls us is the willingness, from time to time, *not* to be used in significant ministry. Jesus modeled this when, having told Peter to bring him some of the fish miraculously caught (as we must consecrate to him the gifts he has given us), he then proceeded apparently to ignore Peter's offering and to feed the disciples from fish he had prepared independently (see Jn 21:9, 13).

Imagine, now, a devoted and gifted Christian woman, whose ministry has been precious to her, finding that for quite a long period the Lord sidelines her so that her potential is not being used. What is going on? Is this spiritual failure? It is probably not spiritual failure at all, but a lesson in Christ's school of holiness. The Lord is reminding her that her life does not depend on finding that people need her. The prime source of her joy must always be the knowledge of God's love for her—the knowledge that though he did not need her, he has chosen to love her freely and gloriously so that she may have the eternal joy of fellowship with him. Regarding her ministry, what matters is that she should be available to him. Then he will decide when and how to put her to service again, and she should leave that with him.

In the spiritual life, what we are always takes priority over what we do. If we lose touch with what we are, and with the reality of God's free mercy as the taproot of our spiritual life, the Lord may have to sideline us until we have learned this lesson again.

4. Empowered Evangelism. *It is right to want to see God's power manifested in a way that has a significant evangelistic effect.*

Holy persons who seek God's honor and glory and their neighbor's good will care deeply about evangelism, the activity that seeks to exalt God in Christ by persuading sinners to turn to him and find new life. They will want to see evangelism done in a way that shows as clearly as possible that the gospel is true, and what is declared about new life in Christ through the power of God is, as we say, "for real." They will want to see the reality of moral and spiritual transformation by the Holy Spirit proclaimed by speakers whose manner and style indicate that they are personally living in the power of the great change they are talking about. They will be very comfortable with the current vogue for describing evangelistic activity as designed, under God, to bring about a "power encounter" between the sinner and the Savior. They will want to share in the activity themselves.

A line of thought about evangelism discussed recently seems to say that public preaching of the gospel is not all it should be, unless it is accompanied by a particular kind of physical manifestation (signs, wonders, miracles). These, it is implied, give the message credibility that it could not otherwise have and trigger the "power encounter" that the verbal message alone would hardly induce. By biblical standards, however, that seems to me a gross overstatement and indeed a real error.[5] Also, it sets those who proclaim the gospel in public on a very slippery path. The temptation to manipulate people and situations to make it appear that the power of God is producing the desired manifestations is likely to prove irresistible. The backlash that comes when investigations show that God was not acting to the evangelist's order is likely to prove inescapable.

We cannot institutionalize and harness the power of God, either in converting souls or in supplying miracles. God uses us, but not we him. It is a spiritual lapse, however well-meant, every time we try to make him dance to our tune. This is not to imply that the God of all grace will not use human ventures in evangelism that are misconceived in this way. My point is only that evangelism is one of the activities covered by the old adage: **if a thing is worth doing, it is worth doing right.** Perhaps it is relevant to note that most if not all of yesterday's greatest evangelists—men like Richard Baxter, John Wesley, George Whitefield, Dwight L. Moody, Charles Spurgeon—impressed their contemporaries as, not indeed sinless, but certainly holy men. This was recognized as having much to do with the power of their ministry.

5. Real Righteousness. *It is right to want to be divinely empowered for righteousness, for moral victories, for deliverance from bad habits, for loving God and for pleasing God.*

The good news here is that through the means of grace—Scripture, fellowship, prayer, and church worship—all Christians may be so empowered. Through the Spirit, whose power we come to know as we discipline ourselves to use these means, we may "put to death the misdeeds of the body" (Rom 8:13), grow in the fruit of the Spirit (Gal 5:22-26), and find strength for the specifics of living to God (1 Cor 16:13; Eph 6:10; Phil 4:13; Col 1:11; 1 Tm 1:12; 2 Tm 2:1, 4:17). Diligence in using the means of grace is the prime secret of deepening holiness and ongoing usefulness. Through this we enter into the momentous process envisaged in Paul's prayer—"that you... may have power... to grasp how wide and long and high and deep is the love of Christ... that you may be filled to the measure of all the fullness of God" (Eph 3:17-19).

The sanctifying process operates from the inside out. Grasping and being grasped by the love of Christ (cf. 2 Cor 5:14) is right at its heart. Partially, unevenly, and incompletely, but nonetheless really, effectively, and sometimes dramatically, Christians prove in experience that the power of God changes lives. This is what real Christians want and seek, and this is what they find.

The Intensity of God's Holiness. A further point, however, needs to be made here, or my upbeat last paragraph will have to be censured as facile and naive for only telling half the story. The spiritual growth process opens the eyes of the Christian's heart to see more clearly not only the greatness of God's love, but also the intensity of his holiness. We have already noted that "holiness" is the biblical label for all that sets God apart from humanity, with direct focus on his majestic potency and his moral purity. Here, the focus is on the latter.

Clearer perceptions of God's purity have a reflex effect, as if that purity were a light shining into the recesses of the self and showing up all that has been lurking in the dark there. As a result, Christians come to see in themselves sinful motives and attitudes, failures, shortcomings, and deficiencies, of which they were unaware before, simply because until now their consciences had not assessed their conduct by so bright a light from God. The things they see include:

- stubborn habits of sin;
- chronic patterns of moral evasion;
- weaknesses of moral character;
- cravings that are really vicious;
- attitudes that are really arrogant;
- behavioral flaws due to temperament;
- inclinations to self-aggrandizement, self-indulgence, and self-pity;
- built-in self-protectiveness because of past hurts;
- moral quirks due to scars of abuse and layers of fear.

All of these faults and many more like them are now thrown into relief, as it were. One has to face them. The meaning of moral perfection—perfect love, humility, joy, peace, goodness, patience, gentleness, wisdom, fidelity, reliability, courage, fair-mindedness, and so on—is etched on the mind more clearly. The distance between that perfection and our own performance, looked at from the standpoint both of motivation and of execution, is perceived willy-nilly. Personal limitations for which we once made excuses to ourselves now seem indefensible. We wince, maybe even weep, at our own former crassness on moral matters.

Like Isaiah in the temple, so with Christians everywhere. The more vividly they see how holy God is, the more poignantly they feel how sinful and corrupt they are themselves. Because spiritual advance thus enlarges insight into the depths of one's own fallenness, those going forward in holiness often feel they are going backward. Their deepened awareness of how sinful they still are, despite their longing to serve God flawlessly, weighs them down. As we have seen already, it calls forth from them their own "wretched man" heart-cry, echoing Paul's in Romans 7:24. Over and over again they dare to hope that they have overcome the downdrag of sin in some area of life. Over and over again God humbles them by letting them discover that it is not yet so. To feel that one's reach is always exceeding one's grasp is distressing. Though knowledge of gospel grace brings them joys in abundance, they are from this standpoint distressed.

This does not, however, mean that they are in an unhealthy spiritual state. Paul's own "wretched man" outburst is the word of the dynamic, spiritually healthy man who is dictating the letter to the Romans. His argument has led him to review what the law tells him about himself as he walks the path of new life in Christ (see Rom 6:1-14, 7:4-6, 8:1-39). From the fact that he could not feel healthy, or claim to be healthy, as he groaned under the burden of not yet being morally perfect as he wanted to be (see Rom 7:22, 8:23), some have inferred that either he really was not healthy or that in Romans 7:14-25 he was not writing about himself at all, despite his use of "I" and the present tense. They have taken for granted that no spiritually healthy person could feel about himself the way Paul does. But this is not so.

Intense distress at one's continuing imperfection, in the context of an intense love of goodness as God defines it and an intense zeal to practice it, is the clearest possible sign of the holiness of heart that is central to spiritual health. The paradox —too hard a nut, it seems, for some to crack—is that increase of real holiness always brings increase of real discontent, because of what has not yet been achieved. The truth is that the sense of frustrated longing which the "wretched man" heart-cry expresses belongs to the experience of all those who seek to live in the power of the Spirit and so please their Savior-God.

But this is not the most important thing about them, nor is their continued sense of sin the best indicator of the power of the Spirit in their lives. The clearest sign is, quite simply, love for God and other people: love that, with or without much strength of feeling (for we cannot always command strong feelings), actively honors God by grateful praise and active service of others by helpful care. Love that constantly says "no" to what, the Puritan Richard Baxter called the "carnal self" in order constantly to say "yes" to its own selfless calling is the strongest proof of the Spirit's power that anyone can imagine.

This book has said things about love already which make further discussion of it needless now. All that is needed here is the above reminder that love framed by truth is the surest verification of the power of God at work in a person, plus the further reminder that the power to love is rooted in the ability to receive love from others—in the first instance, from the Father and the Son.

... that you... may have power... to grasp... the love of Christ.... **Eph 3:17-18**

Christ's love compels us. 2 Cor 5:14

(God) loved us and sent his Son as an atoning sacrifice for our sins.... Since God so loved us, we also ought to love one another. 1 Jn 4:10-11

We love because he first loved us. 1 Jn 4:19

A PANORAMA OF GOD'S POWER

The present chapter has taken us across country that is tricky to traverse these days. But now, once again, we are approaching the head of the pass, the place where the panoramic view unfolds. In light of what has been said so far, the panoramic account of the power of God in human lives, ours and those of others, comes out like this:

The Power of God Is God Himself in Action. Most modern talk of power has to do with impersonal forces in nature or society, or human prerogatives of control, but our present theme is not either of these. We are talking about the divine energy that brought the universe into existence when nothing but God himself was in existence; the energy that upholds the universe in being every moment (for no created thing is self-sustaining), and that orders, controls, and directs everything that happens within the universe at any time. Our immediate concern is with the operation of this energy in the vast complexity of our human lives—both in the intricacies of our bodily functions and in the greater intricacies of our conscious personal being. These intricacies include our thinking, planning, decision-making, and maintaining of commitments; our habits and behavior patterns; our actions and reactions; our use of our skills, natural and acquired, and of our creativity; our hopes, fears, joys, pains, and what they do to us; our relational, moral, and aesthetic experiences; all our ups and downs of feeling, from exuberance to exhaustion, from ecstasy to apathy, and from delight to depression; and so on. All these facets of our life are touched by the energy of God.

Most particularly, we are focusing on God's exercise of his energy in redemptive grace. By this he regenerates, assures, sanctifies, alters our disposition, changes our character through moving us to practice Christlike virtues, equips us to serve others, and enables us to do and be for God what, left to ourselves, we never could have been or have done. The power here is not the sort of power that we humans can grab hold of and manipulate. It is power that belongs to God, and that he alone manages. Just as my will is me in action, so God's power is God in action. When God acts upon human beings they are under his control, but he is not under theirs. God's power is sovereign power, sovereignly employed.

As God exerted great power in creation, and exerts great power in his providential upholding and shaping of things, so he has committed himself to exert great power in the saving and upbuilding of his people. In Ephesians 3:10, Paul, having declared that the riches of Christ are unsearchable, explains the divine intent in the economy of grace as "that now, through the church, the manifold wisdom of God should be made known to the rulers and authorities in the heavenly realms."

The vivid picture that these words conjure up is one of the church as God's display area, where he shows an audience of watching angels what a breathtaking variety of wonderful things he can do in and through sin-damaged human beings. My three Greek dictionaries render the Greek word translated "manifold" (πολυποικιλος /polupoikilos) as much-variegated, very many-sided, and of greatly differing colors—which renderings give us some idea of the range and resourcefulness of God's ongoing work of power in the church. This word, writes John Stott, "was used to describe flowers, crowns, embroidered cloth and woven carpets. The simpler word *poikilos* was used in the LXX [Greek Old Testament] of the 'coat of many colours' (AV) or 'richly ornamented robe' (NIV) which Jacob gave to his youngest son Joseph (Gn 37:3, 23, 32). The church as a multiracial, multicultural community is like a beautiful tapestry."[6] Yes—and also as a multirepair shop, where disordered and broken-down lives, made ugly by sin, are being reconstructed in Christlike shape. The wisdom of God that Paul has in view is not just the wisdom that brings Jew and Gentile together in the body of Christ, but is also the wisdom that directs the power that quickens the spiritually dead and makes new creatures of them in a new and lovely fellowship of holiness and love (Eph 2:1-10, cf. 4:20-24).

Great is the power of God in the lives of the people of God! Paul's stupendous prayer that follows, asking God that his readers might be empowered to know the full dimensions of the love of Christ so that they might be filled to all the fullness of God, and his great doxology after that, celebrating the fact that God can do "immeasurably more than all we ask or imagine" (Eph 3:20), further confirm the point. The potential of God's power in our lives is incalculable. Do we reckon with this fact?

The Power of God Is the Power of the Holy Spirit. The personal distinctness of the Holy Spirit is part of the New Testament revelation of the triune nature of God. His personal ministry since Pentecost as the second Paraclete (Jn 14:16) is part of the New Testament revelation of the tripersonal God in loving and saving action. "Paraclete" is a Greek term to which no single word in English does justice; it means counselor, helper, advocate, supporter, comforter in the sense of encourager, in short anyone who sustains another in any connection at all. Jesus himself was the first paraclete, and it is his place as care-giver that the Holy Spirit takes. The personal indwelling of the Holy Spirit as the source, guide, and enabler of our new life in Christ, the inner intercessor who makes up for deficiencies in our praying (Rom 8:26) and the resident within us who is grieved when we dirty his home (Eph 4:30), is highlighted in the New Testament (Jn 14:17; Rom 8:9-11).

The power of God that operates in human lives in connection with the gospel is more than once identified as the power of the Holy Spirit (Rom 15:13, 19; cf. 1 Cor 2:4; 1 Thes 1:5).

"Power," as we noted, is a word associated in everyday English with impersonal forces, but the power of the Holy Spirit is the effective agency of a person, who personally relates himself to those in whose lives he works. "Even when the New Testament speaks of the Spirit in impersonal images, the chief of which are wind, fire and water," writes Tom Smail, "the images are used dynamically to show that they are pointing to one who has the will and the power to control us rather than to something we ourselves can control".[7] The Holy Spirit is not an impersonal force put at our disposal or harnessed to our wills; rather, the Spirit is a sovereign person who at his own will, which is also the will of the Father and the Son, disposes of us.

The Spirit operates in and through:

- our thinking (he convinces us of God's truth);
- our decision-making (he leads us to will the will of God); and
- our affections (he draws forth from us love and hate, hope and fear, joy and sorrow, and other feeling-laden dispositions, all responding to the realities of the gospel).

His blessing on the Bible we read, and on the Christian instruction we receive, persuades us of the truth of Christianity. He shows us how God's promises and demands bear on our lives. His new-creative action at the center of our personal being so changes and energizes us that we do in fact obey the truth. The persuasion at conscious level is powerful. The heart-changing action that produces Christian commitment is almighty. First to last, however, the power exercised is personal. The Holy Spirit is a living person, not a mere force.

To be sure, he is, so to speak, shy and faceless. His ministry is to focus our attention on the Father and the Son, to teach us to say "Lord" (divine master) to Jesus and "Abba" (beloved

Father) to the Sender of Jesus, and to know that when we say it we mean it (see Rom 8:15, 10:8-13; 1 Cor 12:3; Gal 4:6). He does not call attention to himself. Most of the time there is nothing humanly abnormal about our experience to force on us any awareness that the Spirit is at work in us—not, at least, until we look back on what we said and did, and see that mere nature cannot account for it. For the truth is that, as the hymn says,

> Every virtue we possess,
> And every victory won,
> And every thought of holiness
> Are his alone.

So, too, in all our service of others, from the simplest forms of practical help to the most delicate spiritual guidance and the most forthright dissuasives from sin, we are activated by the Spirit—whether we know it or not. It is the Spirit's power that generates all the goodness of the Christian's good works.

Something of the range of the Spirit's ministry to the saints appears in Romans 8:4-16, where in the space of thirteen verses Paul speaks of

1. believers living according to the Spirit, with the Spirit driving them on toward God (Rom 8:4-6);
2. believers being inhabited by the Spirit here and now (Rom 8:9);
3. believers having their mortal bodies quickened by the Spirit when the day of resurrection comes (Rom 8:11);
4. believers putting to death (mortifying) their vices "by the Spirit" (Rom 8:13);
5. believers being moved constantly to say—indeed, to cry— "Abba (Father)" to God, under the prompting of the Spirit as he witnesses to their adoption (v. 15).

All this shows the aptness of Tom Smail's title for his book on the Holy Spirit, *The Giving Gift.* The Spirit (the gift of the Father and the Son to us who now believe) gives us what it takes to give ourselves back to God in the grace-taught gratitude that is sparked and fed by grace-given assurance. Thus the Spirit by his power engineers our return to God, from whom we first fell.

The Father and the Son have given us the Spirit, we might say, so that he may give us back to the Father and the Son by sovereignly inducing us to give ourselves back, as the free and resolute determination of hearts now freed from sin's dominion. The test, therefore, of whether a paranormal physical condition, or state of consciousness, is Spirit-wrought is whether it points and pulls us along the road of biblically defined self-giving to God, in humility, love, zeal, praise, and thanksgiving. As a tour guide showing a building always leads sightseers along a set route, so no manifestation of any sort of power that lacks this directional thrust should ever be ascribed to the Spirit, whose agenda is always to lead us to the divine throne.

The Power of God Is Exerted in Accordance with God's Purpose. Scripture is full of references to the power of God. We are told of its working

- in creation;
- in providence (natural regularities, meaningful coincidences, miraculous deliverances);
- in grace (the quickening and enabling of individuals for faith, repentance, righteousness, service and witness; also, the reviving of the church); and
- in the future glory that Christ's return will usher in (the remaking of the cosmos, the bodily resurrection of every dead person, and the bodily transformation of every living person).

In all these acts of power, we are told, God shows himself sovereign. He is working out his own purpose for each individual person, human or angelic, and for the history of the universe, over which he rules and which he directs towards its climax according to his eternal plan.

With regard to the history of this world, the church is at the center. The Bible tells us what the essence of the plan is: Jesus Christ, already this world's reigning Lord, will continue to reign until, one way or another (opinions among believers differ as to just how), all created rational beings come to acknowledge his Lordship. In the broadest sense, God is exerting his power here and now in order, step by step, to bring about this final consummation.

God has made his purpose a matter of promise to us. The Bible is full of particular promises in which aspects of that purpose are spelled out as a basis for our responsive trust. Were it not so, you could hardly call our contact with God a personal relationship at all. Real personal relationships always involve personal commitments, and promises are the utterances that regulate such commitments. A promise is a word that reaches into the future, creating a bond of obligation on the part of the one who gives it and of expectation on the part of the one who receives it. In this sense it is what logicians call a "performative" word, one that brings about a new state of affairs for those by whom and to whom it is spoken. That our mighty Creator should have bound himself to use his power fulfilling promises to us—"very great and precious promises," as 2 Peter 1:4 puts it—is one of the wonders of biblical religion.

All God's promises relate, one way or another, to his purpose of glorifying himself by blessing his human creatures. There are announcements of his purpose of:

- preserving earth's natural order for humanity until history ends (Gn 9:8-17);
- maintaining an abiding covenant relationship with Abraham and his descendants, including all who are in Christ (Gn 17:1-8; Gal 3:7-9, 14, 22-29);
- bestowing particular benefits on his people here and now according to their needs—forgiving their sins, delivering them from evils, strengthening them in their weakness, comforting them in their sorrows, guiding them in their perplexities, and so on;

- sending Christ back to this world in glory, to create new heavens and a new earth, and to bring his people into a final state of joy with their Savior compared with which, as C.S. Lewis says somewhere, "the highest raptures of earthly lovers will appear as mere milk and water."

All God's universal promises to his people relate to the fulfilling of his saving purpose for them. He wants us to see this and be glad of it.

Scripture also tells of God giving and miraculously fulfilling many specific promises to many special people—promises of progeny to particular childless wives, for instance (Gn 17:15-19, 18:10-15, 30:22; Jgs 13; 1 Sm 1:9-20; Lk 1:7-20), and to the virgin Mary (Lk 1:26-38). We need to be careful in the lessons we draw from such stories. Because these miraculously born children each had a special role in the fulfilling of God's purpose for the world, we must not read these narratives as constituting a divine promise of pregnancy to all childless wives who pray.

Nor, to give another example, may we treat narratives of Jesus' miraculous healings in Palestine, where he evidenced his messianic claims (see Mt 11:2-6), as constituting a promise of similar healing to any and all who pray for it today.

Nonetheless, all biblical stories of specific promises fulfilled by God's power, and of particular gracious displays of that power in blessing, remind us of what God can do. They encourage us to rely on his omnipotence and trust him to fulfill his purpose in each Christian's life in the way he sees best.

Questions about the power of prayer—the relationship between our praying and God's using of his power in the situations we pray about—constantly arise to perplex us. What has been said suggests the way to resolve them.

Prayer and God's Will. First, can we by petitionary prayer control and direct God's power? Is that the meaning of Jesus' words about moving mountains by prayer (Mt 17:20, 21:21; Mk 11:22-24; cf. 1 Cor 13:2)? Is this the lesson for us of Elijah's stopping and starting the rain by prayer (Jas 5:16b-18)? The short answer is: no, we cannot manipulate God into doing our will when our will is not his. Yet he regularly wills to give blessings in answer to the prayers which, through incentives from Scripture and the burdening of our hearts by his Spirit, he prompts us to make.

By this means he achieves two goals together: giving of good gifts to his children, which he loves to do; and enriching of their relationship with him through the special joy and excitement of seeing that the good things were given in response to their petitions. Moreover, there are times—not many, but they do occur—when God gives great assurance as to what to pray for, and great confidence before the event that the prayer will be answered (as he did in Elijah's case). The memory of such occasions (one does not forget them!) remains as a strong incentive to pray confidently and expectantly about the next need that appears.

I cannot claim to know much about this. But I recall a day of prayer for a Christian institution, for which I had some responsibility, that out of the blue had been told to close. Two hours into our praying I knew that I was being shown exactly what to ask for—a pattern of survival involving seven items. All of them at that moment seemed impossible to achieve, but all of them within eight months became reality. I recall too a morning when I walked home praying for a person facing a cancer operation the next day. As I neared home, the load of care lifted. I had a strange sense of being told I had been heard, and need not pray any more. Many others were praying for this person, and I do not know whether any of them had any such experience. All I know is that next day the surgeon could find no trace of cancer. Such precise intimations from God in advance as to how he plans to use his power are (I believe) very rare. But others have told similar stories of how God took them into his confidence, so to speak, while they were praying to him to use his power and show forth his glory in particular situations. As I said above, these things happen, and we should recognize and rejoice that they do.

The truth here is not that prayer changes God's mind or twists his arm, but rather that our prayer, generated and sustained as it is by God himself, becomes the means of our entering into God's mind. We end up asking him to do what he had planned all along to do, once he had brought us to the point of asking him to do it with an appropriately felt seriousness of concern. If we want to see the power of God at work answering our prayers (and there is something wrong with us if we do not), our task is not to screw ourselves up to a self-induced certainty that what we have chosen to ask for is going to happen, just because we have assured ourselves that it will. Our task is, rather, to seek God's mind about the needs that press on us and to allow him to show us (with as much or as little detail as Scripture and the Spirit may suggest to us in each case) how we should pray "thy will be done"—thus following Jesus' path of prayer in Gethsemane.

Miracles. Second, is it ever right to ask God to show his power by a miracle? Provided that the bottom line of our prayer is "thy will—not mine as against thine—be done," there is nothing improper in our telling God when we think that a miracle—a spectacular coincidence, or a display of the power of the new creation in, for instance, organic healing—would advance his glory and the hallowing of his name. Paul prayed for miraculous healing of his thorn in the flesh. He was not wrong to do so, although as it turned out a miracle was not God's answer to his prayer (see 2 Cor 12:9). We only go wrong if, when we ask for a miracle, we are not prepared to find that God has other ideas. But his power remains undiminished; and although we must recognize that miracles are always unlikely, we need to remember that they are never impossible.

Our hope to see miracles must, however, always be tempered by a grasp of this next point.

The Power of God Is Shown Most Fully in Human Weakness.
There are many sorts of weakness. There is the bodily weak-

ness of the invalid or cripple; there is the character weakness of the person with besetting shortcomings and vices; there is the intellectual weakness of the person with limited ability; there is the weakness brought on by exhaustion, depression, stress, strain, and emotional overload. God sanctifies all these forms of weakness by enabling the weak to be stronger (more patient, more outgoing, more affectionate, more tranquil, more joyful, and more resourceful) than seemed possible under the circumstances. This is a demonstration of his power that he delights to give.

Paul states the principle thus: "We have this treasure (knowledge of God in Christ) in jars of clay to show that this all-surpassing power is from God and not from us. We are hard pressed on every side, but not crushed; perplexed, but not in despair; persecuted, but not abandoned; struck down, but not destroyed. We always carry around in our body the death of Jesus, so that the life of Jesus may also be revealed in our body. So then, death is at work in us" (2 Cor 4:7-12). In a self-centered, pleasure-oriented, self-indulgent world like ours today, this sounds most brutal and chilling. But it is, in fact, the true meaning of the time-honored, much-applauded dictum, "Man's extremity is God's opportunity." Opportunity for what?—to show his power, the power of his grace, now displayed for the praise of his glory.

Being weak, and feeling weak, is not in itself fun, nor can it be a condition of what the world would see as maximum efficiency. One might have expected God to use his power to eliminate such weakness from the lives of his servants. In fact, however, what he does again and again is to make his weak servants into walking wonders—sometimes, of course, in the physical sense, immobilized wonders—of wisdom, love, and helpfulness to others despite their disability. It is thus that he loves to show his power. This is a truth that is vitally important to understand.

Paul himself learned this lesson very thoroughly through his interaction with the Corinthians. Paul was not a man for half measures, or self-effacement, or standoff relationships. He was naturally a "ball of fire," as we say, imperious, combative, brilliant, and passionate. Conscious of his apostolic authority and very sure that his teaching was definitive and health-giving, he spent himself unstintingly in the discipling of his converts. He felt and expressed deep affection for them because they were Christ's, and naturally looked not only for obedience but also for affection in return.

In the case of the Corinthians, however, the obedience was wavering and grudging, and the affection was virtually nil. This, as Paul's letters to them illustrate, was partly because Paul did not come up to their conceited expectation that any teacher worth his salt would throw his intellectual weight about in order to impress them. It was partly too because other teachers, who did throw their weight about, had secured their loyalty, and partly also because they had embraced a triumphalist view of spiritual life that valued tongue-speaking and uninhibitedness above love, humility, and righteousness. They thought of Christians as persons set free by Christ to do just about anything, with no regard for the consequences. They looked down on Paul as "weak"—unimpressive in presence and in speech (2 Cor 10:10), and possibly wrong in some of his doctrinal and moral teaching. They were very critical of his personal style and behavior.

Anyone in Paul's position would find this painful to a degree, and it is clear from his letters to the Corinthians, with their expressions of anguished love and their alternations of pain, anger, disappointment, frustration, and sarcasm, that Paul himself did find it exceedingly painful. His response, however, was magnificent. He embraced weakness—not the weakness of ministry alleged by the Corinthians, but the weakness of a sick body, a servant role, and a hurting heart—as his calling here on earth. "If I must boast," he wrote, "I will boast of the things that show my weakness" (2 Cor 11:30). "I will not boast about myself, except about my weaknesses" (2 Cor 12:5). And he suited the action to the word:

To keep me from becoming conceited... there was given me a thorn in the flesh, a messenger of Satan, to torment me. Three times I pleaded with the Lord to take it away from me. But he said to me, "My grace is sufficient for you, for my power is made perfect in weakness." Therefore I will boast all the more gladly about my weaknesses, so that Christ's power may rest on me. That is why, for Christ's sake, I delight in weaknesses, in insults, in hardships, in persecutions, in difficulties. For when I am weak, then I am strong.

2 Cor 12:7-10

What was the thorn? We do not know. But it must have been a personal disability, some malfunctioning in his make-up, or he would not have said it was in his "flesh" (meaning his created humanity). And it must have been painful, or he would not have called it a "thorn."

Why was Paul given it (by God, in providence)? For discipline, as the apostle recognized, to keep him humble—no mean agenda, let it be said, when a man had such an enormous ego as did Paul.

In what sense was Paul's thorn a messenger of Satan? It sparked thoughts of resentment at God, pity for himself, and despair about the future of his ministry—the sort of thoughts that Satan specializes in stirring up within us all. Anything that prompts such thinking thereby becomes a messenger of Satan to our souls.

Why did Paul pray specifically to the Lord Jesus about his thorn? Because Jesus was the healer, who had wrought many miraculous cures in the days of his flesh and some through Paul during Paul's years of missionary ministry (see Acts 14:3, 8-10, 19:11). Now Paul needed Christ's healing power for himself, so in three solemn seasons of prayer he sought it.

Why was healing withheld? Not for lack of pure-hearted prayer on Paul's part, nor for lack of sovereign power on Christ's part, but because the Savior had something better in view for his servant. (God always reserves the right to answer our requests in a better way than we make them.) Jesus' response to Paul's prayer could be expanded like this: "Paul, I will tell you what I am going to do. I am going to display my strength in your continuing weakness, in such a way that the things you fear—the ending or enfeebling of your ministry, the loss of your credibility and usefulness—will not occur. Your ministry will go on in power and strength as before, though in greater weakness than before. You will carry this thorn in the flesh with you as long as you live. But in that condition of weakness, my strength will be made perfect. It will become more obvious than ever that it is I who keep you going." The implication was that this state of things would be more to Paul's personal blessing, more to the enriching of his ministry, and more to the glory of Christ the enabler, than an immediate cure would be.

What should we make of Paul's reaction? Clearly he understood and accepted what Christ had communicated to him as he prayed. Clearly he saw it as defining his own vocation. It is natural to suppose that one reason why he narrated it so fully was that he knew he was being made a model for others to imitate. His experience certainly is a model to which again and again we find ourselves required to conform.

The pattern is that the Lord first makes us conscious of our weakness, so that our heart cries out, "I can't handle this." We go to the Lord to ask him to remove the burden that we feel is crushing us. But Christ replies: "In my strength you *can* handle this, and in answer to your prayer, I will *strengthen* you to handle it." Thus in the end our testimony, like Paul's, is: "I can do everything through him who *gives me strength*" (Phil 4:13); "The Lord stood at my side and *gave me strength*" (2 Tm 4:17). And we find ourselves saying, with Paul: "Praise be to the God and Father of our Lord Jesus Christ, the Father of compassion and the God of all comfort, who comforts us in all our troubles, so that we can comfort those in any trouble with the comfort we ourselves have received from God. For just as the sufferings of Christ flow over into our lives, so also through Christ our comfort overflows" (2 Cor 1:3-5).

By "comfort," Paul means the encouragement that invigorates, not the relaxation that enervates. It is in that sense that we join him in testifying to the comfort of God. We find ourselves living (if I may put it this way) baptismally, with resurrection-out-of-death as the recurring shape of our experience. And we realize with ever-growing clarity that this is the fullest and profoundest expression of the empowered Christian life.

It appears, then, that being divinely empowered so that one grows stronger in Christ has nothing necessarily to do with performing spectacularly or, by human standards, successfully (whether or not one performs so is for God to decide). It has everything to do, however, with knowing and feeling that one is weak. In this sense, we only grow stronger by growing weaker. The world means by strength (of character, mind, and will) a natural endowment, the ability to press ahead, undistracted and undiscouraged, towards one's goals. God-given strength or power is however a matter of being enabled by Christ himself through the Spirit to keep on keeping on in:

- personal holiness before God;
- personal communing with God;
- personal service of God; and
- personal action for God.

One keeps on however weak one feels. One keeps on even in situations where what is being asked for seems to be beyond one, and one does so in the confidence that this is how God means it to be. For only at the point where the insufficiency of natural strength is faced, felt, and admitted does divine empowering begin.

So the power path is humble dependence on God to channel his power to the depths of our being so as to make and keep us faithful to our calling in sanctity and service. With that we depend on him to channel his power through us into others' lives to help them move forward at their points of need. The power pitfall is self-reliance and failure to see that without

Christ we can do nothing that is spiritually significant, however much we do quantitatively, in terms of energetic activity. The power principle—God's power scenario, we might call it—is that divine strength is perfected in conscious human weakness. The power perversions suppose that God's power is something we can possess and control, or that we may look to him to empower us for service when we are not looking to him to empower us for righteousness; but those ideas, as we have seen, are utterly wrong.

If I could remember, each day of my life, that the way to grow stronger is to grow weaker, if I would accept that each day's frustrations, obstacles, and accidents are God's ways of making me acknowledge my weakness, so that growing stronger might become a possibility for me, if I did not betray myself into relying on myself—my knowledge, my expertise, my position, my skill with words, and so on—so much of the time, what a difference it would make to me!

I wonder how many others, besides myself, need to concentrate on learning these lessons? If you have read thus far, I urge you to pause, and ask yourself how firmly they are anchored in your heart. They need to be anchored there very firmly indeed, and I fear that in many Christian hearts today they are not. May God in his great mercy weaken us all!

Hard Gaining: The Discipline of Endurance

When all kinds of trials and temptations crowd into your lives, my brothers, don't resent them as intrud - ers, but welcome them as friends! Realize that they come to test your faith and to produce in you the quality of endurance. But let the process go on until that endurance is fully developed, and you will find you have become men of mature character with the right sort of independence. **Jas 1:2-4, Phillips**

Endure hardship as discipline; God is treating you as sons. **Heb 12:7**

RUNNING THE RACE WITH EYES FIXED ON JESUS

Do you know the phrase, "hard gaining?" I did not till my son took up body-building and brought home one of the magazines that cater to this interest. Then I found that "hard gaining" is virtually a technical phrase in the body-builders' world, covering all the muscle-developing and chest-expanding routines that those desiring Samsonic stature must buckle down to as means to the hoped-for effect—the impressive physique that will be the end-product.

Following the routines is hardly fun, and it cannot be classified as no sweat, but I observe that it pays off. My son, who works in the prison system, is shorter than I am, but now he weighs more. Even the most casual observer can see that his extra bulk is mostly muscle. Through hard discipline ("no pain, no gain," they say) he has gained; there are no two ways about that.

Christian maturity, which is holiness full-grown, is the promised end-product of another hard-gaining discipline, namely *endurance*—both passive (*patience*) and active (*perseverance*). The New Testament uses two pairs of Greek words, each consisting of a noun and a related verb, to express this idea. The two pairs are virtually synonymous, though the verbal form of the one (*hupomonē, hupomeno*) gives the thought of standing firm under pressure while the verbal form of the other (*makrothumia, makrothumeo*) suggests rather staying cool under provocation and not quickly cracking. In fact, the two ideas shade into each other, and the habit of endurance calls for both. The colloquial English word for endurance is "stickability." Its North American counterpart is "stick-to-it-iveness." The notion is summed up by the motto of the first Christian institution in which I taught: "Be right and persist."

The four Greek words occur all told over seventy times, for endurance is a major New Testament theme. And patience (the passive mode of endurance, whereby pain, grief, suffering, and disappointment are handled without inner collapse) is named as one facet, if we may so speak, of the fruit of the Spirit (Gal 5:22-23). This means that it is not a natural endowment but a supernatural gift, a grace of character which God imparts to those whom he is transforming into the likeness of Christ.

To say this is not, however, to contradict our statement above—that endurance is wrought in us through a discipline of hard gaining. Each aspect of the fruit of the Spirit that Paul mentions is, in fact, a matter of divine command, as well as of divine gift. Each is a habit of reaction that is most strikingly seen in situations where, humanly speaking, a different reaction would have been expected. Thus, love shines brightest when exercised for Jesus' sake toward the unlovely and seemingly unlovable; joy, when we rejoice in our salvation and our Savior even though sad things surround us; peace, when, sure of God's sovereign providence, we stay calm instead of panicking or getting frazzled.

In the same way, patient endurance is most apparent when we stand steady under pain and pressure instead of cutting and running, or crumpling and collapsing. But hanging tough in this way is a habit that takes some learning. The hardness of the gaining that produces Christian character must not be minimized: to endure Christianly (which means, in fruit-of-the-Spirit terms, lovingly, joyfully, peacefully, kindly, without loss of goodness, faithfulness, gentleness, and self-control) is no casual agenda. Many of us have hardly begun to tackle it as yet. Integral to our holiness, our maturity and our Christ-likeness, however, is this habit of enduring. Forming the habit, and making sure we never lose it, is a necessary discipline for those who are Christ's.

The letter to the Hebrews is evidently addressed to a Jewish Christian church that was undergoing ill-treatment from fellow Jews who resented its Christian faith. The believers were thinking that a return to official Judaism might be a smart move, losing them nothing and gaining them an end to persecution. The letter was written to urge them to stand firm in their Christianity. To make his point, the writer expounds systematically and in detail the way in which the Old Testament order of grace—such as it was, under the Mosaic version of God's covenant—has been superseded and cancelled through the high priestly mediation and atoning death of Jesus Christ, the incarnate Son of God. His argument thus demonstrates that if they relapsed into the Judaism from which they came, they would gain nothing of significance, and lose everything that mattered, since they would forfeit their salvation and expose themselves to horrific judgment for their unfaithfulness. So they must at all costs stand firm.

Hebrews is the classic New Testament treatment of endurance, and the weightiest of its many weighty words on the subject is as follows, at the opening of chapter 12:

> Since we are surrounded by such a great cloud of witnesses (i.e., the Old Testament heroes of faith described in chapter 11, all of whom grasped the rightness and worthwhileness of standing firm), let us throw off everything that hinders and the sin that so easily entangles (clearly, the desire for ease that was tempting them to apostasy), and let us run with perseverance (*hupomonē*) the race marked out for us. Let us fix our eyes on Jesus, the author and perfecter of our faith, who for the joy set before him endured (*hupomeno*) the cross, scorning its shame, and sat down at the right hand of the throne of God. Consider him who endured (*hupomeno*) such opposition from sinful men, so that you will not grow weary and lose heart. **Heb 12:1-3**

From this passage two truths about endurance jump out at us.

1. The Life of Christian Endurance Is Like a Long-Distance Race. The race picture, here as elsewhere in the New Testament (see 1 Cor 9:24-27; Gal 5:7; Phil 2:16; 2 Tm 4:7), is telling us two things: first, that perseverance is the only path to the prize of final glory and, second, that what perseverance requires is a sustained exertion of concentrated effort day in and day out—a single-minded, whole-hearted, self-denying, flat-out commitment to praising and pleasing the Father through the Son as long as life lasts. As successful competitors in cross-countries, marathons, and triathlons pace themselves into a winning rhythm, so it is meant to be with Christians. As some athletes were, as we say, born to run, so all who are born again are called to run, in the sense of putting all their energy into steady godliness as their life-strategy. Keeping up the winning rhythm in the Christian life, as in the Boston Marathon, is constantly demanding and sometimes agonizing. But the very meaning of perseverance and patient endurance is that you do it anyway, because you are God's child running on what, in the profoundest sense, is for you the home stretch.

This sustained inward effort, raised to the limit of what you can do with the brains, gifts and energy God has given you, is one central aspect of Christian holiness, one without which a person's supposed holiness would degenerate into self-ndulgent softness. But true holiness is neither self-indulgent nor soft. It is tough. It is virile. It has backbone and guts, and a face set like flint. It is fueled by a heart of joy as the winning-post appears ahead. Real Jesus-likeness, as the writer points out, means this—nothing less—and real holiness means real Jesus-likeness, as we have said before.

2. The Life of Christian Endurance Is Lived by Fixing Our Eyes on Jesus. "Fixing our eyes" is a good translation. The Greek word implies that one looks away from everything else in order to concentrate on one's object of attention. The imperative need to do this in relation to Jesus is central to what the text tells us. Christians are surrounded, sometimes almost deafened, by the siren-songs of those who want them to stop being awkward customers who behave Christianly and become worldly wimps who only do what those around them are already doing. Christians must learn to disregard these distracting noises. We cannot follow Christ in holiness unless we are willing to stand out from the crowd and swim against the stream.

The secret of endurance, says the writer, is to concentrate on Jesus himself: "look to" him, as the older translations put it; "gaze steadily at him" is the thought that is being expressed. What the letter has said already gives the phrase its meaning. To start with, we are to gaze at Jesus as our model and standard of godliness. "Consider him who endured such opposition (v. 3), who "learned obedience from what he suffered" (5:8)— who was, and is, "faithful to the one who appointed him… as a son over God's house" (3:2, 6); who "has been tempted in every way, just as we are—yet was without sin" (4:15); who "suffered when he was tempted" (2:18). He is the great exemplar of saying "no" to sin at all costs, even at the cost of life itself. His example is there for us to follow (cf. 12:4).

The most vital truth for the life of holy endurance is not, however, that Jesus is our standard, momentary as that truth is. The most vital truth is, rather, that Jesus is our sustainer, our source of strength to action, our sovereign grace-giver (see 2:18, 4:16), "the author and perfecter of our faith" (v. 2). As the writer's just-completed tour through the Old Testament heroes' gallery, filling chapter 11, has shown, faith for him ("being sure of what we hope for and certain of what we do not see," as he defines it in 11:1) is a compound of knowing, trusting, hoping, and stubbornly persisting in trustful hope against all odds. Faith can do this, the writer implies throughout, because the One who has graciously brought us to faith, and whom we now trust, helps us to do it. "God has said, 'Never will I leave you; never will I forsake you' [Dt 31:6-7]. So we say with confidence, 'The Lord is my *helper...*' [Ps 118:6]," (13:5-6). "Let us then approach the throne of grace with confidence, so that we may receive mercy and find grace to help us in our time of need" (4:16).

This confident, expectant approach is faith in action. It is precisely the glorified Lord Jesus, who by his Word and Spirit brought our faith into being and keeps it in being (that is the meaning of "author and perfecter"), who now helps us to stand steady as we gaze on him and cling to him by means of our focused, intentional, heartfelt prayer. It is often said that "help!" is the best prayer anyone ever makes. When directed to the Lord Jesus, it is certainly the most effective. And that last statement (be it said) remains as true for us now as ever it was for anyone, since, as the writer goes on to say, "Jesus Christ is the same yesterday and today and forever" (13:8).

Two further truths about Christian endurance now become plain. First, the fact that Jesus is our model shows that the resolute perseverance to which we are called is not the practice of *stoicism*. Our word, stoicism, refers to the moral ideal of the Stoics, an influential school of Greek philosophers in New

Testament times. The Stoic ideal was self-sufficiency and the stiff upper lip. Stoicism saw it as beneath human dignity to give way to feelings of sorrow, pain, grief, regret, or any kind of hurt. In any rough situation, said the Stoics, proper pride should lead you to grin and bear it, and not let it get you down. Turn your mind inward and bite the bullet. Draw on the resources of your humanity to take life as it comes and to keep yourself from lapsing into tears, complaints, moans, groans, or any other expressions of weakness. To show distress is shameful and contemptible. Big boys must learn not to cry. If, however, you regularly act as if you did not feel distress, you will progressively become the sort of person who does not feel it. That will be an aspect of virtue as well as an achieving of strength.

Certainly, there is a sort of heroism in this ideal. But it is the perverse heroism of self-sufficient, self-glorifying pride, the sick heroism of Milton's Satan in *Paradise Lost.* And it is at the opposite extreme from the obedient, dependent heroism of Jesus, the perfect man, who "offered up prayers and petitions with loud cries and tears to the one who could save him from death, and... was heard because of his reverent submission" (5:7). Yet he ended his prayer facing the fact that he was not to be saved from death and accepting that fact as the good will of his Father. (The reference is to Gethsemane.) Accordingly, strengthened through his prayer, Jesus walked straight into the jaws of death, and "learned obedience"—that is, learned both the practice and the cost of it—"from what he suffered" (5:8). He was shamed, and scourged, and he died on the cross, in an agony that felt like agony every moment until the ordeal was over.

Holy endurance of this Christ-like sort is an expression, not of pride, but of humility; not of defiant self-reliance, but of ready obedience; not of tight-lipped fatalism in a bleak, uncaring universe, but of resolute, though often pained and aching, submission to a loving Lord, of whom it has been truly said, "Christ leads me through no darker rooms/Than he went through before." Our crucified Savior's promise of "grace to help us in our time of need" (4:16) stands forever. How thankful we should be for that!

Second, the fact that Jesus is our model in holy endurance shows that the channel through which power to endure flows, subjectively speaking, is *hope*, which as we saw is faith's forward look (11:1). Reviewing the appalling and glorious twenty-four hours from the upper room through Gethsemane and the show trials to the degradation and torment of Golgotha, the writer proclaims that Jesus "for the joy set before him endured the cross, scorning its shame;" after which, he triumphantly rose and ascended, sitting down (as executive ruler of everything) "at the right hand of the throne of God" (v. 2). What we are being told here is that Jesus was sustained by hope. His sure and certain hope of glory led him to the cross, and through the cross, to the triumph beyond.

We too, as the writer has already said, are to be upheld by our hope, the sure and certain hope of glory promised to us in the gospel—the glory to which a life of faithful endurance is guaranteed to lead us. "We have this hope as an anchor for the soul, firm and secure" (6:19). Anchored ships stay steady. Anchored Christians do the same. And the anchor that can and does hold us steady is the hope that is ours in Christ.

ENDURANCE INSPIRED BY HOPE

Here we touch on a truth on which modern theology dwells much. God made us hoping creatures, creatures who live very much in their own future, creatures whose nature it is to look forward, and to get excited about good things that we foresee, and to draw joy and strength to cope with the present from our expectations of future fulfillment and delight. Life is always richer when you have something to look forward to. We say, "While there's life, there's hope." But the deeper truth is that while there is hope, there is life, because in the absence of anything exciting to look forward to, existence itself becomes a burden and life no longer feels worth living.

One of the saddest things today is the number of elderly people who, not being believers, have nothing to look forward to. Their life is fading away. Their bodies are getting feeble and breaking down. They cannot do what they used to do, and will never be able to do it again. They feel they are moving deeper and deeper into a dark cave, with the darkness thickening around them, and no light, or way out, for them at the end. They find living without hope to be an unrelieved burden. They get bitter in heart, and sunk in self-pity and nostalgia. If they become (as, alas, they sometimes do) a misery to others, it is because they first became in this way a misery to themselves. Hopelessness wastes the spirit.

I remember inquiring of someone who had recently visited my one-time headmaster, a brilliant scholar then aged ninety-one, how the old man was. "Terribly gloomy," was the reply; "I asked him what he was doing these days, and all he would say was, 'Waiting for the end.'" As I knew, he had rejected Christianity in his youth and embraced a sort of Buddhism. This was the result. To be without hope is a tragic thing, the more so because it is needless. God never intended humankind to live without hope, and he has, in fact, given Christians the most magnificent hope that ever was.

The New Testament presents this hope in various ways, but the basic assertion is that which breaks surface when Paul announces himself an apostle by the command "of Christ Jesus, our hope" (1 Tm 1:1), and when he identifies the "glorious riches" of the "mystery" (his gospel message) as "Christ in you, the hope of glory" (Col 1:27). Jesus Christ himself, to whom we who believe are united even now, is the Christian's hope. Our union with him is not an absorbing and abolishing of our personhood, like the union with the divine that Hinduism envisages (escape from pain, no doubt, but no joy otherwise). It is, rather, a love-relationship analogous to that of spouses, whose love for each other, and union in that love, makes each one more alive and more joyful than before. Yes,

Christ himself is our hope. Each of us is traveling along a path that he has appointed for us to an eternity of joy in which he will be the center, the focus, and the source of our endless delight.

This is the "living hope" for which Peter gives praise in 1 Peter 1:3, the "grace to be given you when Jesus Christ is revealed" (v. 13). It generates present joy in anticipation and present patience under pressure. Paul scores a beautiful verbal bull's-eye when, writing to the Thessalonians, he celebrates "your work produced by faith, your labor prompted by love, and your *endurance inspired by hope* in our Lord Jesus Christ" (1 Thes 1:3). This trio of responsive energies, or should I say, this threefoldness of energetic response, should be visible in every Christian's life: faith, love, hope; work, exertion, endurance—all together. (What God has joined, let not man separate!) This is Christ-like living. This is holiness in the round.

At the end of 1 Thessalonians, Paul, having earlier declared: "It is God's will that you should be sanctified" (4:3), prays: "May God himself... sanctify you through and through. May your whole spirit, soul, and body be kept blameless at the coming of our Lord Jesus Christ" (5:23). He means, let it be faith, love, hope, work, exertion, endurance—all to the very end.

His form of words confirms for us three truths that should now be evident to us. First, it is always right for Christians to focus on their future hope, never mind how much mockery they incur for looking beyond this world to "pie in the sky when you die." Second, it is always right for Christians to center their hoping on Jesus' promised return (which will certainly occur, though we cannot now date it or imagine it), never mind how satirically the world may deride our expectation. Third, we must always be ready for Christ's appearing, which means that we must always be actively cooperating with God's work of sanctifying us and actively resisting all persuasions and pressures to use our energy doing something else.

All of this, too, belongs to holiness in the round: hope and holiness go together. "Dear friends, now we are children of

God, and what we will be has not yet been made known. But we know that when he appears, we shall be like him, for we shall see him as he is. Everyone who has this hope in him purifies himself, just as he is pure" (1 Jn 3:2-3). Christians who are not pursuing holiness are suspect with regard to their hope. Pastorally the question of what they are hoping for may well be the best entry-point to help them to a better mind regarding their way of life. Hope and holiness truly form a pair.

MODERN UNREALITY ABOUT SUFFERING

Christian endurance, as we have seen, means living lovingly, joyfully, peacefully, and patiently under conditions that we wish were different. There is an umbrella-word that we use to cover the countless variety of situations that have this character, namely the word *suffering*. Suffering is in the mind of the sufferer, and may conveniently be defined as getting what you do not want while wanting what you do not get. This definition covers all forms of loss, hurt, pain, grief, and weakness—all experiences of rejection, injustice, disappointment, discouragement, frustration, and being the butt of others' hatred, ridicule, cruelty, callousness, anger, and ill-treatment—plus all exposure to foul, sickening, and nightmarish things that make you want to scream, run, or even die. Suffering in some shape or form is everyone's lot from earliest days, though some know far more of it than others. I shall try to be explicit now about how suffering and holiness relate to each other.

How much credibility can at this point attach to the words of one who has lived so comfortable and straightforward a life, with such good health and so many good friends, as I have, I do not know. Suffering is one of the many things I feel I know very little about. But here anyway are the truths to which I hope to hold, with God's help, through whatever sufferings—trivial discomforts or major distresses—my "golden years," as old age is now called, may bring me.[1] They are the truths about suffering that every Christian needs, and none of us dare forget.

First, I remind myself that ours is not a good time for any sort of realism about suffering—indeed, any sort of realism about God,[2] about Christianity, about virtue, about relationships, about death and dying, or about anything else except matters of technology. In our Western world fantastic technical skills are wedded to an extreme emotional childishness and immaturity, which bogs us all down deeper in sin's legacy of self-centeredness, self-absorption, and self-pity than any generation has ever sunk since Christianity entered the world.

Moreover, this is a post-Christian age intellectually, in which little sense of God's greatness and holiness remains, while unworthy fancies concerning him abound. We think of him as everyone's heavenly grandfather, there to lavish gifts upon us and enjoy us the way we are. In the absence of any sense of the sinfulness of our sins, we expect VIP treatment from him all the time. It is our everyday habit to manipulate the idea of equality or fairness to ensure that we get as much of what we want as the next person does. We cherish a sense of cosmic unfairness whenever one person suffers as others do not—especially if that person is ourself. Sacrifice for the good of others—parents for children, husbands and wives for each other, business managers for their employees and shareholders, political leaders for the community they claim to serve—is almost unheard of nowadays. Society has largely become a jungle in which we are all out hunting for pleasure, profit, and power, and are happy to shoot others if that is the way to get what we want.

Meantime, as compared with all Christians of up to about a generation ago, we have shockingly little sense of the reality, pervasiveness, shame, and guilt of sin. We cherish shockingly strong illusions about having a right to expect from God health, wealth, ease, excitement, and sexual gratification. We are shockingly unaware that suffering Christianly is an integral aspect of biblical holiness, and a regular part of business as usual for the believer.

When I seek sanity about suffering, I am heavily handicapped by these cultural cross-currents. They infect the air I breathe, and work in my spiritual system as a potent low-level poison. They are certainly part of the reason why I find it so hard to control my thoughts and feelings, and experience so much childish fury, when minor discomforts and wrist-slappings come my way.

SUFFERING MUST BE EXPECTED

Second, I remind myself that suffering as defined (getting what one does not want while wanting what one does not get) is specified in Scripture as part of every Christian's calling, and therefore of mine as much as of anyone else's. (Authors who write about life are not therefore excused from the task of actually living it!) Suffering must be expected, and even valued, by all believers without exception.

God does not shield Christians from the world's ill-will. Just by living as they do, finding their dignity and delight in pleasing God and dissociating themselves from the self-serving rat-race which the devotees of pleasure, profit, and power spend their whole life running, Christians condemn the world (see Eph 5:8-14; Heb 11:7). The world, stung, retaliates with anti-Christian anger. "The world cannot hate you," Jesus told his unbelieving siblings, "but it hates me because I testify that what it does is evil" (Jn 7:7). So to his disciples he says: "If the world hates you, keep in mind that it hated me first. If you belonged to the world, it would love you... but I have chosen you out of the world. That is why the world hates you" (Jn 15:18-19; see 1 Pt 4:4; 1 Jn 3:13). Whether the world's hostility is casual or focused, whether it is contemptuous and cool or flaming and ferocious, whether it is expressed in official persecution or informal cold-shouldering and social ostracism, it is always there as a more or less resentful reaction to people who—because of their prior loyalty—decline, albeit peacefully, to fit into the conventions, lifestyle, and value-system that are felt in some way to hold the community together.

"For example," writes Thomas Schmidt, "a businessman is attempting to follow Jesus in the way he conducts himself at work. His superiors ask him to falsify data for the sake of a client. He is cajoled, harassed, and finally insulted, but he refuses.... He accepts abuse in quiet confidence that he answers to Someone much higher on the Organizational Chart. The result? Admiration? Remorse on the part of his superiors, a new moral climate in the office? Hardly. Instead, he is passed over for promotion for not being a 'team player'."[3] Ideologically-based persecution may not overtake us as it overtook Christians in the first four centuries and as it has overtaken so many Third World and Iron Curtain Christians in our own time, but the kind of thing Schmidt describes happens in the West every day. "Everyone who wants to live a godly life in Christ Jesus will be persecuted," says Paul (2 Tm 3:12). This is one of the forms that persecution takes.

Nor is it only the secular world that sticks a knife into the Christian's ribs. It is startling to see how malice and arrogance within the church conspire to make Christians suffer. People who know they are called to live in love with their neighbor, doubly so when he or she is a fellow believer, make exceptions of those with whom they disagree. Seeing themselves as fighting the Lord's battle for truth and wisdom, they display their dislike of untruth and unwisdom by personal attacks on those whose ideas seem to them untrue and unwise. "Even my close friend, whom I trusted, he who shared my bread, has lifted up his heel against me," complains the psalmist (Ps 41:9), and his experience was far from unique. In May, 1991, I read the following news item:

LONDON—The new Archbishop of Canterbury, George Carey, faced an extraordinary attack Sunday from a priest who called in a newspaper article for the clergy to sideline him. Headlined "Deliver us, Lord, from this man," the article was printed opposite the editorial page in *The Sunday Telegraph*. The right-wing newspaper said it was "necessarily anonymous." The national church of England... was in danger, the article said, and the church would be well advised "to marginalize the archbishop before he marginalizes the rest of us." Carey, 55, is on the evangelical wing of the Church of England, mother church of the world's 70 million Anglicans. He has vowed to try to revive the church, steadily losing members, with a decade of evangelism.

Chicago Tribune **Wire Service**

Thus was George Carey—a Bible-believing, Christ-loving, charismatic activist—publicly stabbed in the back four weeks after his installation in archiepiscopal office. The secular world, one feels, could scarcely be more brutal.

But this is a pattern of things that recurs again and again in the church. Having myself known what it is to be the object of a vendetta mounted by fellow Anglicans, I felt for Dr. Carey, but I was not really surprised by the assault itself. Invoking the Lord's support for an attack on the Lord's servant is a frequent form of perversity that goes back to Caiaphas at least. And (my present point) it causes pain, which those attacked have to learn to endure.

Nor does God shield his children from personal traumas and troubles: losses and crosses, as the Puritans used to call them. On the contrary! In this fallen world, where the entry of sin has put everything out of joint, Jesus the Redeemer experienced trouble—an uncomprehending family, a hostile civil authority, friends who failed him—and the redeemed who follow him now find themselves in the same boat. Christians, like Jesus, get betrayed and victimized, as we have seen already. Christians get swindled and forced into bankruptcy, like others. Christians have family troubles, as others do. All seems well, then suddenly someone has cancer, someone is jailed, someone has become permanently and agonizingly dependent, someone who should not be pregnant is pregnant, someone has AIDS, one's child dies, one's spouse walks out on one. That is just a sample list of things that happen. One is left feeling that the roof has fallen in, and one is utterly alone and ruined, much as Job must have felt on his ash-heap. (And Christians, too, find themselves, like Job, having to endure at such times the censures of self-righteous know-alls, which make the pain worse.)

Other burrs under our saddle come, not from our relational involvements, but from our lack of a healthy body or a healthy mind. There are, for instance, Christians who battle throughout their adult lives with homosexual cravings which they know it is wrong to indulge, but which nag incessantly. The three great lies of our culture are that self-gratification is life's true goal—that it is very bad for you to thwart your own strong desires—and that any behavior you feel comfortable with is all right. Christian homosexuals who reject these lies feel as isolated from other gays who have swallowed them as they do from even celibate heterosexuals, and find their sense of isolation permanently painful. In the same way, constant struggling with any other obsessive urge that others do not share (sadism, for instance, or the passion to pilfer) is painful. But we were never promised that living uprightly would be an easy business. Ease is for heaven, not earth. Life on earth is fundamentally out of shape and out of order by reason of sin. The God who loves and saves sinners has chosen to let life go on that way most of the time. So strains, pains, disappointments, traumas, and frustrations of all sorts await us in the future, just as they have overtaken us already in the past. Suffering is to be expected, and we must prepare for it. It is a biblically predicted fact of every Christian's life that our joys will be punctuated with bad experiences to the very end.

SUFFERING MUST BE VALUED

Does that thought startle you? It should not. The world, of course, does not find value in suffering. It has no reason to. But Christians are in a different position, for the Bible assures us that God sanctifies our suffering to good ends. We are not to pretend, out of stoical pride, that we feel no pain or distress. Equally, however, we are not to spend all our time brooding on how we suffer, for that is sinful self-absorption. In any case, there are more important things to do. Our task is to take suffering in stride, not as if it is a pleasure (it isn't), but in the knowledge that God will not let it overwhelm us and that he will use it, by his own supernatural alchemy, to three good ends, at least.

1. Our Suffering Produces Character. God makes our hurts a means of our moral transformation into the image of our Savior. "We can be full of joy here and now even in our trials and troubles," writes Paul. "Taken in the right spirit these very things will give us patient endurance; this in turn will develop as mature character, and a character of this sort produces a steady hope" (Rom 5:3 ff.; Jas 1:2-4). How this works is explained in Hebrews 12:5-11, a passage we glanced at before. The writer, having urged his readers to run life's race with eyes fixed on Jesus and no yielding to sin, goes on to tell them that their pains and griefs are their heavenly Father's moral training, inflicted not out of brutal indifference but in order to lick them into a holy shape. "Endure hardship as discipline; God is treating you as sons. For what son is not disciplined by his father?... God disciplines us for our good, that we may share in his holiness. No discipline seems pleasant at the time, but painful. Later on, however, it produces a harvest of righteousness and peace for those who have been trained by it" (Heb 12:7, 10-11). Scars tie in with sanctity. Pain has an educational effect.

Educational pain? How savage it sounds! But how realistic the point really is! "What son is not disciplined by his father?" Parents who love their children take time out to discipline them when young, so that they may one day be adults that the parents can be proud of. This is simply true. What is the alternative? "If you are not disciplined... then you are illegitimate children and not true sons" (v. 8). The unhappy scenario in which the biological father will not take responsibility for the welfare of his illegitimate offspring (and his legitimate off-spring too, sometimes) was as familiar in the ancient world as it is today. The fact is that without the holiness that comes through God's discipline, "no one will see the Lord" (v. 14). But if God is taking the trouble to train us up in righteousness here and now, that shows that he is preparing us for an eternity of joy with our Lord Jesus at his right hand. This is how our holy Father in heaven works for our good.

The divine education that is in view here has two sides. One was expressed by George Whitefield, the eighteenth-century evangelist, who spoke somewhere of our kindly Lord putting thorns in all our beds lest, like the disciples in Gethsemane, we be found sleeping when we need to be watching and praying. As bodily discomfort keeps us awake physically, so lack of situational ease and contentment will keep us awake spiritually.

The other side is revealed by Jesus' summons to every would-be disciple to "deny himself and take up his cross daily and follow me" (Lk 9:23, cf. 14:27). The only persons in Jesus' day who carried their own crosses were condemned criminals from the slave and non-Roman-citizen classes who had to walk to the place of their crucifixion. These were persons who had lost their civil rights, whom society had decreed that it wanted dead, and at whose imminent sufferings—and crucifixion, remember, was the cruelest form of execution ever devised—no one was going to turn a hair. Jesus, at the end of his life, literally joined that category. But what he was saying in the words quoted was that morally he was in it already, by virtue of people's negative attitude of heart toward him. His followers, then, must clear-headedly accept a similar outcast relationship to the community around them, because that is all they can expect if they are loyal to him.

This is what self-denial really means—not a mere cutting back on some bit of private self-indulgence, but totally surrendering one's natural wish for acceptance and status and respect. It means preparing to be rejected as worthless and dispensable, and to find oneself robbed of one's rights.

Schmidt hammers this home, and rightly so. I quote:

> In his first epistle Peter writes, "If you suffer for doing good and you endure it, this is commendable before God" (2:20). He begins the next verse by saying, "For you have been called for this purpose" (NASB), and he goes on to describe Christ's example. Constructive suffering, or educational pain, is central to a life of faith.
>
> The idea is expressed strongly by Paul as well. In Romans 8:17, he makes suffering the condition of eternal inheritance, calling believers "co-heirs with Christ, if indeed we share his sufferings in order that we may also share in his glory." In Philippians 1:29 Paul writes that "it has been *granted* to you on behalf of Christ not only to believe in him, but also to suffer for him."[4]

Suffering is thus seen as a vocation, one that prepares us for glory with Christ by drawing us deeper into the sanctity of being like Christ in our reaction to the experience of wanting what we do not have while having what we do not want.

The Greek word that Phillips, the New International Version, and many others translate as "character" in Romans 5:4 is *dokimē* (δοκιμή). Strictly speaking, this term expresses the complex thought of proven quality recognized and approved as such by an interested party—in this case, God himself. The reason why *dokimē* brings hope (confidence that joy and glory with Christ will be one's ultimate inheritance) is not that persons who have stood fast through thick and thin may now pass votes of confidence in themselves, but that the God whom they serve generates within them an awareness that in his strength they have passed tests that he himself imposed. Their patience in showing loyalty to him under the pressure they endured was his own gift to them, and it has left them stronger than they were before. Christians who have gone through hardship for their Lord's sake are tested products of proven quality. *Dokimē* signifies this state of triumphant testedness, with God's seal of approval marking it.

Now *dokimē*, says Paul, produces hope. Our sense of the glory of the life to come is sharpened, and our longing for it is intensified, both as a spontaneous spin-off of the knowledge of God's present approval and as a direct fruit of knowing that the agony has actually enlarged our capacity to enjoy the final glory when it comes. Paul is explicit about this in 2 Corinthians 4:17-18, where writing out of a spell of life-threatening experiences (see 1:8-10), he says, not in irony, but expressing his honest retrospective assessment of what he had been through: "Our light (!) and momentary troubles are achieving for us an eternal glory that far outweighs them all. So we fix our eyes not on what is seen, but on what is unseen. For what is seen is temporary, but what is unseen is eternal." Paul does not, of course, mean that suffering earns glory in the way that work earns wages, nor that it creates glory in the way that chiseling creates a statue. He means only to imply that suffering makes one more able to enjoy the coming glory than one was before, just as one enjoys renewed bodily health more when it has been preceded by much sickness and pain. Romans 8 contains a similar assessment and a similar testimony: "I consider that our present sufferings are not worth comparing with the glory that will be revealed in us.... we ourselves, who have the firstfruits of the Spirit, groan inwardly as we wait eagerly for our adoption as sons, the redemption of our bodies.... if we hope for what we do not yet have, we wait for it patiently" (vv. 18, 23, 25). Integral to the Christlikeness of character that the refiner's fire of suffering induces is a deepening passion of joyful hope, and hopeful joy.

This passion, which was in Christ and in Paul so strongly, was in Moses too. "By faith Moses... refused to be known as the son of Pharaoh's daughter. He chose to be mistreated along with the people of God rather than enjoy the pleasures of sin for a short time. He regarded disgrace for the sake of Christ as of greater value than the treasures of Egypt, *because he was looking ahead to his reward"* (Heb 11:24-26; emphasis mine). Let Moses be an example to us of living in terms of our hope, of finding, as did Paul, that as absence makes one's heart grow fonder, so pressure makes one's hope glow brighter. When Christians endure hardship in the power of the Holy Spirit, brighter hope is one regular result.

2. Our Suffering Glorifies God. He sanctifies it to this end in two ways, corresponding to the double sense of "glory" and "glorify God" in the Bible. The double sense is as follows. First, "glory" means God's display to his creatures of the perfections that are his—the wisdom, power, uprightness, and love that, singly and combined, make him praiseworthy. Further, he is "glorified" when by word and deed he shows these qualities to his rational creatures. Second, "glory" also means the praise that our thanks, trust, adoration, submission, and devotion give to God, for the praiseworthiness we have now seen in him. He is "glorified" when we exalt him responsively in these ways. In Ephesians 1:3 Paul plays on the similar two senses of "bless," "Blessed be God... who has blessed us...." God is blessed by our words of praise. God blesses us by his word of power. The thought would have been essentially the same if Paul had said: *"Give* glory to God for *showing* his glory in the blessings he has now given us in Christ."

In times of weakness and woe, Christianly handled, God is glorified in both senses. On the one hand, he reveals the glorious riches of his resources in Christ by keeping us going, so that overwhelming pressures do not overwhelm us, even when they look like doing so. Paul celebrates the fact that he and his apostolic associates are "hard pressed on every side, but not crushed; perplexed, but not in despair; persecuted, but not abandoned; struck down, but not destroyed; dying, and yet we live on; beaten, and yet not killed; sorrowful, yet always rejoicing" (2 Cor 4:8-9, 6:9-10). And he explains that God's purpose in these pressures is to make apparent to all the supernatural power of Christ's risen life and gracious enabling, whereby saints are kept going in situations where it seemed impossible that anyone could keep going. A British brand of light bulb has long been advertised by the slogan "still keeps going when the rest have stopped." Paul is telling us that one way God glorifies himself in his saints is by keeping them going when anyone else would have had to stop.

Of God's self-glorifying action in saints who suffer, Paul writes: "We have this treasure (knowledge of the glory of God in the face of Christ) in jars of clay to show that this all-surpassing power is from God and not from us... we always carry around in our body the death of Jesus, so that the life of Jesus may also be revealed in our body. For we who are alive are always being given over to death for Jesus' sake, so that his life may be revealed in our mortal body. So then, death is at work in us..." (4:7, 10-12). Similarly, with reference to the mysterious "thorn in my flesh" he writes, as we saw: "He said to me, *'My grace is sufficient for you, for my power is made perfect in weakness.'* Therefore I will boast all the more gladly about my weaknesses, so that Christ's power may rest on me. That is why, for Christ's sake, I delight in weaknesses, in insults, in hardships, in persecutions, in difficulties. For when I am weak, then I am strong" (12:9-10, emphasis mine). When natural resources fail God's servants, supernatural support comes into play.

Nor is this a special experience reserved for special people in the family of God. On the contrary, it is a matter of promise to all God's people. That is implied by Paul's earlier word to the Corinthians: "No temptation has seized you except what is common to man. And God is faithful; he will not let you be tempted beyond what you can bear. But when you are tempted, he will also provide a way out so that you can stand up under it" (1 Cor 10:13). Temptations are places and times of decision in which Satan works to bring us down in an experience of defeat while God acts to build us up through an experience of overcoming. The pain, grief, self-hatred, disappointment, fear, and inner exhaustion that are so often part of the temptation experience isolate us from the seemingly untroubled. They make us feel that what we face and experience is worse than what has ever confronted anyone else before. But it never is so; and there will always be "grace to help us in our time of need" whenever we seek it (Heb 4:16). Whatever the burden, the power is there to keep the Christian from crumpling. Through God's faithfulness in supplying supernatural strength to those who are in Christ, they endure hardship, overcome temptation, and keep going as before, and in them God glorifies himself mightily.

The other side of the matter is modeled by psalm after psalm (look at 4, 5, 6, 7, 22, 34, 38, 40, 41, 42, 43, for starters) and by Paul and Barnabas singing hymns in their cell with their feet in the stocks after their flogging at Philippi (Acts 16:23-25). The proper response to pressure is praise plus prayer. The fiercer the opposition, the stronger the praise should be. It is through praise no less than through petition that help comes. It is by praise over and above petition that we most directly honor and glorify God, out of the depths and in the fire no less than at quieter times. Praise brings strength to endure, even as it gives glory to God our strengthener. Well does Richard Baxter's hortatory poem (now a familiar hymn) say:

> Ye saints, who toil below,
> Adore your heavenly King,
> And onward as ye go
> Some joyful anthem sing.
> Take what he gives
> And praise him still,
> Through good and ill,
> Who ever lives!
>
> My soul, bear thou thy part,
> Triumph in God above,
> And with a well-tuned heart
> Sing thou the songs of love!
> Let all thy days
> Till life shall end,

Whate'er he send,
Be filled with praise!

Baxter was an English Puritan, and like most of the English Puritans, he suffered for much of his life through bad housing and bad health, community hostility, social ostracism, political, ecclesiastical, and economic upsets, and actual persecution. The Puritans grasped (as many of us today do not) that Christians are not called to be the nicest people in the world according to the world's idea of what a nice person is like. Instead, they are to be the Lord's counterculture, living with different motives, purposes, and values from those of the world because of their loyalty to God. When Christians behave in a way that society finds odd and judgmental (and Christians do not have to be actually judgmental before they are felt to be such), society will soon gang up against them in one way or another. The Puritans experienced this—hence the malicious stereotypes of Puritans that still go the rounds among people who ought to know better—and consistent Christians experience it still. We saw how John Geree, describing the character of an old English Puritan in 1646, pictured this model man as having for his motto *Vincit qui patitur*, "he who suffers conquers."[5] It really does seem that of all Protestants since the Reformation the Puritans had as hard a furrow to plough as any. But Baxter was not the only Puritan who, following the lead of David in Psalm 34:1, praised the Lord at all times, and who by this discipline (which was also, for the Puritans, a delight, as it can be for us too) persistently glorified God. In doing so he found strength to stand fast in his serve.

3. Suffering Fulfills the Law of Harvest. That law can be stated thus: before there is blessing anywhere, there will first be suffering somewhere. Scripture does not explain this, but simply sets it before us as a fact. Jesus first announced the law when he declared, speaking of his own ministry, "Unless a kernel of wheat falls to the ground and dies, it remains only a single seed. But if it dies, it produces many seeds" (Jn 12:24). The many seeds in his case were the many millions for whom his cross would mean new life. Then, having said (v. 25) that following him requires willingness to lay down one's life, he declares: "Whoever serves me must follow me" (v. 26). The natural implication is that he requires all who are his to live by the same law of harvest that he lived by himself, becoming the seed that dies to bring forth fruit. Every experience of pain, grief, frustration, disappointment, and being hurt by others is a little death. When we serve the Savior in our worldly world, there are many such deaths to be died. But the call to us is to endure, since God sanctifies our endurance for fruitfulness in the lives of others.

Paul's grasp of this principle is reflected in several of his remarks about his own ministry. "I rejoice in what was suffered for you" ("my sufferings for your sake," RSV). Also, he says, "I fill up in my flesh what is still lacking in regard to Christ's afflictions, for the sake of his body, which is the church" (Col 1:24). That these afflictions are edificatory rather than propitiatory in effect will not, I think, be disputed. Paul is affirming a link between his troubles (he was writing from prison) and the furtherance of Christ's work of building his church. In a parallel letter, also from prison, Paul calls himself "the prisoner of Christ Jesus for the sake of you Gentiles" (Eph 3:1). To the Corinthians he writes: "Death is at work in us, but life is at work in you" (2 Cor 4:12). To Timothy he writes: "I endure everything for the sake of the elect, that they too may obtain the salvation that is in Christ Jesus, with eternal glory" (2 Tm 2:10). In each of these texts, the reality of a connection between his own suffering and others being blessed is made clear, though the nature of the connection is not precisely defined.

Part of the meaning of the principle, surely—even if not all—is that through the pounding we experience we are, so to speak, broken up small so that each bit of what we are may become food for some hungry soul: food, that is, in the sense of empathetic insight and supportive wisdom. In ministry to others it is often decisively helpful when we can say: "I know how you are feeling. I've been there myself. And God met me there and taught me lessons and saw me through—let me tell you about it." As Jesus once explained that the reason a man was born blind was not punishment for anyone's past sin, but God's present purpose of displaying divine power by healing him (Jn 9:1-3), so the true answer to the question, "Why is this happening to me?" will often be: It is not chastening or correction for yesterday's moral lapses. It has nothing to do with the past at all. It has to do only with the use God plans to make of you tomorrow, and how you need to be prepared for that. The hard and bitter experiences that now ravage you, like the death of a loved one (one example), are fitting you to be a channel of God's life to someone else. So you should expect hardship in some form to continue all your days, according to Jesus' own declaration: "Every branch [in me, the vine] that does bear fruit he [the Father] prunes so that it will be even more fruitful" (Jn 15:2). That is how the law of harvest works.

We see that law further illustrated in Isaiah 50:4-9, one of the servant-songs that point prophetically ahead to the suffering and glory of Jesus. This song is in the first instance Isaiah's own testimony. It begins: "The sovereign LORD has given me an instructed tongue, to know the word that sustains the weary." It continues: "I offered my back to those who beat me, my cheeks to those who pulled out my beard; I did not hide my face from mocking and spitting.... It is the sovereign LORD who helps me...." The implication is that the word which sustains the weary only comes to be known through the experience of others' hatred and brutality. Isaiah juxtaposes these two things because they are parts of a single package.

Even more clearly is the fruitfulness of suffering for ministry illustrated by the experience of our Lord Jesus himself. Jesus "has been tempted in every way, just as we are—yet was without sin" (Heb 4:15), and now as a result "is able to help those who are being tempted" (2:18). Over and above the saving significance of his perfect obedience to the Father as the second head of our race, the strain he underwent in enduring temptation (think of his days in the desert at the start of his ministry, and his hours in Gethsemane at its end) has fitted him to minister help to our harried souls in a way that would not otherwise be a reality. If this was the way the master went, it is less wonder that his servants should find themselves treading it too.

William Booth, founder and General of the Salvation Army, once gave the Army as a motto for the year the one word, "Others." No one could ever devise a more Christian, indeed Christlike, motto than that. But serving the Lord by being there to seek the good of others, and to help them where they need help, will involve us in being ground up small in the mill of God's providence for others' sake. Augustine expressed this by saying that God's servants have to be "broken and distributed" to feed the hungry; a thought that Oswald Chambers somewhere elaborated by declaring that God turns his agents into broken bread and poured-out wine. Thus it goes, and we must be ready to endure it. True holiness, which is Christ-centered and others-oriented, accepts this without demur.

Paul was a holy man, and so, far from resenting his many hardships (see 2 Cor 11:23-33), he rejoiced publicly that he could see this principle actually being worked out in his own life. "Blessed be the God and Father of our Lord Jesus Christ … the God of all consolation who consoles us in all our affliction, so that we may be able to console those who are in affliction with the consolation with which we ourselves are consoled by God.… If we are being afflicted, it is for your consolation… if we are being consoled, it is for your consolation…" (1:3-6, NRSV). Paul was content to be ground up small in the mill for others.

The way to deal with suffering in any form—from the mildest irritation to the mental and physical agony that so absorbs and overwhelms you that you groan and scream—is to offer it to the God who has permitted it, telling him to make what he wills of it, and of us through it. Contemplative prayer is often pictured as the loving look Godward, without at that moment either spoken words or active thoughts. It is contemplative prayer also when the Godward look is submissive, at a time when all power of thought and speech has been swamped by pain. Jesus on the cross is the model for this. The Father, we learn, sanctified Jesus' suffering as a ransom-price for us (Mt 20:28; 1 Cor 6:20), as our example of innocence victimized (1 Pt 2:20-23), and as the experience of our forerunner learning in practice what obedience costs (Heb 5:8). In a similar way the Father now sanctifies our suffering, as we have seen, for the ripening and refining of our Christian character, for a demonstration in us of the reality of supernatural empowering, and for our actual fruitfulness in serving others. One facet of Jesus' holiness was his willingness to suffer all kinds of pain for his Father's glory and others' good. One facet of holiness in Jesus' disciples is willingness to be led along a parallel path.

FORTITUDE: COURAGE WITH ENDURANCE

Poor Rocky. He has lost his nerve.

You might think from his name that Rocky is a strong man—a boxer or a bodyguard or a member of some other tough-guy profession. But no; he is a small black dog, barrel-shaped, low-slung, and slightly shaggy, with a rolling gait, a narrow nose, and a great fan tail almost as big as himself. My son, who brought him home from school when he was about four inches long, identifies him as a Norwegian Barge Dog. The rest of us think he is a mixture of—well, this and that. In a manner reminiscent of Christopher Robin's Pooh Bear, he is a dog of very little brain. Not that one holds that against him, but it needs to be borne in mind. He was a spirited small creature, until the time when he walked on water or, more precisely, failed to walk on water. But then his morale collapsed, and he has run scared ever since, with swiveling frightened eyes betokening a fear-filled heart. Poor Rocky.

The first time, he had his head in the air. He was chasing a bird. The lakeside was a few inches above water level. Clearly he had not noticed how the land lay, and he ran full tilt off the edge. For a moment, so the watchers told me, his front legs went wild, and there was a look of surprise on his face such as you do not often see. Then, like Piglet in the story, he found himself entirely surrounded by water, and scrambled out shaken to the core. The second time he was busily moving across the seaside rocks, and walked out on the green weed between two of them supposing it to be solid ground. But it wasn't, so down he went once again. Now he suspects the universe, and thinks of water as perilous stuff, not to be trusted in any form. This goes far beyond hating to be bathed, though indeed he does hate to be bathed, and always did. But today, when a storm rages outside the house, particularly a thunderstorm, he has to huddle, quivering, at someone's feet. When he is in the car and it is raining, or when the car splashes through puddles, he shivers, shakes, and whimpers like a soul in torment. It is clear that his nerve is gone. He lacks fortitude. Again I have to say, poor Rocky.

Fortitude, the fourth of the four cardinal virtues in medieval moral theology, is bravery and more. Bravery can be fitful and can fade, but fortitude is a compound of courage and endurance. It lasts. Faith fosters fortitude by holding before us our promised hope, of which we were thinking a few pages back (see 1 Cor 15:58; Heb 3:6, 6:19-20, 10:23-25, 12:1-13). The idea of fortitude comes from Aristotle, but power to practice it comes only from the gospel, through the exercise of faith and hope in Jesus Christ.

Faith also fosters fortitude by realistically receiving God's assurances that pain and strife must be expected in our pilgrimage, and then by inducing purity of heart in those who are actually under pressure and suffering distress. As Kierkegaard declared in a book title, "purity of heart is to will one thing"—that thing being the command and glory of God. This purity, which is also referred to in Scripture as the simplicity of a united heart and a single eye, is advanced by the experience of affliction. Dr. Samuel Johnson, the eighteenth-century wiseacre of England, once observed that when a man knows he is going to be hanged in a fortnight it concentrates his mind wonderfully. For Christians an awareness that the life God is leading them into is the spiritual counterpart of Winston Churchill's "blood, toil, tears, and sweat" has a similar effect. The world's allurements become much less alluring, and they know with great clarity of mind that a close walk with the Father and the Son, leaning hard on them and drawing strength from them through the Holy Spirit, is both what they need and what they want. Thus in situations of suffering faith purifies the heart.

Three verses from Psalm 119 testify to this. "Before I was afflicted I went astray, but now I obey your word" (v. 67). Rough experiences, which could in themselves indicate divine displeasure, challenge us to repent of past thoughtlessness and carelessness and to become more conscientious in doing our Father's will. "It was good for me to be afflicted so that I might learn your decrees" (v. 71). As if to say: I did not see clearly what you want for my life, nor what the behavioral model that the Bible spells out for me really involves, until trouble struck me. But I understand it better now. And finally: "I know, O LORD, that… in faithfulness you have afflicted me" (v. 75). God's faithfulness consists in his unwillingness that his children should lose any of the depths of fellowship with himself that he has in store for them. So he afflicts us to make us lean harder on him, in order that his purpose of drawing us into closest fellowship with himself may be fulfilled.

John Newton expressed this side of sanctification unforgettably:

> I asked the Lord that I might grow
> In faith, and love, and every grace,

Might more of his salvation know
And seek more earnestly his face.

'Twas he who taught me thus to pray,
And he, I trust, has answered prayer;
But it has been in such a way
As almost drove me to despair.

I hoped that in some favoured hour
At once he'd answer my request,
And by his love's constraining power
Subdue my sins, and give me rest.

Instead of this, he made me feel
The hidden evil of my heart,
And let the angry powers of hell
Assault my soul in every part.

Yea, more, with his own hand he seemed
Intent to aggravate my woe,
Crossed all the fair designs I schemed,
Blasted my gourds, and laid me low.

"Lord, why is this?" I trembling cried,
"Wilt thou pursue thy worm to death?"
"'Tis in this way," the Lord replied,
"I answer prayer for grace and faith.

"These inward trials I employ
From self and pride to set thee free,
And break thy schemes of earthly joy,
That thou mayest seek thy all in me."

Two examples of the fortitude that is integral to holiness
may be given as I close. The first is Mabel, a blind, deaf, dis-
ease-ridden, and cancerous old lady of eighty-nine whom Tom
Schmidt met in a convalescent home where she had been bed-
ridden for twenty-five years. He asked her what she thought
about as she passed her lonely days and nights. "She said, *I*

think about Jesus.... I asked, *What do you think about Jesus?* She replied slowly and deliberately as I wrote. And this is what she said: *'I think about how good he's been to me. He's been awfully good to me in my life, you know.... I'm one of those kind who's mostly satisfied.... Lots of folks wouldn't care much for what I think. Lots of folks would think I'm kind of old-fashioned. But I don't care. I'd rather have Jesus. He's all the world to me.'*[6] Schmidt affirms, and truly, that Mabel had power—the kind of power Paul prayed that the Ephesians might have, power to "grasp how wide and long and high and deep is the love of Christ" (Eph 3:18). I cite Mabel, equally truly I think, as an example of fortitude— courage with endurance. Power and fortitude are two main ingredients in authentic Christian holiness. "No pain, no gain," but through pain, great gain.

My second example is Terry Waite, the British hostage released at the end of 1991 after nearly five years of solitary confinement in Lebanon, chained to the wall of his room for almost twenty-four hours daily. In an interview he said: "I have been determined in captivity, and still am determined, to convert this experience into something that will be useful and good for other people. I think that's the way to approach suffering. It seems to me that Christianity doesn't in any way lessen suffering. What it does is enable you to take it, to face it, to work through it, and eventually to convert it."[7] Here, too, is a clear testimony to that gain through pain that belongs to authentic holiness.

This is a soft age in the West, an age in which ease and comfort are seen by the world as life's supreme values. Affluence and medical resources have brought secular people to the point of feeling they have a right to a long life, and a right to be free of poverty and pain for the whole of that life. Many even cherish a grudge against God and society if these hopes do not materialize. Nothing, however, as we now see, could be further from the true, tough, hard-gaining holiness that expresses true Christianity.

Paul, as I said earlier, was a truly holy man. He shall have the last word, as he lays himself on the line with regard to the Christian way to live:

> I consider everything a loss compared to the surpassing greatness of knowing Christ Jesus my Lord, for whose sake I have lost all things. I consider them rubbish, that I may gain Christ.... I want to know Christ and the power of his resurrection and the fellowship of sharing in his sufferings, becoming like him in his death, and so... to attain to the resurrection from the dead....
>
> I press on to take hold of that for which Christ Jesus took hold of me. Brothers, I do not consider myself yet to have taken hold of it. But one thing I do: Forgetting what is behind and straining toward what is ahead, I press on toward the goal to win the prize for which God has called me heavenward in Christ Jesus. All of us who are mature should take such a view of things.   Phil 3:8, 10-15

Mature...? Oh... yes, I see. And I am a silly child who stumbles and fumbles and tumbles every day. Holy Father, Holy Son, Holy Spirit, I need your help. Lord, have mercy; hold me up, and hold me steady—please, starting now. Amen.

N O T E S

ONE
What Holiness Is, and Why It Matters

1. See also J.I. Packer, *God's Words: Studies of Key Bible Themes* (Leicester, IVP 1981), ch. 14, "Holiness and Sanctification," 169–79; *Keep in Step with the Spirit* (Leicester, IVP 1984), chs. 3–4, 94–169.
2. J.C. Ryle, *Holiness* (Welwyn: Evangelical Press, 1979 [Centenary Edition]), 34–37.
3. Richard Baxter, *Poetical Fragments* (1681).
4. G.W. Allport, *Pattern and Growth in Personality* (New York: Holt, Rinehart and Winston, 1961), 34.
5. Chris Brain and Robert Warren, "Why Revival *Really* Tarries—Holiness," *Renewal*, 181 (June 1991), 35; quoting James Philip, *Christian Maturity* (London: Inter-Varsity Press, 1964), 70. I have attempted to make the same point briefly in *Knowing Man* (Exeter Paternoster 1978) and more fully with Thomas Howard in *Christianity: the True Humanism* (Berkhamsted: Word Books, 1985).
6. Philip, *Christian Maturity*, 65.
7. Philip, *Christian Maturity*, 67–69.
8. See John MacArthur, Jr., *You Call Me Lord* (London: Marshall Pickering 1989); Richard P. Belcher, *A Layman's Guide to the Lordship Controversy* (Southbridge: Crowne Publications, 1990); J.I. Packer, "Understanding the Lordship Controversy," in *Table Talk* (Ligonier Ministries), (May 1991), 7.

TWO
Explorating Salvation: Why Holiness Is Necessary

1. Lane Adams, *How Come It's Taking Me So Long to Get Better?* (Wheaton: Tyndale House, 1975).
2. See *Keep in Step with the Spirit*, 94–169, especially 145–64; John MacArthur, Jr., *Our Sufficiency in Christ* (Milton Keynes: Word Publishing), 191–209.
3. See Rom 5:1, 10; Eph 4:32; Col 1:13; 1 JN 1:3.
4. See J.I. Packer, *Keep in Step with the Spirit*, 170–234; "Charismatic Renewal: Pointing to a Person and a Power," *Christianity Today* (March 7, 1980), 16–20; "Piety on Fire," *Christianity Today* (May 12, 1989), 18–23.
5. J.R.W. Stott, *The Epistles of John* (London: Tyndale Press and Grand Rapids: Eerdmans, 1964), 119. He quotes from Robert Law, *The Tests of Life* (Edinburgh: T. & T. Clark, 1909).

FOUR
Holiness: The Panoramic View

1. Stephen Neill, *Christian Holiness* (London: Lutterworth Press, 1960), 114.
2. Neill, *Christian Holiness*, 118.
3. *Keep in Step with the Spirit*, 93–115.
4. See Kenneth Leech, *Soul Friend: The Practice of Christian Spirituality* (London: Sheldon Press, 1977; San Francisco: Harper & Row, 1980); Tilden H. Edwards, *Spiritual Friend: Reclaiming the Gift of Spiritual Direction* (New York: Paulist Press. 1980).
5. My own criticism of these formulations is scattered through *Keep in Step with the Spirit*; see especially 132–45, 202–28.
6. John Calvin, *Institutes of the Christian Religion*, I. xi.
7. See Regin Prenter, *Spiritus Creator* (Philadelphia: Muhlenberg Press, 1953); Paul Althaus, *The Theology of Martin Luther* (Philadelphia: Fortress Press, 1966), Index, s.v. God the Holy Spirit.
8. See J.I. Packer, *Among God's Giants* (Eastbourne: Kingsway, 1991); Leland Ryken, *Worldly Saints* (Grand Rapids: Zondervan, 1986).
9. John Owen, *Of the Mortification of Sin in Believers: Works,* ed. William H. Gould (London: Banner of Truth Trust, 1966), VI.79.
10. *Keep in Step with the Spirit,* passim.
11. R. Kent Hughes, *Disciplines of a Godly Man* (Wheaton: Crossway Books, 1991), 206.
12. John Geree, *The Character of an Old English Puritane or Nonconformist* (1646); quoted from Gordon Wakefield, *Puritan Devotion* (London; Epworth Press, 1957), x.

FIVE
Growing Downward to Grow Up: The Life of Repentance

1. *Writings of John Bradford: Sermons, etc.* (Cambridge: Parker Society, 1848), 30.
2. *Writings of John Bradford: Sermons, etc.*, 32–35.
3. *Writings of John Bradford: Sermons, etc.*, 36. John Foxe the martyrologist, writing, it seems, independently, says that Bradford's last audible words as he took his place at the stake were, ''O England, England, repent thee of thy sins'': *Acts and Monuments* (London: Seeley & Burnside, 1836–47), VII. 194.
4. *Writings of John Bradford: Sermons, etc.*, 33.
5. *Writings of John Bradford: Sermons, etc.*, 36.
6. *Writings of John Bradford: Sermons, etc.*, 224.
7. Compare Cranmer's congregational confession that opens his services of Morning and Evening Prayer: ''We have erred and strayed from thy ways like lost sheep . . . there is no health in us. But thou, O Lord, have mercy upon us, miserable offenders. Spare thou them, O God, which confess their faults. Restore thou them that are penitent.'' Compare too his Ash Wednesday collect: ''Create and make in us new and contrite hearts, that we worthily [i.e., in a fit manner] lamenting our sins, and acknowledging our wretchedness, may obtain of thee, the God of all mercy, perfect remission and forgiveness.''
8. *Writings of John Bradford: Sermons, etc.*, 35.
9. *Writings of John Bradford: Sermons, etc.*, 34.
10. *Writings of John Bradford: Sermons, etc.*, 14.
11. *Writings of John Bradford: Sermons, etc.*, 22.

12. *Writings of John Bradford: Letters, etc.* (Cambridge: Parker Society, 1848), 10, 20, 31, 34.

13. *Westminster Shorter Catechism*, answer 87. Compare *Westminster Confession*, XV, "Of Repentance Unto Life." "Repentance unto life in an evangelical grace, the doctrine whereof is to be preached by every minister of the Gospel, as well as that of faith in Christ, But it, a sinner, out of the sight and sense not only of the danger, but also of the filthiness and odiousness of his sins, as contrary to the holy nature, and righteous law of God; and upon the apprehension of his mercy in Christ to such as are penitent, so grieves for, and hates his sins, as to turn from them all unto God. . . . repentance . . . is of such necessity to all sinners, that none may expect pardon without it" (i-iii).

14. Preface, *Commentary on the Psalms* (1557).

15. *Institutes of the Christian Religion*, III. iii. 5.

16. *Westminster Confession*, XV.v.

17. For fuller discussion of Rom 7:7–25, see *Keep in Step with the Spirit*, 127, 159, 263.

18. For examples of such meditation, see my *Knowing God* (London: Hodder & Stoughton).

19. *Christian Holiness*, 128.

SIX
Growing into Christ-likeness: Healthy Christian Experience

1. Ryle, *Holiness*, 82–84. Ryle confirms his point with words from the Puritan, Thomas Watson: "True grace is progressive, of a spreading, growing nature. It is with grace as it is with light: first, there is the daybreak; then it shines brighter to the full noonday. The saints are not only compared to stars for their light, but to trees for their growth (Is 61:3; Hos 14:5). A good Christian is not like Hezekiah's sun that went backwards, nor Joshua's sun that stood still, but is always advancing in holiness, and increasing with the increase of God."

2. Ryle, *Holiness*, 199ff.

3. Ryle, *Holiness*, 144.

4. Eric Liddell, *Disciplines of the Christian Life* (London: Triangle, 1985), 21.

5. J.M. Barrie, *Peter Pan* (London: Hodder & Stoughton, 1928), 111, 155.

SEVEN
Growing Strong: The Empowered Christian Life

1. See *Keep in Step with the Spirit*, 191–209.

2. Some argue that the lack of any such promise is a virtual assurance that they will not continue: see, e.g, B.B. Warfield, *Counterfeit Miracles* (London: Banner of Truth, 1976).

3. C.S. Lewis, *Miracles* (London: Geoffrey Bles, 1947), title of ch. 16.

4. See H.G. Haile, *Luther: an Experiment in Biography* (Princeton: Princeton University Press, 1979), 123.

5. See J.I. Packer, "The Means of Conversion," *Crux*, XXV.4 (December 1989): 20.

6. J.R.W. Stott, *God's New Society: the Message of Ephesians* (Leicester InterVarsity Press, 1979), 123.

7. Tom Small, *The Giving Gift* (London: Hodder & Stoughton, 1988), 35.

EIGHT

Hard Gaining: The Discipline of Endurance

1. See, on this, Peter Kreeft, *Making Sense out of Suffering* (Ann Arbor: Servant Books, 1986); Elisabeth Elliot, *A Path through Suffering* (Cambridge: Crossway Books 1991); Joni Eareckson, *A Step Further* (Basingstoke: Pickering & Inglis 1979).

2. I have tried to correct some of the mistaken ideas about God in *Knowing God* (Downers Grove: InterVarsity Press, 1973).

3. Thomas Schmidt, *Trying to be Good* (Grand Rapids: Zondervan, 1990), 131.

4. Schmidt, *Trying to be Good*, 130ff.

5. Packer, *A Quest for Godliness*, 151.

6. Schmidt, *Trying to be Good*, 182.

7. *Church Times*, December 27, 1991, 2.